ST THOMAS AQUINAS

SUMMA

THEOLOGIÆ

Latin text and English translation,
Introductions, Notes, Appendices
and Glossaries

NON NISI TE

PIÆ MEMORIÆ
JOANNIS
PP. XXIII
DICATUM

IN AN AUDIENCE, 13 December 1963, to a group representing the Dominican Editors and the combined Publishers of the New English *Summa*, His Holiness Pope Paul VI warmly welcomed and encouraged their undertaking. A letter from His Eminence Cardinal Cicognani, Cardinal Secretary of State, 6 February 1968, expresses the continued interest of the Holy Father in the progress of the work, 'which does honour to the Dominican Order, and the Publishers, and is to be considered without doubt as greatly contributing to the growth and spread of a genuinely Catholic culture', and communicates his particular Apostolic Blessing.

ST THOMAS AQUINAS

SUMMA THEOLOGIÆ

VOLUME 45

PROPHECY AND OTHER CHARISMS

(2a2æ. 171–8)

Latin text. English translation, Introduction, Notes,
Appendices & Glossary

ROLAND POTTER O.P.

CAMBRIDGE UNIVERSITY PRESS
Cambridge, New York, Melbourne, Madrid, Cape Town, Singapore, São Paulo

Cambridge University Press
The Edinburgh Building, Cambridge CB2 2RU, UK

Published in the United States of America by Cambridge University Press, New York

www.cambridge.org
Information on this title: www.cambridge.org/9780521393928

This digitally printed first paperback version 2006

A catalogue record for this publication is available from the British Library

ISBN-13 978-0-521-39392-8 hardback
ISBN-10 0-521-39392-2 hardback

ISBN-13 978-0-521-02953-7 paperback
ISBN-10 0-521-02953-8 paperback

CONTENTS

ix

EDITORIAL NOTES

THE TEXT AND TRANSLATION

THE TRANSLATION, which matches the order of sentences in the original, was made from the Leonine text, which, somewhat reparagraphed and repunctuated, is followed in the main by this volume: the few variations are shown. Scriptural references are to the Vulgate.

FOOTNOTES

Those signified by a superior number are usually the references given by St Thomas and tracked down by the Leonine Commission, with the exception of no. 1 to each article which refers to parallel texts in his writings. Those signified alphabetically are editorial references and explanatory remarks.

REFERENCES

Biblical references are to the Vulgate; Patristic references to Migne (PG, Greek Fathers; PL, Latin Fathers). When the English titles are well known, references to the works of St Thomas and Aristotle are in English. Titles of St Thomas's works are abbreviated as follows:

Summa Theologiæ, without title. Part, question, article, reply; e.g. 1a. 70, 1 ad 2. 2a2æ. 25, 4.

Summa Contra Gentiles, CG. Book, chapter; e.g. *CG* 11, 14.

Scriptum in IV Libros Sententiarum, Sent. Book, distinction, question, article, solution or *quæstiuncula*, reply; e.g. 11 *Sent.* 15, 1, 1, ii ad 3.

Compendium Theologiæ, Compend. theol.

Scriptural commentaries (*lecturæ, expositiones reportata*): Job, *In Job*; Psalms, *In Psal.*; Isaiah, *In Isa.*; Jeremiah, *In Jerem.*; St Matthew, *In Matt.*; St John, *In Joann.*; Epistles of St Paul, e.g. *In 1 Cor.* Chapter, verse, *lectio* as required.

Philosophical commentaries: Aristotle, *Peri Hermeneias, In Periherm.*; Posterior Analytics, *In Post. Anal.*; Physics, *In Phys.*; De Cælo et Mundo, *In de Cæl.*; De Generatione et Corruptione, *In de Gen. et Corr.*; De Anima, *In de Anima*; Metaphysics, *In Meta.*; Nichomachean Ethics, *In Ethic.*; Politics, *In Pol.* Book, chapter, *lectio* as required, 1, also for

references to Dionysius, *De divinis Nominibus, In de Div. Nom.* References
to Aristotle include the Bekker numbering.

Quæstiones quodlibetæ,Quodl.

Complete titles are given for other works.

˙Where did the view of seeing prophecy
as interpretation come from if
med. and even fathers view prophecy
as knowledge.

˙Does Cal. betray both views?

˙Is there explicit discussion of the two ^ views?

˙Cal clings to idea: prophets as interpreters
of the law, where did get that?

˙Check Aquinas on / Cor. Does he say same?

˙Check Greek comm. Theophylact!! also
chrysostom

– Need to read Cassiodorus

˙How are the inspired penmen of scr. treated by
Calvin !??

INTRODUCTION

THE root principle of all that is treated in the following Questions is God's free gift, just as the root principle of all true mysticism is God's free gift. He intervenes in men's souls by redeeming and by granting the fruits of redemption, which are sanctification leading to eternal unity with him. In a progressively egalitarian society it becomes more difficult to realize that God favours some more than others, and that these differences are all to the glory of God and to the detriment of no man at all.

St Thomas, with all Catholic tradition, assumes that some men are more favoured by God. In particular these have received special 'charisms'— which is going to be our rendering of the rather tautological Latin of the medievals, i.e. *gratiæ gratis datæ*. He then proceeds to investigate these special graces from an intellectualist standpoint. In this he is a child of his age by giving speculative knowledge pride of place. For him the rôle of a prophet is a sublime act of knowledge, receiving from God truths above all human capacities and transmitting these to men. Modern scholars and theologians would stress that, for a Semite, knowing is an activity of the whole being; and that in the Bible hearing is more important than seeing.

Certainly if St Thomas were alive today, he would make the needful adaptations and embody the valid findings in Semitic studies. But it could be argued that he himself was aware of the limitations of prophecy as a bare communication of truth. Tongues, speech and miracles all have a part to play—yet that part is always the conveyance of truth in what might be called the more medieval sense. Another and earlier section of the *Summa* (1a2æ. 98–105, The Old Law, Vol. 29 of this series, together with its lead-in discussions to the New Law of the Gospel) corresponds more fully to the modern desire for straight Biblical Theology. In this section on Prophecy, we let St Thomas speak for himself in his own way.

POSTQUAM DICTUM EST de singulis virtutibus et vitiis, quæ pertinent ad omnium hominum conditiones et status, nunc considerandum est de his quæ specialiter ad aliquos homines pertinent.

Invenitur autem differentia inter homines secundum ea quæ ad habitus et actus animæ rationalis pertinent, tripliciter.

Uno quidem modo secundum diversas gratias gratis datas, quia, ut dicitur,[1] *divisiones gratiarum sunt: et alii datur per spiritum sermo sapienti, alii sermo scientiæ,* etc.

Alia vero differentia est secundum diversas vitas, activam scilicet et contemplativam, quæ accipitur secundum diversa operationum studia: unde et ibidem dicitur quod *divisiones operationum sunt.*[2] Aliud enim est studium operationis in Martha, quæ *sollicita erat, et laborabat circa frequens ministerium,* quod pertinet ad vitam activam; aliud autem est in Maria, quæ *sedens secus pedes Domini audiebat verbum illius,* quod pertinet ad contemplativam, ut habetur.[3]

Tertio modo, secundum diversitatem officiorum et statuum, prout dicitur,[4] *Et ipse dedit quosdam cuidem apostolos, quosdam autem prophetas, alios vero evangelistas, alios autem pastores et doctores,* quod pertinet ad diversa ministeria, de quibus dicitur, *Divisiones ministrationum sunt.*[5]

Est autem attendendum circa gratias gratis datas, de quibus occurrit consideratio prima, quod quædam earum pertinent ad cognitionem, quædam vero ad locutionem, quædam vero ad operationem. Omnia vero quæ ad cognitionem pertinent, sub *prophetia* comprehendi possunt. Nam prophetica revelatio se extendit non solum ad futuros hominum eventus, sed etiam ad res divinas, et quantum ad ea quæ proponuntur omnibus credenda, quæ pertinent ad *fidem* et quantum ad altiora mysteria, quæ sunt perfectorum, quæ pertinent ad *sapientiam.* Est etiam prophetica revelatio de his quæ pertinent ad spirituales substantias, a quibus vel ad bonum vel ad malum inducimur; quod pertinet ad discretionem spirituum. Extendit etiam se ad directionem humanorum actuum, quod pertinet ad scientiam, ut infra patebit.[6] Et ideo primo occurrit considerandum de prophetia et de raptu, qui est quidam prophetiæ gradus.

De prophetia autem quadruplex consideratio occurrit: quarum prima est de essentia ejus; secunda de causa ipsius; tertia de modo propheticæ cognitionis; quarta de divisione prophetiæ.

---

[1] *I Corinthians* 12, 4
[2] ibid 6
[3] *Luke* 10, 39

HAVING TREATED of particular virtues and vices which relate to all men generally in every condition and walk of life, we must now consider what relates to some only and specially.

Men differ in three ways as regards the lasting dispositions and activities of a rational being.

The first is by reason of charisms or gratuitous graces, because *there are diversities of graces, and to one is given through the Spirit a word of wisdom, to another a word of knowledge,* and so forth.[1]

A second arises from the difference between active and contemplative lives. This is gauged in terms of a differing bent of activity. So in the same text we read *there are varieties of working.*[2] One thing is the zeal for activity in Martha who was *anxious and troubled about many things,* which is characteristic of the active life, another is that of Mary *who sat at the Lord's feet and listened to his teaching,*[3] which is characteristic of the contemplative life.

A third arises from differences in offices and states; thus *his gifts were that some should be apostles, some prophets, some evangelists, some pastors and teachers.*[4] Such are the *varieties of service* of which St Paul speaks.[5]

Charisms or gratuitous graces are our present concern. Some of these relate to knowledge (171-5), others to speech (176-7), others again to action (179). All the gifts relating to knowledge can be listed under the heading of *prophecy.* Prophetic revelation not only ranges out to future happenings among men, but also to divine realities, both with respect to what is proposed for the belief of all, which constitutes *faith*; and also with respect to higher mysteries, an appanage of the perfect, and constituting *wisdom.* Prophetical revelation also deals with spiritual substances as inclining us to good or evil, and this constitutes *discernment of spirits.* Finally, prophetic revelation extends to the direction of human acts: here we have the gift of *knowledge,* as we shall see later.[6] So our first reflections will be about prophecy, and then about ecstasy, which is a kind of grade of prophecy (175).

Prophecy calls for four considerations, the nature of prophecy (171), its causality (172), the mode of prophetic knowledge (173), the divisions of prophecy (174).

---

[4]*Ephesians* 4, 11
[5]I *Corinthians* 12, 5
[6]2a2æ. 177, 1

Quæstio 171. de prophetia

Circa primum quæruntur sex:

1. utrum prophetia pertineat ad cognitionem;
2. utrum sit habitus;
3. utrum sit solum futurorum contingentium;
4. utrum propheta cognoscat omnia prophetabilia;
5. utrum propheta discernat ea quæ divinitus percipit, ab eis quæ proprio spiritu videt;
6. utrum prophetiæ possit subesse falsum.

articulus 1. *urum prophetia pertineat ad cognitionem*

AD PRIMUM sic proceditur:[1] 1. Videtur quod prophetia non pertineat ad cognitionem. Dicitur enim[2] quod *corpus Elisæi mortuum prophetavit;* et infra dicitur[3] de Joseph quod *ossa ipsius visitata sunt, et post mortem prophetaverunt.* Sed in corpore vel in ossibus post mortem non remanet aliqua cognitio. Ergo prophetia non pertinet ad cognitionem.

2. Præterea, dicitur,[4] *Qui prophetat, hominibus loquitur ad ædificationem.* Sed locutio est effectus cognitionis, non est autem ipsa cognitio. Ergo videtur quod prophetia non pertineat ad cognitionem.

3. Præterea, omnis cognoscitiva perfectio excludit stultitiam et insaniam. Sed hæc simul possunt esse cum prophetia; dicitur enim,[5] *Scitote, Israel, stultum prophetam et insanum.* Ergo prophetia non est cognoscitiva perfectio.

4. Præterea, sicut revelatio pertinet ad intellectum, ita inspiratio videtur pertinere ad affectum, eo quod importat motionem quamdam. Sed prophetia dicitur esse *inspiratio* vel *revelatio,* secundum Cassiodorum.[6] Ergo videtur quod prophetia non magis pertineat ad intellectum quam ad affectum.

SED CONTRA est quod dicitur,[7] *Qui enim Propheta dicitur hodie, olim vocabatur Videns.* Sed visio pertinet ad cognitionem. Ergo prophetia ad cognitionem pertinet.

RESPONSIO: Dicendum quod prophetia primo et principaliter consistit in cognitione, quia videlicet prophetæ cognoscunt ea quæ sunt procul et remota ab hominum cognitione. Unde possunt dici prophetæ a *pro,* quod est *procul, phanos,* quod est *apparitio,* quia scilicet eis aliqua quæ sunt

---

[1]cf 3a. 7, 8. *De veritate* XII, 1. *In Isaiam* 1. *In* 1 *Cor.* 14, *lect.* 1. *In Hebr.* 11, *lect.* 7
[2]*Ecclesiasticus* 48, 13

Question 171. the nature of prophecy

Here there are six points of inquiry:

1. is prophecy a matter of knowledge?
2. is it a steady disposition?
3. is it only concerned with future contingents?
4. does a prophet know all that can be prophetically conveyed?
5. can a prophet distinguish what is divinely revealed from what he grasps by his own mental capacity?
6. can error beset prophecy?

article 1. is prophecy a matter of knowledge?

THE FIRST POINT:[1] 1. Prophecy is apparently not a form of knowledge, for we read of Elisha, *when he was dead his body prophesied,*[2] and a little further on it is said of Joseph, *his bones were visited and they prophesied.*[3] But after death neither bones nor bodies are capable of knowledge.

2. St Paul says that *he who prophesies speaks to men for their upbuilding and encouragement and consolation.*[4] But speech is an effect of knowledge and not knowledge itself. Neither then is prophecy a form of knowledge.

3. All perfection of knowledge excludes foolishness and insanity. Yet foolishness and insanity are at times associated with prophecy: *Israel shall know it: the prophet is a fool, the man of spirit is mad.*[5] Thus prophecy is not a perfection in the order of knowledge.

4. Since revelation relates to the intelligence, inspiration would seem to relate to an affective impulse, for it implies some sort of motion. Now Cassiodorus tells us that prophecy is an *inspiration* or a *revelation.*[6] Thus prophecy no more belongs to the intelligence than to the will.

ON THE OTHER HAND I *Samuel*[7] tells us that he who *is now called a prophet was formerly called a seer.* Now vision is an act of knowledge; thus prophecy is of an intellectual order.

REPLY: Prophecy is firstly and principally a knowledge; prophets in fact know realities which are remote from the knowledge of men. Perhaps we can say that they are called prophets from *pro* for *procul*, far off, and *phanos*, appearance, because some realities which are far away appear

---

[3] ibid 49, 18   [4] I *Corinthians* 14, 3   [5] *Hosea* 9, 7
[6] *Expositio in Psalterium*, prol. PL 70, 12   [7] I *Samuel* 9, 9

procul apparent. Et propter hoc, ut Isidorus dicit,[8] *in veteri Testamento appellabantur Videntes, quia videbant ea quæ cæteri non videbant, et prospiciebant quæ in mysterio abscondita erant.* Unde et gentilitas eos appellabat *Vates a vi mentis,* ut ibidem præmittit.[9]

Sed quia, ut dicitur ad *Cor.,*[10] *Unicuique datur manifestatio spiritus ad utilitatem;* et infra, dicitur,[11] *Ad ædificationem Ecclesiæ quærite ut abundetis;* inde est quod prophetia secundario consistit in locutione, prout prophetæ ea quæ divinitus edocti cognoscunt, ad ædificationem aliorum annuntiant, secundum illud *Isa.,*[12]*Quæ audivi Domino exercituum, Deo Israel, annuntiavi vobis.* Et secundum hoc, ut Isidorus dicit,[13] possunt dici *Prophetæ,* quasi *Præfatores,* eo quod porro fantur, idest a remotis fantur, et de futuris vera prædicunt.

Ea autem quæ supra humanam cognitionem divinitus revelantur, non possunt confirmari ratione humana quam excedunt, sed operatione virtutis divinæ, secundum illud,[14] *Prædicaverunt ubique, Domino cooperante, et sermonem confirmante sequentibus signis.* Unde tertio ad prophetiam pertinet operatio miraculorum, quasi confirmatio quædam propheticæ enuntiationis. Unde dicitur,[15] *Non surrexit Propheta ulta in Israel sicut Moyses, quem nosset Dominus facie ad faciem in omnibus signis atque portentis.*

1. Ad primum ergo dicendum quod auctoritates illæ loquuntur de prophetia quantum ad hoc tertium, quod assumitur ut prophetiæ argumentum.

2. Ad secundum dicendum quod Apostolus ibi loquitur quantum ad propheticam enuntiationem.

3. Ad tertium dicendum quod illi qui dicuntur prophetæ insani et stulti non sunt veri prophetæ, sed falsi: de quibus dicitur,[16] *Nolite audire verba prophetarum, qui prophetant vobis, et decipiunt vos: visionem cordis sui loquuntur, non de ore Domini;* et,[17] *Hæc dicit Dominus, Væ prophetis insipientibus, qui sequuntur spiritum suum, et nihil vident.*

4. Ad quartum dicendum quod in prophetia requiritur quod intentio mentis elevetur ad percipienda divina. Unde dicitur,[18] *Fili hominis, sta super pedes tuos, el loquar tecum.* Hæc autem elevatio intentionis fit Spiritu Sancto movente: unde ibidem subditur, *Et ingressus est in me spiritus, et statuit me super pedex meos.*[19] Postquam autem intentio mentis elevata est ad superna, percipit divina: unde subditur ibidem, *Et audivi loquentem*

---

[8]*Etymologies* VII, 8. PL 82, 283   [9]ibid VIII, 7. PL 82, 308   [10]I *Corinthians* 12, 7
[11]ibid 14, 12   [12]*Isaiah* 21, 10   [13]loc cit note 9
[14]*Mark* 16, 20   [15]*Deuteronomy* 34, 10   [16]*Jeremiah* 23, 16
[17]*Ezekiel* 13, 3   [18]ibid 2, 1   [19]ibid 2, 2
[a]Quasi fore-speakers. St Thomas borrows his definition from Isidore of Seville, but is misled by his authority, and makes the word prophet *prophētēs* derive from a

close to them. That is why Isidore writes,[8] *In the Old Testament they were termed seers because they perceived what others could not perceive, and grasped what was shrouded in mystery.* In the pagan world prophets were called *diviners* because of *their power of mind.*[9]

But because 1 *Corinthians* says,[10] *To each is given the manifestation of the Spirit for the common good,* and,[11] *strive to excel for the building up of the Church,* it follows that prophecy secondarily consists of utterance or speech, in so far as the prophets know what they have been divinely taught, and they proclaim this knowledge for the edification of others; as is said in *Isaiah,*[12] *What I have heard from the Lord of hosts, the God of Israel, I announce to you.* In this way, as Isidore says, prophets can be termed *quasi fore-speakers,* since they proclaim what is remote, and speak truly of what is future.[13a]

Those truths which surpass all human knowledge and which are revealed from God cannot find confirmation in that human reasoning which they transcend, but only in the working of divine power, as is said,[14] *They went forth and preached everywhere while the Lord worked with them and confirmed the message by the signs that attended it.* We also read in *Deuteronomy,*[15] *And there has not arisen a prophet since in Israel like Moses whom the Lord knew face to face . . . for all the signs and wonders which the Lord sent him to do.*

Hence 1. The authorities cited refer to prophecy in the third sense just mentioned, which regards the proof of prophecy.

2. St Paul is referring here to the proclamation of the prophetic message.

3. Those who are called raving or mad prophets are not true prophets but false. Jeremiah speaks of them:[16] *Do not listen to the words of the prophets who prophesy to you, filling you with vain hopes: they speak of visions of their own minds, not from the mouth of the Lord.* And Ezekiel writes,[17] *Thus says the Lord, Woe to the foolish prophets who follow their own spirit and have seen nothing.*

4. In prophecy it is needed that the capacity of a mind should be raised to the point of perceiving divine truth, as is said,[18] *Son of man stand on your feet and I will speak with you.* This raising of a mind's capacity is brought about by a movement of the Holy Spirit: thus we read, *The Spirit entered into me and set me upon my feet.*[19] After the capacity of mind was raised to things above, he perceived divine truths, hence, *I heard him*

Greek *porro* which is impossible. The real derivation is from *pro* in place of, instead of, etc; and the rest of the word is not from *phainein* = appear, but from *phemi, phanai* = speak or say. The prophet is one who speaks on behalf of or for another. Etymologically there is no suggestion of futurity; and in fact a prophet does not necessarily predict the future. He is more often 'man of God' revealing God's very present will for the people of God.

7

ad me. Sic igitur ad prophetiam requiritur inspiratio quantum ad mentis elevationem, secundum illud,[20] *Inspiratio Omnipotentis dat intelligentiam;* revelatio autem quantum ad ipsam perceptionem divinorum, in quo perficitur prophetia, et per ipsam removetur obscuritatis et ignorantiæ velamen, secundum illud,[21] *Qui revelat profunda de tenebris.*

articulus 2. utrum prophetia sit habitus

AD SECUNDUM sic proceditur:[1] 1. Videtur quod prophetia sit habitus, quia, ut dicitur in *Ethic.*,[2] *tria sunt in anima, potentia, passio et habitus.*[a] Sed prophetia non est potentia, quia sic inesset omnibus hominibus, quibus potentiæ animæ sunt communes. Similiter etiam non est passio, quia passiones pertinent ad vim appetitivam, ut supra habitum est;[3] prophetia autem pertinet principaliter ad cognitionem, ut dictum est.[4] Ergo prophetia est habitus.

2. Præterea, omnis perfectio animæ quæ non semper est in actu est habitus. Sed prophetia est quædam animæ perfectio, non autem semper est in actu; alioquin non diceretur dormiens propheta. Ergo videtur quod prophetia sit habitus.

3. Præterea, prophetia computatur inter gratias gratis datas. Sed gratia est habituale quoddam in anima, ut supra habitum est.[5] Ergo prophetia est habitus.

SED CONTRA, *habitus est quo quis agit cum voluerit,* ut dicit Commentator.[6] Sed aliquis non potest uti prophetia, cum voluerit; sicut patet de Elisæo,[7] *quem cum Josaphat de futuris requireret, et prophetiæ spiritus ei deesset, psaltem fecit applicari, ut prophetiæ ad hunc spiritus per laudem psalmodiæ descenderet, alque ejus animum de venturis repleret,* ut Gregorius dicit.[8] Ergo prophetia non est habitus.

RESPONSIO: Dicendum quod, sicut Apostolus dicit,[9] *Omne quod manifestatur, lumen est,* quia videlicet sicut manifestatio corporalis visionis fit per lumen corporale, ita etiam manifestatio visionis intellectualis fit per

---

[20]*Job* 32, 8   [21]ibid 12, 22
[1]cf 1a2æ. 68, 3 ad 3; 2a2æ. 176, 2 ad 3. *De veritate* XII, 1. *CG* III, 154. *De potentia* VI, 4.*Quodl.* XII, 17, 1. *In* 1 *Cor.* 14, *lect.* 6
[2]*Ethics* II, 5. 1105b20   [3]1a2æ. 22, 2
[4]above art. 1   [5]1a2æ. 109, 6 & 9; 110, 2
[6]Commentary on *De Anima* 18   [7]II *Kings* 3, 15
[8]*On Ezekiel* I, 1. PL 76, 793   [9]*Ephesians* 5, 13
[a]'Steady disposition', a rendering of St Thomas's *habitus*, Aristotle's *hexis*, and for which there is no exact equivalent in English. *Habitus* is a lasting quality in an ability or power whereby this acts naturally, promptly, firmly and pleasurably.

speaking to me. And so prophecy calls for an inspiration that will raise a mind's capacities, as is said in *Job*,[20] *But it is the breath of the Almighty that makes him understand*; and prophecy calls for revelation as regards the actual perception of divine truths. This is a high point in prophecy, since revelation brings about the removal of the veils of ignorance and obscurity. It is God *who uncovers the deeps out of darkness, and brings deep darkness to light.*[21]

article 2. is prophecy a steady disposition?

THE SECOND POINT:[1] 1. It is suggested that prophecy is a steady disposition. Aristotle tells us[2] of three things in the soul, potency, emotion, and steady disposition.[a] But prophecy is not a potency, because if it were it would be in all men, for potencies of the soul are common to all. Nor is it emotion, because emotions relate to affective qualities, as we have seen.[3] But prophecy is primarily a matter of knowledge, as we have agreed.[4] Thus prophecy is a steady disposition.

2. All perfections of a soul which are not constantly actualized are steady dispositions. But prophecy is a sort of perfection of soul, and is not constantly actualized—otherwise we could never say that a prophet sleeps. So it seems that prophecy is a lasting disposition.

3. Prophecy is reckoned among the charisms, or gratuitous graces. But grace is something habitually in the soul.[5] So prophecy is a lasting disposition.

ON THE OTHER HAND, a steady disposition, *habitus*, is that by which a person acts when he wishes to, as Averroes says.[6] Now none can take to prophecy when he wills, as is clear from the story of Elisha;[7] as Gregory puts it,[8] *When Jehoshaphat inquired about future happenings, and the spirit of prophecy gave out in Elishah, Jehoshaphat caused a harp to be played, so that the spirit of prophecy might come down upon him and fill his mind with future realities.* Thus prophecy is not a lasting disposition.

REPLY: As St Paul says,[9] *When anything is exposed by the light it becomes visible, for anything which becomes is light,* because, for instance, just as material light makes for the manifestation of material vision, so too intellectual light makes for the manifestation of intellectual vision. Accordingly

---

He who has a *habitus* uses it when he wills and as he wills; thus if he knows something thoroughly well, he has knowledge of it 'producible at will'. He has in fact a habitus of that knowledge.

For a tractate on *habitus* cf 1a2æ. 49–54, Vol. 22 of this series.

lumen intellectuale. Oportet ergo quod manifestatio proportionetur lumini per quod fit, sicut effectus proportionatur suæ causæ.

Cum ergo prophetia pertineat ad cognitionem quæ supra naturalem rationem existit, ut dictum est,[10] consequens est quod ad prophetiam requiratur quoddam lumen intellectuale excedens lumen naturalis rationis. Unde *Mich.*,[11] *Cum sedero in tenebris, Dominus lux mea est.*

Lumen autem dupliciter alicui inesse potest: uno modo per modum formæ permanentis, sicut lumen corporale est in sole et in igne; alio modo per modum cujusdam passionis, sive impressionis transeuntis, sicut lumen est in aëre. Lumen autem propheticum non inest intellectui prophetæ per modum formæ permanentis; alias oporteret quod semper prophetæ adesset facultas prophetandi: quod patet esse falsum. Dicit enim Gregorius,[12] *Aliquando prophetiæ spiritus deest prophetis, nec semper eorum mentibus præsto est, quatenus cum hunc non habent, se hunc cognoscant ex dono habere, cum habent.* Unde Elisæus dixit de muliere Sunamite,[13] *Anima ejus in amaritudine est, et Dominus celavit a me, et non indicavit mihi.*

Et hujus ratio est, quia lumen intellectuale in aliquo existens per modum formæ permanentis et perfectæ perficit intellectum principaliter ad cognoscendum principium illorum quæ per illud lumen manifestantur; sicut per lumen intellectus agentis præcipue intellectus cognoscit prima principia omnium illorum quæ naturaliter cognoscuntur. Principium autem eorum quæ ad supernaturalem cognitionem pertinent, quæ per prophetiam manifestantur, est ipse Deus, qui per essentiam a prophetis non videtur; videtur autem a beatis in patria, in quibus hujusmodi lumen inest per modum cujusdam formæ permanentis et perfectæ, secundum illud,[14] *In lumine tuo videbimus lumen.*

Relinquitur ergo quod lumen propheticum insit animæ prophetæ per modum cujusdam passionis vel impressionis transeuntis; et hoc significatur *Exod.*,[15] *Cumque transibit gloria mea, ponam te in foramine petræ,* etc.; et *Reg.*, dicitur ad Eliam,[16] *Egredere, et sta in monte coram Domino; et ecce Dominus transit,* etc. Et inde est quod sicut aër semper indiget nova illuminatione ita etiam mens prophetæ semper indiget nova revelatione, sicut discipulus, qui nondum est adeptus principia artis, indiget ut de singulis instruatur. Unde et *Isa.* dicitur,[17] *Mane erigit mihi aurem, ut audiam quasi magistrum.* Et hoc etiam ipse modus loquendi prophetiam designat, secundum quod dicitur quod locutus est Dominus ad talem vel talem prophetam; aut quod factum est verbum Domini, sive manus Domini super eum.

---

[10]above art. I   [11]*Micah* 7, 8
[12]loc cit note 8. PL 76, 792

there must be a proportion between the light and what the light makes visible, as between a cause and its effect.

Now as prophecy pertains to a knowledge which surpasses natural reason,[10] it follows that prophecy calls for a certain light which surpasses the light of natural reason. Hence we read,[11] *When I sit in darkness the Lord will be a light to me.*

Light can inhere in a being in two ways, either by way of a permanent form, as material light is in the sun or in a fire, or by way of a kind of transient passion or impression, as light is in the air. Now prophetical light does not inhere in the mind of a prophet as a permanent form—for then the prophet would always have the faculty of prophesying, which is patently false. As Gregory says,[12] *Sometimes the spirit of prophecy fails the prophets, and is not at all times present to them. So much so that when they do not have the gift they are brought to acknowledge that it is a sheer gift when they do have it.* So too Elishah said of the Sunamite woman,[13] *She is in bitter distress and the Lord has hidden it from me and has not told me.*

The reason for this is that an intellectual light, inhering in someone as a permanent and perfect form, adds perfection to the intellect, chiefly leading it to know the principle of all the truths manifested by that light: just as by the light of active intellect the mind chiefly knows the first principles of all that is naturally knowable. But the principle of all that relates to supernatural knowledge and of all that is manifested by prophecy, is God himself, who in his essence cannot be known by the prophets. Yet God will be seen by the blessed in heaven, because in these the light inheres by way of a permanent and perfected form: *In thy light we shall see light.*[14]

It remains then that prophetical light inheres in the soul of a prophet by way of a transient passion or impression. This is shown in *Exodus*,[15] *While my glory passes by, I will put you in the cleft of a rock,* and in *Kings* we read,[16] *Go forth and stand upon the mount before the Lord, and behold the Lord passed by.* So too just as the atmosphere ever needs to be newly lighted up, so too the prophet's mind ever needs new revelation, just as a pupil who has not mastered the principles of his art needs instruction about each single point. *Isaiah* says,[17] *Morning by morning he awakens . . . he wakens my ear.* So too the very wording of Scripture is descriptive of prophecy, as when we read 'the Lord has spoken' to one or other prophet, or that the 'word of the Lord' was heard, or that 'the hand of the Lord was upon him'.

---

[13]II *Kings* 4, 27   [14]*Psalms* 35, 10
[15]*Exodus* 33, 22   [16]I *Kings* 19, 11
[17]*Isaiah* 50, 4

Habitus autem est forma permanens. Unde manifestum est quod prophetia, proprie loquendo, non est habitus.

1. Ad primum ergo dicendum quod illa divisio Philosophi non comprehendit absolute omnia quæ sunt in anima, sed ea quæ possunt esse principia moralium actuum: qui quandoque fiunt ex passione, quandoque autem ex habitu, quandoque autem ex potentia nuda, ut patet in his qui ex judicio rationis aliquid operantur, antequam habeant habitum.

Potest autem prophetia ad passionem reduci, si tamen nomen passionis pro qualibet receptione accipiatur, prout Philosophus dicit,[18] quod *intelligere pati quoddam est.* Sicut enim in cognitione naturali intellectus possibilis patitur ex lumine intellectus agentis, ita etiam in cognitione prophetica intellectus humanus patitur ex illustratione divini luminis.

2. Ad secundum dicendum quod, sicut in rebus corporalibus, abeunte passione, remanet quædam habilitas ad hoc quod iterum patiantur, sicut lignum semel inflammatum facilius iterum inflammatur, ita etiam in intellectu prophetæ, cessante actuali illustratione, remanet quædam habilitas ad hoc quod facilius iterato illustretur: sicut etiam mens semel ad devotionem excitata, facilius postmodum ad devotionem pristinam revocatur. Propter quod Augustinus dicit[19] esse necessarias crebras orationes, *ne concepta devotio totaliter extinguatur.*

Potest tamen dici quod aliquis dicitur propheta, etiam cessante actuali prophetica illustratione, ex deputatione divina, secundum illud *Jer.,*[20] *Et prophetam in gentibus dedi te.*

3. Ad tertium dicendum quod omne donum gratiæ hominem elevat ad aliquid quod est supra naturam humanam, quod quidem potest esse dupliciter. Uno modo quantum ad substantiam actus, sicut miracula facere, et cognoscere incerta et occulta divinæ sapientiæ, et ad hos actus non datur homini donum gratiæ habituale. Alio modo est aliquid supra naturam humanam quantum ad modum actus, non autem quantum ad substantiam ipsius; sicut diligere Deum et cognoscere eum in speculo creaturarum, et at hoc datur donum gratiæ habituale.

articulus 3. utrum prophetia sit solum futurorum contingentium

AD TERTIUM sic proceditur:[1] 1. Videtur quod prophetia sit solum futurorum contingentium. Dicit enim Cassiodorus[2] quod *prophetia est inspiratio vel revelatio divina, rerum eventus immobili veritate denuntians.* Sed eventus

---

[18]*De Anima* III, 4. 429a14
[19]*Epist.* 130. *Ad Probam* 9, PL 33, 501
[20]*Jeremiah* 1, 5

A steady disposition is an abiding form. So it is clear that prophecy, properly speaking, is not a lasting disposition.

Hence: 1. The division here given by Aristotle is not exhaustive; it does not simply include all that is found in the soul, but just those elements which can come to be principles of moral action. These moral actions can issue sometimes from passion, sometimes from lasting disposition, sometimes from mere potency, as is manifest in those who act from a judgment of reason before they have an ingrained habit.

Yet prophecy could be reduced to 'passion', provided this be taken in the sense of any kind of receptivity. As Aristotle says,[18] *Understanding is a kind of passivity.* For just as in natural knowledge mind as passivity is affected by the light of active mind, so too in prophetic knowledge the human mind is affected by the glow of divine light.

2. As in material creatures, when passion has ceased there remains a certain propensity to be again affected, e.g. when wood has once been lighted, it is the more easily made to flame up again. So in the mind of a prophet: when the divine light ceases, there still remains a certain propensity to be once again enlightened from above. So too a mind which has once been stirred to devotion can subsequently all the more easily be called back to its former devotion. That is why Augustine says[19] that frequent prayers are needful, lest a devotion once kindled in us be totally extinguished.

Yet it is possible, if God so disposes, for someone to be called a prophet, even when the actual prophetic enlightenment has ceased, as in *Jeremiah*,[20] *I appointed you as a prophet to the nations.*

3. Every gift of grace raises a man to something which is above human nature. This can be in two ways. One, as regards the substance of an act, e.g. working miracles or knowing secrets and mysteries of divine wisdom. To accomplish such, a man does not receive the gift of habitual grace. But as regards the mode of an act, and no longer its substance, e.g. loving God and knowing him in the mirror of his creatures: in this instance a habitual grace is given.

article 3. whether prophecy only relates to future contingents

THE THIRD POINT:[1] 1. It would seem that prophecy only relates to future contingents. Thus Cassiodorus says[2] *prophecy is a divine inspiration or revelation which proclaims the outcome of events with unspeakable truth.* But

---

[1]cf *De veritate* XII, 2. *In Isaiam* 1. *In Rom.* 12, lect. 2. *In Psalm.* 50. *CG* III, 159
[2]*Exposition on Psalms*, Prol. PL 70, 12

pertinet ad contingentia futura. Ergo de solis contingentibus futuris fit revelatio prophetica.

2. Præterea, gratia prophetiæ dividitur contra sapientiam et fidem, quæ sunt de divinis; et discretionem spirituum, quæ est de spiritibus creatis; et scientiam, quæ est de rebus humanis, ut patet ad *Cor*.[3] Habitus autem et actus distinguuntur secundum objecta, ut patet per ea quæ supra dicta sunt.[4] Ergo videtur quod de nullo pertinente ad aliquod horum sit prophetia. Relinquitur ergo quod sit solum de futuris contingentibus.

3. Præterea, diversitas objecti causat diversitatem speciei, ut ex supra dictis patet.[5] Si ergo prophetia quædam sit de futuris contingentibus, quædam autem de quibusdam aliis rebus, videtur sequi quod non sit eadem species prophetiæ.

SED CONTRA est quod Gregorius dicit[6] quod *prophetia quædam est de futuro; sicut id quod dicitur Isa.*,[7] '*Ecce virgo concipiet, et pariet filium;*' *quædam de præterito, sicut id quod diciturs Gen.*,[8] '*In principio creavit Deus cœlum et terram;*' *quædam de præsenti, sicut id quod dicitur* 1 ad *Cor.*,[9] '*Si omnes prophetent, intret autem quis infidelis . . . occulta cordis ejus manifesta fiunt.*' Non ergo est prophetia solum de contingentibus futuris.

RESPONSIO: Dicendum quod manifestatio quæ fit per aliquod lumen ad omnia illa se extendere potest quæ illi lumini subjiciuntur; sicut visio corporalis se extendit ad omnes colores, et cognitio naturalis animæ se extendit ad omnia illa quæ subduntur lumini intellectus agentis. Cognitio autem prophetica est per lumen divinum, quo possunt omnia cognosci, tam divina quam humana, tam spiritualia quam corporalia. Et ideo revelatio prophetica ad omnia hujusmodi se extendit; sicut de his quæ pertinent ad Dei excellentiam et angelorum, spirituum ministerio revelatio prophetica facta est; ut *Isa.*,[10] ubi dicitur, *Vidi Dominum sedentem super solium excelsum et elevatum.* Cujus etiam prophetia continet ea quæ pertinent ad corpora naturalia, secundum illud *Isa.*,[11] *Quis mensus est pugillo aquas?* etc. Continet etiam ea quæ ad mores hominum pertinent, secundum illud *Isa.*,[12] *Frange esurienti panem tuum*, etc. Continet etiam ea quæ pertinent ad futuros eventus, secundum illud *Isa.*,[13] *Venient tibi duo in die una subito sterilitas et viduitas.*

Considerandum tamen est quod, quia prophetia est de his quæ procul a nostra cognitione sunt, tanto aliqua magis ad prophetiam pertinent quanto longius ab humana cognitione existunt.

Horum autem est triplex gradus. Quorum unus est eorum quæ sunt procul a cognitione hujus hominis sive secundum sensum, sive secundum

---

[3]1 *Corinthians* 12, 8   [4]1a2æ. 18, 5; 54, 2   [5]loc cit

events are future contingents. So prophetic revelation only applies to future contingents.

2. From St Paul[3] it appears that the grace of *prophecy* is distinguished from *wisdom* and *faith* which relate to divine realities, from *discernment of spirits* which is concerned with created spirits, and from *knowledge*, which is concerned with human realities. Now lasting dispositions and acts are distinguished by their objects, as we have agreed.[4] It would seem that prophecy belongs to none of these objects: accordingly prophecy only relates to future contingents.

3. Diversity of objects establishes a diversity of species, as we have seen.[5] If one sort of prophecy relates to future contingents, and another sort to other realities, it follows that prophecy is not specifically one.

ON THE OTHER HAND Gregory says[6] that *prophecy can apply to the future— Behold a virgin shall conceive and bear a son;*[7] *to the past—In the beginning God created heaven and earth;*[8] *and finally to the present—If all prophesy and an unbeliever or outsider enters, the secrets of his heart are disclosed.*[9] Thus prophecy does not relate only to future contingents.

REPLY: Knowledge caused by an enlightening can relate to all that is revealed by such a light; thus corporeal vision extends to all colours, and knowledge which is natural to the soul extends to all that is subject to the light of an activating intellect. Now prophetic knowledge is brought about by a divine light which makes possible the knowledge of all realities, whether they be human or divine, spiritual or corporeal. And so prophetic revelation extends to all such realities. Thus by the ministry of spirits a prophetic revelation concerning the perfections of God and the angels was made; thus,[10] *I saw the Lord sitting upon a throne high and lifted up.* Isaiah's prophecy also refers to natural bodies: thus,[11] *Who has measured the waters in the hollow of his hand?*; and it refers to human conduct too, thus,[12] *Share your bread with the hungry*, etc; and finally also to future events, thus,[13] *These two things will come to you in a moment, in one day, the loss of children and widowhood.*

Yet we should consider that because prophecy relates to what is far from our range of knowledge, then the more a reality is distant from human knowledge, the more properly will that reality belong to prophecy.

There are three degrees of remoteness from human knowing. The first covers what is hidden from this or that individual, whether in sense or

---

[6]*On Ezekiel* I, I. PL 76, 786 [7]*Isaiah* 7, 14 [8]*Genesis* I, I
[9]I *Corinthians* 14, 24 [10]*Isaiah* 6, I [11]ibid 40, 12
[12]ibid 58, 7 [13]ibid 47, 9

intellectum, non autem a cognitione omnium hominum; sicut sensu cognoscit aliquis homo quæ sunt sibi præsentia secundum locum; quæ tamen alius humano sensu, utpote sibi absentia, non cognoscit. Et sic Elisæus prophetice cognovit quæ Giezi discipulus ejus in absentia fecerat, ut habetur *Reg.*;[14] et similiter cogitationes cordis unius alteri prophetice manifestantur, ut dicitur ad *Cor.*,[15] et per hunc modum etiam ea quæ unus scit demonstrative, alii possunt prophetice revelari.

Secundus autem gradus est eorum quæ excedunt universaliter cognitionem omnium hominum, non quia secundum se non sint cognoscibilia, sed propter defectum cognitionis humanæ; sicut mysterium Trinitatis, quod revelatum est per Seraphim dicentia: *Sanctus, Sanctus, Sanctus,* etc., ut habetur *Isa.*[16]

Ultimus autem gradus est eorum quæ sunt procul ab omnium hominum cognitione, quia in seipsis non sunt cognoscibilia; ut contingentia futura, quorum veritas non est determinata.

Et quia quod est universaliter et secundum se, potius est eo quod est particulariter et per aliud, ideo ad prophetiam propriissime pertinet revelatio eventuum futurorum: unde et nomen prophetiæ sumi videtur. Unde Gregorius dicit quod[17] *cum ideo prophetia dicta sit, quod futura prædicat, quando de præterito vel præsenti loquitur, rationem sui nominis amittit.*

1. Ad primum ergo dicendum quod prophetia ibi definitur secundum id quod proprie significatur nomine prophetiæ: et per hunc etiam modum prophetia dividitur contra alias gratias gratis datas.

2. Unde patet responsio ad secundum. Quamvis possit dici quod omnia quæ sub prophetia cadunt, conveniunt in hac ratione quod non sunt ab homine cognoscibilia nisi per revelationem divinam; ea vero quæ pertinent ad sapientiam et scientiam, et interpretationem sermonum, possunt naturali ratione ab homine cognosci; sed altiori modo manifestantur per illustrationem divini luminis. Fides autem etsi sit de invisibilibus homini, tamen ad ipsam non pertinet eorum cognitio quæ creduntur, sed quod homo per certitudinem assentiat his quæ sunt ab aliis cognita.

3. Ad tertium dicendum quod formale in cognitione prophetica est lumen divinum, a cujus unitate prophetia habet unitatem speciei, licet sint diversa, quæ per divinum lumen prophetice manifestantur.

articulus 4. utrum propheta per divinam inspirationem cognoscat
omnia quæ possunt prophetice cognosci

AD QUARTUM sic proceditur:[1] 1. Videtur quod propheta per divinam inspirationem* cognoscat omnia quæ possunt prophetice cognosci. Dicitur

---

*Piana: *revelationem,* revelation

intellect, yet is not hidden from men in general; just as a man knows by his senses what is adjacent to him in place while another person, with the same senses, fails to know because he is not adjacent. Thus Elishah knew prophetically what Giezi his disciple had done in his absence.[14] So too the thoughts of one person's heart can be manifested prophetically to another.[15] In this way too the knowledge which one has by demonstration can be revealed to us in prophecy.

The second degree is comprised of those truths which universally surpass the knowledge of all men, not because they are intrinsically unknowable, but because of a defect in human knowledge. An example of this is the mystery of the Trinity which was revealed by the Seraphim who cried, *Holy, Holy, Holy.*[16]

Third, and most remote of all, is that which surpasses the knowledge of all men, because the truths concerned are not knowable; such are future contingents whose truth is not determined.

Now because what is universal and self-caused surpasses what is particular and caused by another, so the revelation of future events most properly belongs to prophecy. From this no doubt derives the name 'prophecy'. Thus Gregory could write,[17] *Prophecy whose nature is to foretell the future, loses its full sense when it speaks of the present or the past.*

Hence: 1. Prophecy there is defined in terms of what is more properly signified by the name of prophecy. And in this way too, prophecy is divided from other charisms. This answers the second objection.

2. However all that comes under prophecy coincides in not being knowable by men except from divine revelation. Those truths which relate to *wisdom* and *knowledge* and *discernment of speeches* can be known by man by natural reasoning; but they are revealed at a higher level by the radiance of God's truth. Though *faith* is about what is invisible to man, yet it is not concerned with a knowledge of what is believed: faith's concern is about man's certain assent to truths which are known to others.

3. The formal element in prophetic knowledge is the divine light. It is from this light and its oneness that prophecy derives its own specific unity, despite the diversity of objects manifested to the prophet by that light.

article 4. does a prophet know all that can be prophetically conveyed?

THE FOURTH POINT:[1] 1. It would seem that a prophet, by divine inspiration, knows all that can be known through the medium of prophecy. Thus

---

[14] II *Kings* 5, 26
[16] *Isaiah* 6, 3
[15] I *Corinthians* 14, 25
[17] loc cit, note 6
[1] cf *De Veritate* XII, 1 ad 5, 6. *In Rom.* 14, lect. 3

enim,[2] *Non faciet Dominus Deus verbum, nisi revelaverit secretum suum ad servos suos prophetas.* Sed omnia quæ prophetice revelantur sunt verba divinitus facta. Nihil ergo eorum est quod non reveletur prophetæ.

2. Præterea, *Dei perfecta sunt opera,* ut dicitur *Deut.*[3] Sed prophetia est divina revelatio, ut dictum est art. præc. Ergo est perfecta; quod non esset nisi perfecte omnia prophetabilia prophetice revelarentur, quia *perfectum est cui nihil deest,* ut dicitur.[4] Ergo prophetæ omnia prophetabilia revelantur.

3. Præterea, lumen divinum, quod causat prophetiam, est potentius quam lumen naturalis rationis, ex quo causatur humana scientia. Sed homo qui habet aliquam scientiam, cognoscit omnia quæ ad illam scientiam pertinent; sicut grammaticus cognoscit omnia grammaticalia. Ergo videtur quod propheta cognoscit omnia prophetabilia.

SED CONTRA est quod Gregorius dicit,[5] quod *aliquando spiritus prophetiæ ex præsenti tangit animum prophetantis, et ex futuro nequaquam tangit; aliquando autem ex præsenti non tangit, et ex futuro tangit.* Non ergo propheta cognoscit omnia prophetabilia.

RESPONSIO: Dicendum quod diversa non est necesse esse simul, nisi propter aliquod unum, in quo connectuntur, et a quo dependent, sicut supra dictum est,[6] quod virtutes omnes necesse est esse simul propter prudentiam vel charitatem. Omnia autem quæ per aliquod principium cognoscuntur connectuntur in illo principio, et ab illo dependent. Et ideo qui cognoscit perfecte principium secundum totam ejus virtutem, simul cognoscit omnia quæ per illud principium cognoscuntur. Ignorato autem communi principio, vel communiter apprehenso, nulla necessitas est simul omnia cognoscendi; sed unumquoque eorum per se oportet manifestari; et per consequens aliqua eorum possunt cognosci, et alia non cognosci.

Principium autem eorum quæ divino lumine prophetice manifestantur, est ipsa veritas prima, quam prophetæ in seipsa non vident. Et ideo non oportet quod omnia prophetabilia cognoscant; sed quilibet eorum cognoscit ex eis aliqua secundum specialem revelationem hujus vel illius rei.

1. Ad primum ergo dicendum quod Dominus omnia quæ sunt necessaria ad instructionem fidelis populi, revelat prophetis; non tamen omnia omnibus, sed quædam uni, quædam alii.

2. Ad secundum dicendum quod prophetia est sicut quiddam

---

[2] *Amos* 3, 7   [3] *Deuteronomy* 32, 4
[4] *Physics* III, 6. 207a8

Amos,[2] *Surely the Lord does nothing without revealing his secret to his servants the prophets?* Now all truths revealed through prophecy are words of divine origin. Thus none of these truths fail to be revealed to a prophet.

2. *Deuteronomy* says that *the works of God are perfect.*[3] But prophecy is a 'divine revealing', as was said in the preceding article. Therefore it is perfect; and this would not be unless the whole of 'prophecy-matter' was revealed to a prophet, for what is perfect is lacking in nothing.[4] Therefore all possible matters of prophecy are revealed to a prophet.

3. That divine light which causes prophecy is more powerful than the light of natural reason which is the source of human knowledge. But he who is master of some knowledge knows all that relates to that knowledge: thus a grammarian knows all the principles of grammar. So it would seem that a prophet knows all possible matters of prophecy.

ON THE OTHER HAND Gregory says,[5] *Sometimes the spirit of prophecy touches the mind of the prophet about the present but not about the future, sometimes about the future and not about the present.* So a prophet does not know all the matter of prophecy.

REPLY: Diverse realities are not necessarily made one unless they all find their unity in one reality and are dependent upon it; as we have explained,[6] all virtues must co-exist by reason of prudence and charity. Now all that comes to be known through some principle finds its unity in that principle and depends on it. Thus one who knows a principle in all its effectiveness, knows at the same time all that is knowable through that principle. But when there is ignorance of the common principle, or the commonly-accepted principle, there is nothing to compel simultaneous knowledge of all realities: rather each must of itself be manifested to the knower. And so, some can be known and some cannot be known.

But the principle of those truths which by God's light are prophetically revealed is the very first Truth itself, whose inner being is hidden from the prophets. So it does not follow that they know all matters of prophecy; but each of them knows only some part of the reality, in accordance with a special revelation on some particular point.[a]

Hence: 1. God reveals to prophets all that is needed for the instruction of the believing people of God. Not that each prophet receives all, but some truths are revealed to one, and some to another.

2. Prophecy is as it were something imperfect in the genus of divine revelation; hence we read in *Corinthians, As for prophecies they will pass*

---

[5]*On Ezekiel* I, I. PL 76, 788   [6]1a2æ. 65, 1 & 2
[a]The mystery of God transcends all knowledge, even that of a prophet.

imperfectum in genere divinæ revelationis: unde dicitur[7] quod *prophetiæ evacuabuntur;* et quod *ex parte prophetamus,* id est, imperfecte. Perfectio autem divinæ revelationis erit in patria; unde subditur, *Cum venerit quod perfectum est, evacuabitur quod ex parte est.* Unde non oportet quod propheticæ revelationi nihil desit, sed quod nihil desit eorum ad quæ prophetia ordinatur.

3. Ad tertium dicendum quod ille qui habet aliquam scientiam, cognoscit principia illius scientiæ, ex quibus omnia quæ sunt illius scientiæ, dependent; et ideo qui perfecte habet habitum alicujus scientiæ, scit omnia quæ ad illam scientiam pertinent. Sed per prophetiam non cognoscitur in seipso principium prophetalium cognitionum, quod est Deus. Unde non est similis ratio.

articulus 5. utrum propheta discernat semper quid dicat per spiritum proprium, et quid per spiritum prophetiæ

AD QUINTUM sic proceditur:[1] 1. Videtur quod propheta discernat semper quid dicat per spiritum proprium, et quid per spiritum prophetiæ. Dicit enim Augustinus[2] quod *mater sua dicebat discernere se, nescio quo sapore, quem verbis explicare non poterat, quid interesset inter Deum revelantem et inter animam suam somniantem.* Sed prophetia est revelatio divina, ut dictum est.[3] Ergo propheta semper discernit id quod dicit per spiritum prophetiæ, ab eo quod loquitur spiritu proprio.

2. Præterea, *Deus* snon *præcipit aliquid impossibile,* sicut Hieronymus (Pelagius) dicit.[4] Præcipitur autem prophetis,[5] *Propheta qui habet somnium, narret somnium; et qui habet sermonem meum, loquatur sermonem meum vere.* Ergo propheta potest discernere quid habeat per spiritum prophetiæ ab eo quod aliter videt.

3. Præterea, major est certitudo quæ est per divinum lumen, quam quæ est per lumen rationis naturalis. Sed per lumen rationis naturalis ille qui habet scientiam pro certo scit se habere. Ergo ille qui habet prophetiam per lumen divinum, multo magis certus est se habere.

SED CONTRA est quod Gregorius dicit,[6] *Sciendum est quod aliquando prophetæ sancti, dum consuluntur, ex magno usu prophetandi quædam ex suo spiritu proferunt, et se hoc ex prophetiæ spiritu dicere suspicantur.*

RESPONSIO: Dicendum quod mens prophetæ dupliciter a Deo instruitur:

[7]I *Corinthians* 13, 8–10   [1]cf *CG* III, 154   [2]*Confessions* VI, 13. PL 32, 731
[3]above arts 1 & 3, objections 4 & 1 respectively
[4]Pelagius, *Libellus fidei ad Innocentium.* PL 45, 1718. For the ascription to Jerome, cf PL 30, 32

away, . . . *for our prophecy is imperfect*, and that we *prophesy in part*, that is, imperfectly. However, the perfection of divine revelation will be in heaven; hence St Paul adds, *When the perfect comes the imperfect will pass away*.[7] Hence it is not necessary that nothing should be lacking to prophetic revelation, but simply that nothing should be lacking in what constitutes prophecy's proper object.

3. He who is master of a science knows all the principles of that science: on these principles depend all else in that science. So he who is perfectly master of a science, knows all that relates to that science.[b] But by prophecy we have no intrinsic knowledge of the principles of all prophetic knowledge —which is God. So the comparison breaks down.

article 5. can a prophet always distinguish what he says by his own spirit from what he says by a spirit of prophecy?

THE FIFTH POINT:[1] 1. It seems that a prophet always distinguishes what he says by his own spirit and what by a spirit of prophecy. Augustine says[2] that his mother *used to say that she distinguished, by some mysterious sense, which could not be put into words, the difference between God revealing and the dreams of her own soul*. But prophecy is a divine revelation, as we have agreed.[3] Therefore prophecy always distinguishes between what it proclaims by the spirit of prophecy and what by its own spirit.

2. It is said, *God does not demand the impossible*.[4] Yet it is demanded of the prophets, *Let a prophet who has a dream, tell the dream, but let him who has my word speak my word faithfully*.[5] Thus a prophet can distinguish what he receives through a spirit of prophecy and what by other means.

3. Divine light is the cause of a certitude which is greater than that attained by the light of natural reason. But he who masters a science by the light of natural reason has certitude about his mastery. Therefore he who has prophecy by divine light is even more certain of having it.

ON THE OTHER HAND, Gregory writes,[6] *Sometimes holy prophets, in the frequent exercise of their prophetic ministry put forth, on being consulted, oracles which emanate from their own minds, while they imagine that they pronounce these in virtue of the spirit of prophecy.*

REPLY: The mind of a prophet is instructed by God in two ways: one is by

---

[5]*Jeremiah* 23, 28
[6]*On Ezekiel* I, I. PL 76, 793
[b]A confident attitude towards knowledge, characteristic of the medievals, but not now shared, partly because of the complexities of scientific and technical development.

uno modo per expressam revelationem; alio modo per quemdam instinctum occultissimum, *quem nescientes humanæ mentes patiuntur*, ut Augustinus dicit.[7]

De his ergo quæ expresse per spiritum prophetiæ propheta cognoscit, maximam certitudinem habet, et pro certo habet quod hæc sunt divinitus sibi revelata; unde dicitur,[8] *In veritate misit me Dominus ad vos, ut loquerer in aures vestras omnia verba hæc:* alioquin si de hoc ipse certitudinem non haberet, fides quæ dictis prophetarum innititur, certa non esset. Et signum propheticæ certitudinis accipere possumus ex hoc quod Abraham admonitus in prophetica visione, se præparavit ad filium unigenitum immolandum: quod nullatenus fecisset, nisi de divina revelatione fuisset certissimus.

Sed ad ea quæ cognoscit per instinctum, aliquando sic se habet ut non plene discernere possit, utrum hæc cogitaverit aliquo divino instinctu, vel per spiritum proprium. Non autem omnia quæ cognoscimus divino instinctu, sub certitudine prophetica nobis manifestantur: talis enim instinctus est quiddam imperfectum in genere prophetiæ. Et hoc modo intelligendum est verbum Gregorii. Ne tamen error ex hoc possit accidere, *per Spiritum Sanctum citius correcti, ab eo quæ vera sunt, audiunt; et semetipsos, quia falsa dixerint, reprehendunt*, ut ibidem Gregorius subdit.[9]

Primæ autem rationes procedunt quantum ad ea quæ prophetico spiritu revelantur.

Unde patet responsio ad omnia objecta.

articulus 6. utrum ea quæ prophetice cognoscuntur vel annuntiantur possint esse falsa

AD SEXTUM sic proceditur:[1] 1. Videtur quod ea quæ prophetice cognoscuntur vel annuntiantur, possint esse falsa. Prophetia enim est de futuris contingentibus: ut dictum est.[2] Sed futura contingentia possunt non evenire; alioquin ex necessitate contingerent. Ergo prophetiæ potest subesse falsum.

2. Præterea, Isaias prophetice prænuntiavit Ezechiæ dicens, *Dispone domui tuæ, quia morieris tu, et non vives;* et tamen additi sunt vitæ ejus postea quindecim anni, ut habetur *Reg.* et *Isa.*[3] Similiter et *Jer.*,[4] Dominus dicit, *Repente loquar adversum gentem et adversum regnum, ut eradicem, et destruam, et disperdam illud. Si pænitentiam egerit gens illa a malo suo quod locutus sum adversus eam, agam et ego pænitentiam super malo quod cogitavi ut facerem ei.* Et hoc apparet per exemplum Ninivitarum, secundum illud

---

[7] *Super Genesim ad litt.* II, 17. PL 34, 278
[8] *Jeremiah* 26, 15
[9] loc cit note 6

explicit revelation, the other, according to Augustine, is by a certain inward instinct *which human minds submit to sometimes even unknowingly.*

About what the prophet knows by a spirit of prophecy he has a maximum of certitude, and he is certain that these truths are divinely revealed to him. Hence *Jeremiah*,[8] *In truth the Lord sent me to you to speak all these words in your ears.* Otherwise if the prophet himself did not have certainty, that faith, which rests upon the utterances of the prophets, would not be certain. A sign of prophetic certitude is offered to us in the story of Abraham. He was admonished in prophetic vision, and prepared himself for the sacrifice of his only son; this he would never have done were he not absolutely certain about the divine revelation.[a]

But, for what a prophet knows by instinct, it sometimes happens that he cannot fully discern whether he thought this out by divine impulse or on his own. Not everything which we know by divine instinct is made clear to us by prophetic certitude; for such an instinct is sometimes imperfect in the way of prophecy. This is how we should understand the words of Gregory. To forestall any possible error because of this, he adds in the same passage, *The Holy Spirit speedily corrects the prophets, causing them to hear the truth, and they correct themselves for having made false utterances.*

The first objections relate to those truths which are revealed by a prophetic spirit.

The answer to all the objections is quite clear.

article 6. can realities known or announced prophetically be false?

THE SIXTH POINT:[1] 1. It seems that what is prophetically known or announced can be false. Prophecy relates to future contingents,[2] but future contingents can fail to come to be: otherwise they would necessarily come to be. Thus prophecy can be false.

2. Isaiah warned Hezekiah prophetically and announced to him, *Set your house in order for you are about to die*; and yet, subsequently, fifteen years were added to his life.[3] So too in *Jeremiah* the Lord says,[4] *If at any time I declare concerning a nation or kingdom, that I will pluck up and break down and destroy it, and if that nation concerning which I have spoken, turns from its evil, I will repent of the evil which I intended to do to it.* The example of the Ninevites gives a proof of this, *God repented of the evil which he had*

[1]cf 2a2æ. 172, 5 ad 3; 6 ad 2. *De veritate* XII, 10 ad 7. *CG* III, 154
[2]above art. 3
[3]II *Kings* 28, 6 & *Isaiah* 38, 65
[4]*Jeremiah* 18, 7–8
[a]*Genesis* 22.

Jonæ,[5] *Misertus est Dominus super malitiam quam dixit ut faceret eis, et non fecit.* Ergo prophetiæ potest subesse falsum.

3. Præterea, omnis conditionalis cujus antecedens est necessarium absolute, consequens est necessarium absolute, quia ita se habet consequens in conditionali ad antecedens, sicut conclusio ad præmissas in syllogismo. Ex necessariis autem nunquam contingit syllogizare nisi necessarium, ut probatur in I *Posterior*.[6] Sed si prophetiæ non potest subesse falsum, oportet hanc conditionalem esse veram, 'Si aliquid est prophetatum, erit.' Hujus autem conditionalis antecedens est necessarium absolute, cum sit de præterito. Ergo et consequens erit necessarium absolute, quod est inconveniens, quia sic prophetia non esset contingentium. Falsum est ergo quod prophetiæ non possit subesse falsum.

Sed contra est quod Cassiodorus dicit[7] quod *prophetia est inspiratio ve revelatio divina, rerum eventus immobili veritate denuntians.* Non autem esset immobilis veritas prophetiæ, si posset ei falsum subesse. Ergo non potest ei subesse falsum.

RESPONSIO: Dicendum quod, sicut ex dictis patet,[8] prophetia est quædam cognitio intellectui prophetæ impressa ex revelatione divina per modum cujusdam doctrinæ. Veritas autem cognitionis est eadem in discipulo et in docente, quia cognitio addiscentis est similitudo cognitionis docentis, sicut etiam in rebus naturalibus forma generati est similitudo quædam formæ generantis. Et per hunc etiam modum Hieronymus dicit quod *prophetia est quoddam signum divinæ præscientiæ.*[9] Oportet igitur eamdem esse veritatem propheticæ cognitionis et enuntiationis, quæ est cognitionis divinæ, cui impossibile est subesse falsum, ut in *Primo* dictum est,[10] Unde prophetiæ non potest subesse falsum.

1. Ad primum ergo dicendum quod sicut in *Primo* dictum est,[11] certitudo divinæ præscientiæ non excludit contingentiam singularium futurorum, quia fertur in ea secundum quod sunt præsentia et jam determinata ad unum. Et ideo etiam prophetia, quæ est divinæ præscientiæ similitudo impressa vel signum, sua immobili veritate futurorum contingentiam non excludit.

2. Ad secundum dicendum quod divina præscientia respicit futura secundum duo: scilicet secundum quod sunt in seipsis, inquantum scilicet ipsa præsentialiter intuetur; et secundum quod sunt in suis causis, inquantum scilicet videt ordinem causarum ad effectus. Et quamvis contingentia futura, prout sunt in seipsis, sint determinata ad unum, tamen,

---

[5]*Jonah* 3, 10
[7]*Exposition of the Psalter.* Prol. PL 70, 12

[6]*Posterior Analytics* I, 6. 75a4
[8]above art. 2

said he would do to them; and he did not do it.[5] Thus prophecy can be subject to error.

3. In every conditional proposition, if the antecedent is absolutely necessary, then the consequence is equally necessary. The consequence in such a proposition is related to the antecedent as premises to a conclusion in a syllogism. And Aristotle demonstrates[6] that from necessary premises there can never be anything but a necessary conclusion. Now if prophecy is never to be subject to error, the following conditional proposition must be true, 'If some event has been foretold, it will take place.' The antecedent of the proposition is absolutely necessary, as it relates to the past: the consequence will also be necessary. We cannot admit this, because prophecy would then no longer relate to contingents. So it is false that prophecy cannot be subject to error.

ON THE OTHER HAND: Cassiodorus tells us[7] that *prophecy is an inspiration or divine revelation which proclaims events with unchanging truth.* Now the truth of prophecy would not be unchanging if error could creep in. Thus prophecy cannot be subject to falsehood.

REPLY: As we saw above[8] prophecy is a knowledge which divine revelation engraves in the mind of a prophet, in the form of teaching. Now the truth of knowledge is the same in disciple as in master. The disciple's knowledge is, in effect, a reproduction of that in the master, just as in natural realities the form of an engendered creature is in some sense a likeness of the generator. That is why Jerome speaks of prophecy[9] as *a seal of the divine foreknowledge.* Thus the truth of prophetic knowledge and prophetic proclamation must needs be the same as that of divine knowledge. And falsity, as we have shown in the *Prima Pars*,[10] cannot creep into prophecy.

Hence: 1. As we have seen in the *Prima Pars*,[11] the certitude of divine foreknowledge does not do away with the contingency of particular events in the future: for the divine foreknowledge focuses on these contingents as being present and already determined in their outcome. So too then, prophecy, which is an imprint or seal of divine foreknowledge, by its unchangeable truth, does not exclude the contingency of future events.

2. Divine foreknowledge faces future events in two ways, in themselves in so far as it sees them in their presentiality, and in their cause, in so far as it considers the relationship of causes and their effects. Future contingents, considered in themselves, are already determined in their realization. But if we consider them in their causes, their determination is not

---

[9]*On Daniel*, 2, 10. PL 25, 521   [10]Ia. 16, 8   [11]Ia. 14, 13

prout sunt in suis causis, non sunt determinata, quin possint aliter evenire. Et quamvis ista duplex cognitio semper in intellectu divino conjungatur, non tamen conjungitur semper in revelatione prophetica, quia impressio agentis non semper adæquat ejus virtutem. Unde quandoque revelatio prophetica est impressa quædam similitudo divinæ præscientiæ, prout respicit ipsa futura contingentia in seipsis: et talia sic eveniunt, sicut prophetantur, sicut illud *Isa.*,[12] *Ecce virgo concipiet.* Quandoque vero prophetica revelatio est impressa similitudo divinæ præscientiæ, prout scilicet cognoscit ordinem causarum ad effectus: et tunc quandoque aliter evenit quam prophetetur; nec tamen prophetiæ subest falsum: nam sensus prophetiæ est quod inferiorum causarum dispositio sive naturalium, sive humanorum actuum, hoc habet ut talis effectus eveniat. Et secundum hoc intelligitur verbum *Isa.* dicentis,[13] *Morieris, et non vives;* idest dispositio corporis tui ad mortem ordinatur: et quod dicitur *Jonæ* 3,[14] *Adhuc quadraginta dies, et Ninive subvertetur;* idest hoc merita ejus exigunt ut subvertatur. Dicitur autem Deus pœnitere metaphorice, inquantum ad modum pœnitentis se habet, prout scilicet mutat sententiam, etsi non mutet consilium.

3. Ad tertium dicendum quod quia eadem est veritas prophetiæ et divinæ præscientiæ, ut dictum est.,[15] hoc modo illa conditionalis est vera, 'Si aliquid est prophetatum, erit,' sicut ista, 'Si aliquid est præscitum, erit.' In utraque enim antecedens est impossibile non esse. Unde et consequens est necessarium, non secundum quod est futurum respectu nostri, sed ut consideratur in suo præsenti, prout subditur præscientiæ divinæ, ut in *Primo* dictum est.[16]

---

[12]*Isaiah* 7, 14
[13]ibid 38, 1
[14]*Jonah* 3, 4

such that they cannot have another outcome. This twofold form of knowledge ever exists simultaneously in the divine mind, but we cannot say the same of prophetic revelation. The imprint made by an agent does not always equal its effectiveness. So it comes about that sometimes prophetic revelation is a kind of impress of divine revelation when it considers future contingents in themselves. Such contingents come to pass, as in *Isaiah*,[12] *Behold a virgin*. At other times, prophetic revelation only reproduces from divine foreknowledge a knowledge of the relations of cause to effect. Events in that case can come to pass in a way other than they have been foretold. Yet prophecy is not, because of that, subject to error; for the meaning of such a prophecy is that subordinate causes, whether in nature or in human acts, are so disposed that such and such an effect must come to be. In this way we need to understand Isaiah's prophecy, *You shall die and not live*,[13] i.e. the state of your soul disposes you for death; and this prophecy of Jonah,[14] *Yet forty days and Nineveh will be overthrown* means that Nineveh's sins call for her overthrow. That 'God repents' is a metaphor: God acts after the manner of one who repents, in so far as he changes his decree but does not modify his counsel.

3. The truth of prophecy is the same as that of divine foreknowledge, as we have just explained.[15] Consequently this conditional proposition, 'If some event has been foretold, it will take place,' remains true, just as 'If some event has been foreseen, it will take place.' In both these propositions, it is impossible for the antecedent not to be. The result is that the consequence is necessary: not indeed if we take it as future in relation to ourselves, but if we take it in its presential actualization, as subject to divine foreknowledge, as we have explained in the *Prima Pars*.[16]

---

[15]In corp.
[16]Ia. 14, 13 ad 2

Quæstio 172. de causa prophetiæ

Deinde considerandum est de causa prophetiæ. Circa hoc quæruntur sex:

1. utrum prophetia sit naturalis;
2. utrum sit a Deo, mediantibus angelis;
3. utrum ad prophetiam requiratur dispositio naturalis;
4. utrum requiratur bonitas morum;
5. utrum sit aliqua prophetia a dæmonibus;
6. utrum prophetæ dæmonum aliquando dicant verum.

articulus 1. *utrum prophetia possit esse naturalis*

AD PRIMUM sic proceditur:[1] 1. Videtur quod prophetia possit esse naturalis. Dicit enim Gregorius[2] quod *ipsa aliquando animarum vis sua subtilitate aliquid prævidet;* et Augustinus dicit[3] quod *animæ humanæ, secundum quod a sensibus corporis abstrahitur, competit futura prævidere.* Hoc autem pertinet ad prophetiam. Ergo anima naturaliter potest assequi prophetiam.

2. Præterea, cognitio animæ humanæ magis viget in vigilando quam in dormiendo. Sed in dormiendo quidam naturaliter prævident quædam futura, ut patet per Philosophum.[4] Ergo multo magis potest homo naturaliter futura præcognoscere.

3. Præterea, homo secundum suam naturam est perfectior animalibus brutis. Sed quædam animalia bruta habent præcognitionem futurorum ad se pertinentium, sicut formicæ præcognoscunt pluvias futuras, quod patet ex hoc quod ante pluviam incipiunt grana in foramen reponere; et similiter pisces præcognoscunt tempestates futuras, ut perpenditur ex eorum motu dum loca tempestuosa declinant. Ergo multo magis homines naturaliter, præcognoscere possunt futura ad se pertinentia, de quibus est prophetia. Est ergo prophetia a natura.

4. Præterea, *Prov.* dicitur,[5] *Cum prophetia defecerit, dissipabitur populus;* et sic patet quod prophetia est necessaria ad hominum conservationem. Sed natura non deficit in necessariis. Ergo videtur quod prophetia sit a natura.

SED CONTRA est quod dicitur,[6] *Non enim voluntate humana allata est aliquando prophetia; sed Spiritu Sancto inspirante locuti sunt sancti Dei homines.* Ergo prophetia non est a natura, sed ex dono Spiritus Sancti.

RESPONSIO: Dicendum quod, sicut supra dictum est,[7] prophetica præcognito potest esse du futuris dupliciter: uno modo secundum quod sunt.

---

[1]cf 1a. 86, 4. *CG* III, 154. *De veritate* XII, 3

Question 172. the cause of prophecy

Under this heading we may raise six points of inquiry:

1. is prophecy natural?
2. does it come from God through the medium of angels?
3. does prophecy call for natural dispositions?
4. does it call for good moral conduct?
5. is there a demonic prophecy?
6. do demonic prophets at times proclaim truth?

article 1. whether prophecy can be natural

THE FIRST POINT:[1] 1. Prophecy, it seems, can be natural. Gregory says that[2] *the soul at times possesses such subtlety that it is capable of foreseeing certain events*. Augustine[3] also says that the human soul when abstracted from bodily senses is capable of foreseeing the future. Such however is a rôle of prophecy. Therefore the soul can naturally arrive at prophecy.

2. The knowledge of a human soul is more effective when awake than when asleep. But some people when asleep naturally foresee certain future events, as Aristotle says.[4] All the more then can a man naturally have knowledge of future events.

3. Man is by nature more perfect than brute animals. But certain brute animals have a foreknowledge of future events relating to themselves: thus ants foresee the onset of rain by hoarding their grain in holes; fishes too foresee coming storms, as we gather from their movement to avoid bad weather. All the more then can men naturally foresee the future that interests them. But this is prophecy. Therefore prophecy is natural.

4. *Where there is no prophecy the people cast off restraint.*[5] Thus prophecy is necessary for the safe-keeping of the human race. Now nature does not fail in what is needful to itself. Therefore prophecy is something natural.

ON THE OTHER HAND Peter says,[6] *No prophecy ever came by the impulse of man, but men moved by the Holy Spirit spoke from God.* Prophecy then is not something natural, but proceeds from a giving of the Holy Spirit.

REPLY: As was said above,[7] there can be two sorts of prophetic knowledge

---

[2] *Dialogues* IV, 26. PL 77, 357
[3] *Super Genes. ad litt.* XII, 13. PL 34, 464
[4] *De divinatione per somnum* 2. 464a17
[5] *Proverbs* 29, 18
[6] II *Peter* I, 21
[7] 2a2æ. 171, 6 ad 2

in seipsis; alio modo secundum quod sunt in suis causis. Præcognoscere autem futura, secundum quod sunt in seipsis, est proprium divini intellectus, cujus æternitati sunt omnia præsentia, ut in *Primo* dictum est.[8] Et ideo talis præcognitio futurorum non potest esse a natura, sed solum ex revelatione divina.

Futura vero in suis causis possunt præcognosci naturali cognitione etiam ab homine; sicut medicus præcognoscit sanitatem, vel mortem futuram in aliquibus causis, quarum ordinem ad tales effectus experimento præcognovit.

Et talis cognitio futurorum potest intelligi esse in homine dupliciter a natura. Uno modo sic quod statim anima ex eo quod in seipsa habet, possit præcognoscere futura; et sic, sicut Augustinus dicit,[9] *quidam voluerunt animam humanam habere quamdam vim divinationis in seipsa.* Et hoc videtur esse secundum opinionem Platonis, qui posuit[10] quod animæ habent omnium rerum cognitionem per participationem idearum, sed ista cognitio obnubilatur in eis per conjunctionem corporis; in quibusdam tamen plus, in quibusdam vero minus, secundum corporis puritatem diversam. Et secundum hoc posset dici quod homines habentes animas non multum obtenebratas ex corporum unione, possunt talia futura præcognoscere secundum propriam scientiam. Contra hoc autem objicit Augustinus,[11] *Cur non semper possit vim divinationis habere anima, cum semper velit?*

Sed quia verius esse videtur quod anima ex sensibilibus cognitionem acquirat secundum sententiam Aristotelis, ut in *Primo* dictum est,[12] ideo melius est dicendum alio modo quod præcognitionem talium futurorum homines non habent, sed acquirere possunt per viam experimentalem, in qua juvantur per naturalem dispositionem, secundum quod in homine invenitur perfectio virtutis imaginativæ et claritas intelligentiæ.

Et tamen hæc præcognitio futurorum differt a prima, quæ habetur ex revelatione divina dupliciter: primo quidem, quia prima potest esse quorumque eventuum et infallibiliter; hæc autem præcognitio, quæ naturaliter haberi potest, est circa quosdam effectus, ad quos se potest extendere experientia humana. Secundo, quia prima prophetia est secundum immobilem veritatem; non autem secunda, sed potest ei subesse falsum.

Prima autem præcognitio proprie pertinet ad prophetiam, non secunda, quia, sicut supra dictum est,[13] prophetica cognitio est eorum quæ naturaliter* excedunt humanam cognitionem. Et ideo dicendum est quod

---

*Leonine: *universaliter*, universally
[8]1a. 14, 3; 57, 3; 86, 4

of future events, first knowing the events in themselves, secondly, knowing them in their causes. But to know future events in themselves is proper to the divine intelligence whose eternity is ever present to all things, as was proved in the *Prima Pars*.[8] And so a knowledge of the future of this sort cannot proceed from nature but only from divine revelation.

Yet future events in their causes are open to foreknowledge by natural apprehension, even by man: as a doctor can have foreknowledge of health or death to come in certain cases. This he has because he has experienced a relation of causes to their effects.

This knowledge of the future which a man has by reason of his nature can be taken in two ways. First, when a soul would be immediately capable of knowing the future by reason of an innate sense which is hers. Thus Augustine remarks,[9] *Some were wont to hold that the human soul itself had a power of divination.* This seemingly was an opinion of Plato;[10] according to him souls have a knowledge of all things by participation in ideas. But this knowledge is clouded because souls are united to a body, in varying degrees, according as their bodies are more or less pure. This hypothesis would allow one to say that men whose souls are not too tarnished because of conjunction with a body are capable, in virtue of their own knowledge, of knowing certain future events. But Augustine objects to this theory,[11] *Why cannot the soul always have this power of divination, seeing that it ever desires it?*

Secondly, and it remains more likely, the soul gains its knowledge from the senses: Aristotle teaches this as we saw in the *Prima Pars*.[12] Thus the opinion is preferable that men have no knowledge of such future events, but they can acquire it by way of experiment. They are then helped by their natural dispositions, according as their imaginative power is more perfect and their intelligence more lucid.

Nevertheless this knowledge of future events differs from that which derives from divine revelation in two ways. Knowledge from divine revelation can relate to any event whatever and is infallible: by contrast, naturally acquired knowledge only covers effects within the range of human experience. Supernatural prophecy possesses immutable truth; natural prophecy can be subject to error.

Supernatural knowledge rather than natural properly belongs to prophecy, because, as was stated above,[13] prophetic knowledge relates to what naturally surpasses human knowledge. So we must say that

---

[9]loc cit note 3
[10]cf *Phædo* 79C. *Republic* 508C
[11]loc cit note 3
[12]Ia. 84, 6
[13]2a2æ. 171, 3

prophetia simpliciter dicta non potest esse a natura, sed solum ex revelatione divina.

1. Ad primum ergo dicendum quod anima, quanto abstrahitur a corporalibus, aptior redditur ad percipiendum influxum spiritualium substantiarum, et etiam ad percipiendum subtiles motus, qui ex impressionibus naturalium causarum in imaginatione humana relinquuntur, a quibus percipiendis anima impeditur, cum fuerit circa sensibilia occupata. Et ideo Gregorius dicit,[14] quod *anima, quando appropinquat ad mortem, præcognoscit quædam futura subtilitate suæ naturæ*, prout scilicet percipit etiam modicas impressiones; aut etiam cognoscit futura revelatione angelica, non autem propria virtute, quia, ut Augustinus dicit,[15] *si hoc esset, tunc haberet, quandocumque vellet, in sua potestate futura præcognoscere*; quod patet esse falsum.

2. Ad secundum dicendum quod cognitio futurorum quæ fit in somniis, est aut ex revelatione spiritualium substantiarum, aut ex causa corporali, ut dictum est,[16] cum de divinationibus ageretur. Utrumque autem melius potest fieri in dormientibus quam in vigilantibus, quia anima vigilantis est occupata circa exteriora sensibilia: unde minus potest recipere subtiles impressiones vel spiritualium substantiarum, vel etiam causarum naturalium; quantum tamen ad perfectionem judicii, plus viget ratio in vigilando quam in dormiendo.

3. Ad tertium dicendum quod bruta etiam animalia non habent præcognitionem futurorum eventuum,* nisi secundum quod ex suis causis præcognoscuntur; ex quibus eorum phantasiæ moventur magis quam hominum, quia phantasiæ hominum, maxime in vigilando, disponuntur magis secundum rationem quam secundum impressionem naturalium causarum. Ratio autem facit in homine multo abundantius id quod in brutis facit impressio causarum naturalium; et adhuc magis adjuvat hominem divina gratia prophetias inspirans.

4. Ad quartum dicendum quod lumen propheticum se extendit etiam ad directiones humanorum actuum: et secundum hoc prophetia necessaria est ad populi gubernationem, et præcipue in ordine ad cultum divinum, ad quem natura non sufficit, sed requiritur gratia.

articulus 2. utrum prophetica revelatio fiat per angelos

AD SECUNDUM sic proceditur:[1] 1. Videtur quod prophetica revelatio non fiat per angelos. Dicitur enim *Sap.*[2] quod *sapientia Dei in animas sanctas*

---

*Leonine, *effectuum*, effects
[14]loc cit note 2
[15]loc cit note 3

prophecy, strictly so-called, cannot be from nature, but only from divine revelation.

Hence: 1. When a soul is abstracted from bodily realities it is more adapted to coming under the sway of spiritual substances; it is also more sensitive to those subtle impressions which natural causes leave upon the human imagination. The soul cannot receive any such impressions when it is taken up with sense objects. That is why Gregory says[14] that *a soul when death draws near foresees certain future happenings, thanks to the tenuousness of its own nature,* and it is sensitive to the very least of impressions, and it can even know the future by angelic revelation. Anyway, it is not by its own power, otherwise, as Augustine says,[15] it would be capable of predicting the future whenever it wanted to, which is manifestly false.

2. That foreknowledge of the future which comes in dreams is either from a revelation of spiritual beings or from a bodily cause, as we have explained when we treated of divinations.[16] These modes of knowledge are more active during sleep than when awake, for the soul of one who is awake is taken up with exterior tangible realities, and is accordingly less capable of sensing the delicate impressions made by spiritual beings or even by natural causes. Yet judgment is better disposed, because reason is more rigorous when awake than when asleep.

3. Animals do not foresee future events except in their causalities, thanks to their imagination. In this respect they surpass men. For a man's imagination, especially when awake, acts more in accord with reason than from the impress of natural causes. Now in man reason exercises an impression much fuller in consequence than natural causes do upon an animal. However, divine grace which inspires prophets is, for man, a still more effective means of help.

4. Light from prophecy extends also to the directing of human acts. In this sense prophecy is needed for the ruling of a people, and especially as regards the worship of God. For in this nature is insufficient, and grace indispensable.

article 2. is prophetic revelation mediated by angels?

THE SECOND POINT:[1] 1. It would seem that prophetic revelation is not mediated by angels. Wisdom *passes into holy souls and makes them friends of God and prophets.*[2] Thus it is immediately or without the mediation of

---

[14]2a2æ. 95, 6
[1]cf CG III, 154. *De veritate* XII, 8. *In Isaiam* 6. *In Matt.* 2
[2]*Wisdom* 7, 27

se transfert, et amicos Dei, et prophetas constituit. Sed amicos Dei constituit immediate. Ergo etiam prophetas facit immediate, non mediantibus angelis.

2. Præterea, prophetia ponitur inter gratias gratis datas. Sed gratiæ gratis datæ sunt a Spiritu Santo, secundum illud,[3] *Divisiones gratiarum sunt, idem autem Spiritus.* Non ergo prophetica revelatio fit angelo mediante.

3. Præterea, Cassiodorus dicit[4] quod *prophetia est divina revelatio.* Si autem fieret per angelos, diceretur angelica revelatio. Non ergo prophetia fit per angelos.

SED CONTRA est quod Dionysius dicit,[5] *Divinas visiones gloriosi patres nostri adepti sunt per medias cælestes virtutes.* Loquitur autem ibi de visionibus propheticis. Ergo revelatio prophetica fit angelis mediantibus.

RESPONSIO: Dicendum quod, sicut Apostolus dicit,[6] *quæ a Deo sunt, ordinata sunt.* Habet autem hoc divinitatis ordo, sicut Dionysius dicit,[7] ut infima per media disponat. Angeli autem medii sunt inter Deum et homines, utpote plus participantes de perfectione divinæ bonitatis quam homines. Et ideo illuminationes et revelationes divinæ a Deo ad homines per angelos deferuntur. Prophetica autem cognitio fit per illuminationem et revelationem divinam. Unde manifestum est quod fiat per angelos.

1. Ad primum ergo dicendum quod charitas, secundum quam fit homo amicus Dei, est perfectio voluntatis, in quam solus Deus imprimere potest; sed prophetia est perfectio intellectus, in quem etiam angelus potest imprimere, ut dictum est,[8] et ideo non est similis ratio de utroque.

2. Ad secundum dicendum quod gratiæ gratis datæ attribuuntur Spiritui Sancto, sicut primo principio; qui tamen operatur hujusmodi gratiam in hominibus mediante ministerio angelorum.

3. Ad tertium dicendum quod operatio instrumenti attribuitur principali agenti, in cujus virtute instrumentum agit. Et quia minister est sicut instrumentum, idcirco prophetica revelatio, quæ fit ministerio angelorum, dicitur esse divina.

articulus 3. utrum ad prophetiam requiratur dispositio naturalis

AD TERTIUM sic proceditur:[1] 1. Videtur quod ad prophetiam requiratur dispositio naturalis. Prophetia enim recipitur in propheta secundum dispositionem recipientis, quia super illud Amos,[2] *Dominus de Sion rugiet,*

---

[3]*1 Corinthians* 12, 4
[4]*Exposition on Psalms.* PL 70, 12

angels that men are made friends of God. So it must be the same with prophets.

2. Prophecy is listed among the charisms. Now these come from the Holy Spirit, as St Paul says,[3] *Now there are varieties of gifts but the same spirit.* So prophetic revelation is not through angelic mediation.

3. Cassiodorus tells us[4] that *prophecy is a divine revelation.* But were it accomplished through angels, it would be called an angelic revelation. Therefore it is not mediated through the angels.

ON THE OTHER HAND, Dionysius says,[5] *Divine visions reached our glorious fathers by means of the heavenly powers.* He is speaking there of prophetic visions. So prophetic revelation is mediated through angels.

REPLY: St Paul says,[6] *What comes from God is done in due order,* and it is a law of divine order, according to Dionysius, to govern lesser orders of beings by intermediaries.[7] But angels hold a middle position between God and men. They participate in fact more than men in the perfection of divine goodness. And this is why divine enlightenment and revelations proceed from God to men by means of angels. Moreover prophetic knowledge depends on the enlightenment that comes from divine revelations. It is thus manifest that angels are intermediaries of these.

Hence: 1. Charity which makes a man into a friend of God is a perfection of the will, upon which God alone can act. But prophecy is a perfection of the mind, upon which even an angel can act, as we have said.[8] So we have two different situations.

2. Charisms are attributed to the Holy Spirit, inasmuch as it is a first principle. Nevertheless the Holy Spirit distributes graces among men through the ministry and mediation of angels.

3. The operation of an instrument is attributed to the principal agent whose effectiveness causes the instrument's action. And because a minister is as it were an instrument, therefore prophetic revelation mediated through the angels is said to be divine.

article 3. does prophecy call for natural dispositions?

THE THIRD POINT:[1] 1. One might think that prophecy calls for natural dispositions. Prophecy is received in the prophet in accordance with the dispositions of the recipient. Thus Jerome, commenting on *Amos,*[2] *The*

---

[5]*De cælest. hier.* 4. PG 3, 181   [6]*Romans* 13, 1
[7]*De eccles. hier,* 5. PG 3, 508   [8]Ia. III, I
[1]cf *De veritate* XII, 4   [2]*Amos* 1, 2

dicit *Glossa* Hieronymi,[3] *Naturale est ut omnes qui volunt rem rei comparare, ex eis rebus sumant comparationes quas sunt experti, et in quibus sunt nutriti: verbi gratia, nautæ suos inimicos ventis, damnum naufragio comparant. Sic et Amos, qui fuit pastor pecorum, timorem Dei rugitui leonis assimilat.* Sed quod recipitur in aliquo secundum modum recipientis, requirit naturalem dispositionem. Ergo prophetia requirit naturalem dispositionem.

2. Præterea, speculatio prophetiæ est altior quam scientiæ acquisitæ. Sed indispositio naturalis impedit speculationem scientiæ acquisitæ; multi enim ex indispositione naturali pertingere non possunt ad scientiarum speculamina capienda. Multo ergo magis requiritur ad contemplationem propheticam.

3. Præterea, indispositio naturalis magis impedit aliquem quam impedimentum accidentale. Sed per aliquid accidentale superveniens impeditur speculatio prophetiæ. Dicit enim Hieronymus super *Matt.*[4] quod *tempore illo quo conjugales actus geruntur, præsentia Spiritus Sancti non dabitur, etiamsi propheta esse videatur qui officio generationis obsequitur.* Ergo multo magis indispositio naturalis impedit prophetiam: et sic videtur quod bona dispositio naturalis requiratur ad prophetiam.

SED CONTRA est quod Gregorius dicit,[5] *Implet,* scilicet Spiritus Sanctus *citharædum puerum, et psalmistam facit: implet pastorem armentarium sycomoros vellicantem, et prophetam facit.* Non ergo requiritur aliqua dispositio præcedens ad prophetiam, sed dependent ex sola voluntate Spiritus Sancti: de quo dicitur I ad *Cor.,*[6] *Hæc omnia operatur unus atque idem Spiritus, dividens singulis prout vult.*

RESPONSIO: Dicendum quod, sicut dictum est,[7] prophetia vere et simpliciter dicta est ex inspiratione divina; quæ autem est ex causa naturali non dicitur prophetia nisi secundum quid. Est autem considerandum quod sicut Deus, qui est causa universalis in agendo, non præexigit materiam nec aliquam materiæ dispositionem in corporalibus effectibus, sed simul potest et materiam et dispositionem et formam inducere, ita etiam in effectibus spiritualibus non præexigit aliquam dispositionem; sed potest simul cum effectu spirituali inducere dispositionem convenientem, qualis requiritur secundum ordinem naturæ. Et ulterius posset etiam simul per creationem producere ipsum subjectum, ut scilicet et animam in ipsa sui creatione disponeret ad prophetiam, et daret ei gratiam prophetalem.

1. Ad primum ergo dicendum quod indifferens est ad prophetiam

---

[3]*Glossa ordinaria.* Jerome PL 25, 1041
[4]Jerome, *Epist.* 22. PL 22, 409. cf Origen. PG 12, 610

Lord will roar from Sion, writes,[3] *It is natural that those who want to make comparisons should take their terms from the context of their own experiences or their own education, e.g. sailors compare their enemies to a contrary wind and their loss to a shipwreck. So Amos, who was a shepherd, likens the wrath of God to the roaring of a lion.* Now any receiving according to the mode of the recipient calls for a natural disposition, therefore prophecy does so too.

2. The considerations of prophecy are more lofty than those of acquired science. But a natural indisposition renders impossible speculating with an acquired science. Many indeed from a natural indisposition cannot arrive at a grasp of the speculative points of a science. All the more reason for having natural dispositions for prophetic contemplation.

3. Natural dispositions which are bad are much more of a hindrance than an accidental obstacle. Now prophetic contemplation is impeded by an accidental obstacle, as Jerome says on *Matthew,*[4] *During the time of conjugal acts the Holy Spirit is not given, even if it is apparently a prophet who is fulfilling the duty of procreation.* All the more so then does natural indisposition hinder prophecy. So it would seem that prophecy requires a good natural disposition.

ON THE OTHER HAND Gregory says,[5] *The Holy Ghost fills the harpist boy and makes him a psalmist; makes a shepherd of flocks and plucker of sycamore trees into a prophet.* So no antecedent disposition is required for prophecy. It depends wholly on the will of the Holy Spirit, of whom it is said,[6] *All these are inspired by one and the same Spirit, who apportions to each one individually as he wills.*

REPLY: As was said above,[7] prophecy, in the true and absolute sense of the word, comes of divine inspiration. A prophecy which derives from a natural cause is only called prophecy in a relative sense. We need to reflect that God who is universal cause in the order of action does not antecedently require, in corporeal effects, either matter or any material predisposition. God can immediately cause to be, all at once, matter, disposition and form. So too in spiritual effects God requires no pre-existing disposition, but can, all at once, bring about the spiritual effect, with a suitable disposition of the sort which would be demanded in the order of nature. Furthermore God could by creation, all at once, produce the subject himself, so that the soul in this person would be disposed towards prophecy in its creation and be given a prophet's grace.

Hence: 1. Whatever images are used to express the prophesied reality

---

[5]*In Evang.* 11, 30. PL 76, 1225   [6]*I Corinthians* 12, 11
[7]above art. 1

quibuscumque similitudinibus res prophetica exprimatur. Et ideo homo ex operatione divina non immutatur circa prophetam. Removetur autem divina virtute, si quid prophetiæ repugnat.

2. Ad secundum dicendum quod speculatio scientiæ fit ex causa naturali. Natura autem non potest operari nisi dispositione præcedente in materia: quod non est dicendum de Deo, qui est prophetiæ causa.

3. Ad tertium dicendum quod aliqua naturalis indispositio, si non removetur, impedire potest prophetalem revelationem, puta si aliquis esset totaliter sensu naturali destitutus; sicut etiam impeditur aliquis ab actu prophetandi per aliquam vehementem passionem, vel iræ, vel concupiscentiæ, qualis est in coitu, vel per quamcumque aliam passionem.

Sed talem indispositionem naturalem removet virtus divina, quæ est prophetiæ causa.

articulus 4. utrum bonitas morum requiratur ad prophetiam

AD QUARTUM sic proceditur:[1] 1. Videtur quod bonitas morum requiratur ad prophetiam. Dicitur enim *Sap.*[2] quoc *sapientia Dei per nationes* in animas sanctas se transfert, et amicos Dei et prophetas constituit.* Sed sanctitas non potest esse sine bonitate morum et sine gratia gratum faciente. Ergo prophetia non potest esse sine bonitate morum et gratia gratum faciente.

2. Præterea, secreta non revelantur nisi amicis, secundum illud,[3] *Vos autem dixi amicos, quia omnia quæcumque audivi a Patre meo, nota feci vobis.* Sed prophetis Deus sua secreta revelat, ut dicitur *Amos.*[4] Ergo videtur quod prophetæ sint Dei amici: quod non potest esse sine charitate. Ergo videtur quod prophetia non possit esse sine charitate, quæ non est sine gratia gratum faciente.

3. Præterea, *Matt.* dicitur,[5] *Attendite a falsis prophetis, qui veniunt ad vos in vestimentis ovium, intrinsecus autem sunt lupi rapaces.* Sed quicumque sunt sine gratia, interius videntur esse lupi rapaces. Ergo omnes sunt falsi prophetæ. Nullus est ergo verus propheta, nisi bonus per gratiam.

4. Præterea, Philosophus dicit[6] quod *si divinatio somniorum est a Deo, inconveniens est eam immitti quibuslibet, et non optimis viris.* Sed constat donum prophetiæ esse a Deo. Ergo donum prophetiæ non datur nisi optimis viris.

SED CONTRA est quod *Matt.*,[7] his qui dixerant, *Domine, nonne in nomine tuo prophetavimus?* respondetur, *Nunquam novi vos. Novit* autem *Dominus*

---

*Piana: *per rationes*, through reasons.
[1]cf *De veritate* XII, 5. *In Joan.* 11, *lect.* 7

is a matter of indifference to prophecy. This aspect of the prophet's task is not altered by the divine operation. The divine power makes away with anything repugnant to prophecy.

2. Reflections on a science spring from a natural cause. But nature cannot act unless there is some antecedent disposition in the matter. But this cannot be said of God who is the cause of prophecy.

3. Some natural indispositions, if not removed, could hinder prophetic revelation, e.g. if one were totally destitute of natural perception. So too one can be impeded from actively prophesying by some vehement passion, whether of wrath, or of concupiscence, as in the marriage act, or in any other violent passions.

But the divine power, the cause of prophecy, remedies all such unhelpful dispositions.

article 4. does prophecy call for goodness of life?

THE FOURTH POINT:[1] 1. Goodness of life is seemingly needed for prophecy. Thus we read[2] that the Wisdom of God *in every generation passes into holy souls and makes them friends of God and prophets.* But holiness cannot exist without goodness of life and sanctifying grace. Therefore prophecy cannot exist without goodness of life and sanctifying grace.

2. Secrets are only made known to friends; *I call you my friends, for all that I have learnt of my father, I have made known to you.*[3] Now God *reveals secrets to the prophets.*[4] Therefore prophets are friends of God. This cannot be without charity, and in turn supposes sanctifying grace.

3. *Beware of false prophets who come to you in sheep's clothing, but inwardly are ravening wolves.*[5] But all who are without grace inwardly are like ravening wolves. Therefore are they all false prophets. So no one is a genuine prophet unless he is good by grace.

4. Aristotle says,[6] *If the divining of dreams is from God, it is unfitting that it should be bestowed on any except the good.* But the gift of prophecy is from God. Thus the gift of prophecy can only be attributed to the best of men.

ON THE OTHER HAND, to those who had said, *Have we not prophesied in the name of the Lord?*, our Lord answers, *I have never known you.*[7] St Paul tells

---

[2] *Wisdom* 7, 27
[3] *John* 15, 15
[4] *Amos* 3, 7
[5] *Matthew* 7, 15
[6] *De divinat.* 1. 462b20
[7] *Matthew* 7, 22–3

eos qui sunt ejus, ut dicitur ad *Tim.*[8] Ergo prophetia potest esse in his qui non sunt Dei per gratiam.

RESPONSIO: Dicendum quod bonitas morum potest attendi secundum duo: uno quidem modo secundum interiorem ejus radicem, quæ est gratia gratum faciens; alio autem modo quantum ad interiores animæ passiones et exteriores actiones. Gratia autem gratum faciens ad hoc principaliter datur, ut anima hominis Deo per charitatem conjungatur. Unde Augustinus dicit,[9] *Nisi impertiatur cuique Spiritus Sanctus, ut eum Dei et proximi faciat amatorem, ille a sinistra non transfertur ad dexteram.*

Unde quidquid potest esse sine charitate, potest esse sine gratia gratum faciente, et per consequens sine bonitate morum.

Prophetia autem potest esse sine charitate; quod apparet ex duobus. Primo quidem ex actu utriusque; nam prophetia pertinet ad intellectum, cujus actus præcedit actum voluntatis, quam perficit charitas: unde Apostolus[10] prophetiam connumerat aliis ad intellectum pertinentibus, quæ possunt sine charitate haberi. Secundo ex fine utriusque: datur enim prophetia ad utilitatem Ecclesiæ, sicut et aliæ gratiæ gratis datæ, secundum illud Apostoli,[11] *Unicuique datur manifestatio spiritus ad utilitatem.* Non autem ordinatur directe ad hoc quod affectus ipsius prophetæ conjungatur Deo, ad quod ordinatur charitas. Et ideo prophetia potest esse sine bonitate morum quantum ad propriam radicem hujus bonitatis.

Si vero consideremus bonitatem morum secundum passiones animæ et actiones exteriores, secundum hoc impeditur aliquis a prophetia per morum malitiam. Nam ad prophetiam requiritur maxima mentis elevatio ad spiritualium contemplationem; quæ quidem impeditur per vehementiam passionum, et per inordinatam occupationem rerum exteriorum. Unde et de filiis prophetarum legitur[12] quod *simul habitabant cum Eliseo*, quasi solitariam vitam ducentes, ne mundanis occupationibus impedirentur a dono prophetiæ.

1. Ad primum ergo dicendum quod donum prophetiæ aliquando datur homini et propter utilitatem aliorum, et propter propriæ mentis illustrationem: et hi sunt in quorum animas sapientia divina per gratiam gratum facientem se transferens, amicos Dei et prophetas eos constituit. Quidam vero consequuntur donum prophetiæ solum ad utilitatem aliorum, qui sunt quasi instrumenta divinæ operationis. Unde Hieronymus dicit[13] super *Matt.*, in illud, *Nonne in nomine tuo prophetavimus?*, *Prophetare, et virtutes facere, et dæmonia ejicere, interdum non est meriti ejus qui operatur,*

---

[8]II *Timothy* 2, 19
[9]*De Trin.* xv, 18. PL 42, 1082
[10]I *Corinthians* 13, 1

Timothy,[8] *The Lord knows who are his*. So prophecy can exist in those who do not belong to God by grace.

REPLY: Goodness of conduct can be envisaged in two ways. First, in respect of its inward root which is sanctifying grace; and secondly in respect of the inward stresses of the soul and outward actions. Sanctifying grace is principally given so that a man's soul may be conjoined to God by charity. Hence the words of Augustine,[9] *Unless the Holy Spirit is imparted to each one to make him a lover of God and neighbour, such a man cannot be transferred from left hand to right hand.*

Now all that can exist without charity can be without sanctifying grace, and consequently without goodness of conduct.

Prophecy can be without charity. This is apparent in two ways. Let us argue first from their acts: prophecy is a matter of intellect whose act precedes that of the will which is perfected by charity. Hence St Paul lists prophecy among other intellectual qualities which can exist without charity.[10] Secondly we can argue from the final purpose or ends. Prophecy, as other charisms, is granted for the utility of the Church: *To each is given a manifestation of the Spirit for the common good.*[11] It is not ordered directly so that the prophet's will can be united to God, which is the purpose of charity. That is why prophecy can exist without goodness of conduct, if we bear in mind the first root of all good conduct which is sanctifying grace.

If however we consider goodness of conduct with respect to a soul's stresses and external actions, then moral wickedness can be an obstacle to prophecy. For prophecy calls for a supreme elevation of mind to contemplative and spiritual realities. This is indeed impaired by vehemence of the passions and by inordinate occupation with external affairs. So we read[12] that *the sons of the prophets* lived together with Elishah—living as it were a solitary life lest they should be impeded in the gift of prophecy by worldly occupations.

Hence: 1. The gift of prophecy is granted to a man both for the utility of others and for the enlightenment of his own mind. The latter are they into whose souls divine Wisdom by sanctifying grace 'betakes herself and makes them into friends of God and prophets'. On the other hand there are some who receive the gift of prophecy solely for the benefit of others: they are thus instruments of divine operation. Thus St Jerome writes,[13] *To prophesy, or to work miracles, and to cast out devils, is at times not due to the merits of the one who so acts. But an invocation of the name of Christ*

---

[11]op cit 12, 7
[12]II *Kings* 4, 38
[13]*On Matthew* 7, 27. PL 26, 50

sed vel invocatione nominis Christi hoc agit, vel ob condemnationem eorum qui invocant, et utilitatem eorum qui vident et audiunt, conceditur.

2. Ad secundum dicendum quod Gregorius exponens illud dicit,[14] *Dum audita superna cælestia amamus, amata jam novimus, quia amor ipse notitia est. Omnis ergo eis nota fecerat, quia a terrenis desideriis immutati amoris summi facibus ardebant.* Et hoc modo non revelantur semper secreta divina prophetis.

3. Ad tertium dicendum quod non omnes mali sunt lupi rapaces, sed solum illi qui intendunt aliis nocere. Dicit enim Chrysostomus[15] (alius auctor) quod catholici doctores, etsi fuerint peccatores, *servi quidem carnis dicuntur, non tamen lupi rapaces, quia non habent propositum perdere Christianos.* Et quia prophetia ordinatur ad utilitatem aliorum, manifestum est tales esse falsos prophetas, quia ad hoc non mittuntur a Deo.

4. Ad quartum dicendum quod dona divina non semper dantur optimis simpliciter, sed quandoque illis qui sunt optimi quantum ad talis doni perceptionem. Et sic Deus donum prophetiæ illis dat quibus optimum judicat dare.

articulus 5. utrum aliqua prophetia sit a dæmonibus

AD QUINTUM sic proceditur:[1] 1. Videtur quod nulla prophetia sit a dæmonibus. *Prophetia* enim *est divina revelatio*, ut Cassiodorus dicit.[2] Sed illud quod fit a dæmone non est divinum. Ergo nulla prophetia potest esse a dæmone.

2. Præterea, ad propheticam cognitionem requiritur aliqua illuminatio, ut supra dictum est.[3] Sed dæmones non illuminant intellectum humanum, ut supra dictum est.[4] Ergo nulla prophetia potest esse a dæmonibus.

3. Præterea, non est efficax signum quod etiam ad contraria se habet. Sed prophetia est signum confirmationis fidei: unde super illud *Rom.*,[5] *Sive prophetiam secundum rationem fidei,* dicit Glossa: *Nota quod in numeratione gratiarum a prophetia incipit, quæ est prima probatio, quod fides nostra sit rationabilis, quia credentes accepto Spiritu prophetabant.*[6] Non ergo, prophetia a dæmonibus dari potest.

SED CONTRA est quod dicitur *Reg.*,[7] *Congrega ad me universum Israel in monte Carmeli, et prophetas Baal quadringentos quinquaginta, prophetasque lucorum quadringentos, qui comedunt de mensa Jezabel.* Sed tales erant dæmonum cultores. Ergo vigetur quod etiam a dæmonibus sit aliqua prophetia.

---

[14]*In Evang.* II, 27. PL 76, 1207   [15]Pseudo-Chrysostom. PG 56, 738
[1]cf *CG* III, 154. *In Isaiam* 3   [2]*Expos. in Psalt. Prol.* PL 70, 12

produces the result; or else the gift is for the refutation of those who invoke the name, or again for the benefit of those who see and hear these wonders.

2. Gregory comments[14] on the text from *John: While we love heavenly secrets which are revealed to us, we already know these lovable secrets; for love itself is a sort of knowing. Jesus made all things known to his disciples; because, freed from earthly desires, they burned with the fire of supreme love.* In this sense divine secrets are not always revealed to prophets.

3. Wicked people are not all ravening wolves, but only those who seek to do harm to others. Thus a work ascribed to Chrysostom[15] says that *Catholic doctors, even if sinners, are called slaves of the flesh, but not ravening wolves, because they have no intention of causing the ruin of Christians.* And because prophecy is ordained to the benefit of others, prophets who cause the ruin of others are false prophets; because they have never been sent by God for this purpose.

4. Divine gifts are not always given to the best absolutely speaking, but sometimes to those who are best as regards receiving this or that gift. Thus it is that God confers prophecy upon those he judges best to give it to.

article 5. can prophecy come from demons?

THE FIRST POINT:[1] 1. It seems that no prophecy can come from demons. *Prophecy* is *divine revelation*, as Cassiodorus says.[2] Anything caused by a demon is not divine. Thus no prophecy comes from a demon.

2. Prophetic knowledge calls for some sort of enlightenment, as we have agreed.[3] Also that demons do not enlighten the human mind.[4] So no prophecy is from demons.

3. No sign is effective if it proves contradictories. But prophecy is a sign of faith confirmed. Hence we read in *Romans*[5] of prophecy *in proportion to our faith.*[6] The *Gloss* comments, *Note that the enumeration of graces begins with prophecies, the first of the proofs that our faith is reasonably founded, because those believers who had received the spirit prophesied.* Prophecy then cannot come from demons.

ON THE OTHER HAND there is the text in *Kings,*[7] *Gather all Israel to me at Mount Carmel and the four hundred and fifty prophets of Baal, and the four hundred prophets of Asherah who eat at Jezabel's table.* Now the cult of these people was one of demons. So we must conclude that some prophecy comes from demons.

---

[3]2a2æ. 171, 2 & 3
[5]*Romans* 12, 6
[7]I *Kings* 18, 19
[4]Ia. 109, 3
[6]*Glossa ordinaria.* Ambrosiaster PL 17, 165

RESPONSIO: Dicendum quod, sicut supra dictum est,[8] prophetia importat fognitionem quamdam procul existentem a cognitione humana. Manicestum est autem quod intellectus superioris ordinis aliqua cognoscere potest quæ sunt remota a cognitione intellectus inferioris. Supra intellectum autem humanum est non solum intellectus divinus, sed etiam intellectus angelorum bonorum et malorum secundum naturæ ordinem. Et ideo quædam cognoscunt dæmones etiam sua naturali cognitione, quæ sunt remota ab hominum cognitione, quæ possunt hominibus revelare. Simpliciter autem et maxime remota sunt quæ solus Deus cognoscit.

Et ideo prophetia proprie et simpliciter dicta fit per solam divinam revelationem; sed ipsa revelatio facta per dæmones potest secundum quid dici prophetia. Unde illi quibus aliquid per dæmones revelatur non dicuntur in scripturis prophetæ simpliciter, sed cum aliqua additione puta prophetæ falsi, vel prophetæ idolorum. Unde Augustinus,[9] *Cum malus spiritus arripit hominem in hæc,* scilicet visa, *aut dæmoniacos facit, aut arreptitios, aut falsos prophetas.*

1. Ad primum ergo dicendum quod Cassiodorus ibi definit prophetiam proprie et simpliciter dictam.

2. Ad secundum dicendum quod dæmones ea quæ sciunt hominibus manifestant, non quidem per illuminationem intellectus, sed per aliquam imaginariam visionem, aut etiam sensibiliter colloquendo: et in hoc deficit hæc prophetia a vera.

3. Ad tertium dicendum quod aliquibus signis etiam exterioribus discerni potest prophetia dæmonum a prophetia divina. Unde dicit Chrysostomus (alius auctor)[10] quod *quidam prophetant in spiritu diaboli, quales sunt divinatores, sed sic discernuntur; quoniam diabolus interdum falsa dicit, Spiritus Sanctus nunquam.* Unde dicitur *Deut.,*[11] *Si tacita cogitatione responderis, Quomodo possum intelligere verbum quod Dominus non est locutus? hoc habebis signum: Quod in nomine Domini propheta ille prædixerit, et non evenerit, hoc Dominus non est locutus.*

articulus 6. ultrum prophetæ dæmonum aliquando prædicant verum

AD SEXTUM sic proceditur:[1] 1. Videtur quod prophetæ dæmonum nunquam vera prædicant. Dicit enim Ambrosius sup. illud *Cor., Nemo potest dicere verum,*[2] quod *omne verum, a quocumque dicatur, a Spiritu Sancto est.*[3] Sed prophetæ dæmonum non loquuntur a Spiritu Sancto, quia *non est conventio Christi ad Belial.*[4] Ergo videtur quod tales nunquam vera prænuntiant.

---

[8]2a2æ. 171, 1
[9]*Super Gen. ad litt.* XII. 19. PL 34, 470
[10]Pseudo-Chrysostom on *Matthew* 7, 22. PG 56, 742

REPLY: As we have said,[8] prophecy implies a knowledge of realities which transcend human knowledge. Now it is obvious that a higher intelligence can know that which is hidden from a lower intelligence. Above human intelligence we have not only the divine mind but also, in nature's ordering, the intelligences of good and bad angels. So demons, in virtue of their natural capacity, can know certain things which are hidden from the natural knowledge of men, and they can reveal these to men. But that which is simply and absolutely above us, God alone knows that. That is why prophecy strictly so called can only stem from divine revelation. Nevertheless even a revelation made by demons can in a sense be called prophecy. Hence in Scripture, those who receive a revelation from demons are not simply called prophets, but are always qualified as false prophets or prophets of idols. Hence Augustine writes,[9] *When an evil spirit seizes on men in visions, it produces demoniacs or possessed people or false prophets.*

Hence: 1. Cassiodorus is here defining prophecy in its absolute and proper sense.

2. Demons manifest to men what they know, not by enlightening their intelligences, but by giving them imaginative vision, or even by addressing them in terms of sense impressions. In this way, this type of prophecy falls short of true prophecy.

3. Certain signs, even external signs, make possible the discernment of true prophecy from false. So it is said,[10] *Some prophesy in the spirit of the devil, and these are diviners: but we can distinguish these, because at times the devil proclaims something untrue, the Holy Spirit never.* Hence the words of Deuteronomy,[11] *And if you should say in your heart, How may we know if the Lord has spoken?—when a prophet speaks in the name of the Lord, if this word does not come to pass or come true, that is a word which the Lord has not spoken.*

article 6. do demons at times prophesy truths?

THE FIRST POINT:[1] 1. They can never do so. On 1 *Corinthians*[2] Ambrose writes,[3] *All truths, no matter who utters them, are from the Holy Spirit.* Now demonic prophets do not speak through the Holy Spirit, for what *accord is there between Christ and Belial?*[4] So it seems that demons of this sort never proclaim truth.

---

[11]*Deuteronomy* 18, 21–2
[1]cf 2a2æ. 174, 5 ad 4. *CG* III, 154
[2]1 *Corinthians* 12, 3
[3]Ambrosiaster. PL 17, 258
[4]II *Corinthians* 6, 15

2. Præterea, sicut veri prophetæ inspirantur a Spiritu veritatis, ita prophetæ dæmonum inspirantur a spiritu mendacii, secundum illud *Reg.*,[5] *Egrediar, et ero spiritus mendax in ore omnium prophetarum ejus.* Sed prophetæ inspirati a Spiritu Sancto nunquam loquuntur falsum, ut supra habitum est.[6] Ergo prophetæ dæmonum nunquam loquuntur verum.

3. Præterea, dicitur[7] de diabolo quod *cum loquitur mendacium, ex propriis loquitur: quia diabolus est mendax et pater ejus,* idest mendacii. Sed inspirando prophetas suos, diabolus non loquitur nisi ex propriis: non enim constituitur minister Dei ad veritatem enuntiandam, quia *non est societas luci ad tenebras,* ut dicitur.[8] Ergo prophetæ dæmonum nunquam vera prædicunt.

SED CONTRA est quod *Numss.* 22[9] dicit quædam glossa[10] quod *Balaam divinus erat, dæmonum scilicet ministerio, et arte magica nonnunquam futura prænoscens.* Sed ipse multa prænuntiavit vera, sicut est id quod habetur *Numss.,*[11] *Orietur stella ex Jacob, et consurget virga de Israel.* Ergo etiam prophetæ dæmonum prænuntiant vera.

RESPONSIO: Dicendum quod sicut se habet bonum in rebus, ita verum in cognitione. Impossibile est autem inveniri aliquid in rebus quod totaliter bono privetur. Unde etiam impossibile est esse aliquam cognitionem quæ totaliter sit falsa, absque admixtione alicujus veritatis. Unde et Beda dicit[12] quod *nulla falsa est doctrina, quæ non aliquando aliqua vera falsis intermisceat.* Unde et ipsa doctrina dæmonum, qua suos prophetas instruunt, aliqua vera continet, per quæ receptibilis redditur. Sic enim intellectus ad falsum deducitur per apparentiam veritatis, sicut voluntas ad malum per apparentiam bonitatis. Unde et Chrysostomus (alius auctor) dicit super *Matt.,*[13] *Concessum est diabolo interdum vera dicere, ut mendacium suum rara veritate commendet.*

1. Ad primum ergo dicendum quod prophetæ dæmonum non semper loquuntur ex dæmonum revelatione, sed interdum inspiratione divina; sicut manifeste legitur de Balaam, cui dicitur Dominus esse locutus *Num.*[14] licet esset propheta dæmonum, quia Deus utitur etiam malis ad utilitatem bonorum. Unde et per prophetas dæmonum aliqua vera prænuntiat: tum ut credibilior fiat veritas, quæ etiam ex adversariis testimonium habet, tum

---

[5]I *Kings* 22, 22
[6]above art. 5 ad 3. 2a2æ. 171, 6
[7]*John* 8, 44
[8]II *Corinthians* 6, 14
[9]*Numbers* 22, 20
[10]*Rabanus Maurus.* PL 108, 729

2. If true prophets are inspired by a spirit of truth then demonic prophets are inspired by a spirit of falsehood, as is said in *Kings*,[5] *I will go forth and I will be a lying spirit in the mouth of all his prophets.* Now we know that prophets inspired by the Holy Spirit never teach what is erroneous.[6] Thus demonic prophets never proclaim what is true.

3. The Gospel says of the devil,[7] *When he lies he speaks according to his nature, for he is a liar and a father of lies.* Thus when the devil inspires his prophets, he only speaks according to his nature; he is not in fact constituted a minister of God to proclaim truth, because as St Paul says,[8] *There is no fellowship between light and darkness.* And so demonic prophets never prophesy anything true.

ON THE OTHER HAND we can cite *Numbers* 22,[9] on which a gloss[10] says, *Balaam was a diviner: by the ministration of demons and magical art he sometimes knew the future.* Now he truly predicted many truths, as we read in *Numbers*,[11] *A star shall come forth out of Jacob, and a sceptre shall rise out of Israel.* Thus demonic prophets can foretell some truths.

REPLY: Goodness has the same relation to realities as truth has to knowledge. Now it is impossible to find in creatures anything which is wholly destitute of all good. So too it is impossible for some knowledge to be wholly false to the exclusion of every particle of truth. Hence Bede says,[12] *There is no false doctrine which does not at times mingle truth with falsehood.* Hence this very teaching of demons, in the instruction of their own prophets, contains some elements of truth, and this makes the teaching acceptable. The mind indeed is led to falsity by an appearance of truth—as the will is inclined to evil by a specious good. Hence Chrysostom, or another, says,[13] *It is granted to the devil at times to proclaim the truth, so that his mendacities may be commended by small touches of truth.*

Hence: 1. Demonic prophets do not always speak from a demonic revelation, but sometimes by divine inspiration, as is clearly stated of Balaam, to whom it is said the Lord spoke,[14] although he was a prophet of demons. Because God uses even the wicked for the benefit of the good. So through demonic prophets he foretells certain truths. Partly so that truth should appear yet more credible because finding support even from adversaries. Partly because when men believe such sources, they are led yet

---

[11]*Numbers* 24, 17
[12]*On Luke* 17, 12. PL 92, 542. cf Augustine PL 35, 1354
[13]Pseudo-Chrysostom, on *Luke* 7, 22. PG 56, 742
[14]*Numbers* 22, 8

etiam quia cum homines *talibus* credunt per eorum dicta magis ad veritatem inducuntur. Unde etiam Sibyllæ multa vera prædixerunt de Christo.

Sed etiam quando prophetæ dæmonum a dæmonibus instruuntur, aliqua vera prædicunt: quandoque quidem virtute propriæ naturæ, cujus auctor est Spiritus Sanctus; quandoque etiam revelatione bonorum spirituum, ut patet per Augustinum.[15] Et sic etiam illud verum quod dæmones enuntiant, a Spiritu Sancto est.

2. Ad secundum dicendum quod verus propheta semper inspiratur a Spiritu veritatis, in quo nihil est falsitatis, et ideo nunquam dicit falsum; propheta autem falsitatis non semper instruitur a spiritu falsitatis, sed quandoque etiam inspiratur a spiritu veritatis. Ipse etiam spiritus falsitatis quandoque enuntiat vera, quandoque falsa, ut dictum est.[16]

3. Ad tertium dicendum quod propria dæmonum dicuntur esse illa quæ habent a seipsis, scilicet mendacia et peccata; quæ autem pertinent ad propriam naturam, non habent a seipsis, sed a Deo. Per virtutem autem propriæ naturæ quandoque vera prænuntiant, ut dictum est.[17] Utitur etiam eis Deus ad veritatis manifestationem per ipsos fiendam dum divina mysteria eis per angelos revelantur, ut dictum est ibid.

---

[15] *Super Gen. ad litt.* XII, 19. PL 34, 470
[16] In corp. & ad 1   [17] ad 1
a Sibyl was the name given in antiquity to a whole series of prophetesses, sisters or daughters or priestesses of Apollo. The Sibylline Oracles were a collection of writings which existed long before the Christian era. Oracles of the inspired Sibyl could make known the will of the gods and show men what to do in grave situations. Prophetesses of this type, under various names, were celebrated from Babylonia to Italy. The Cumæan Sibyl played an important part in Roman history, and figures prominently in Vergil's *Aeneid* Book VI as conductor of the poet into the realm of the shades.

Meanwhile a sibylline collection was devised in Egypt by the Jews for further towards truth. So too the Sibyl predicted much that was true of Christ.[a]

Moreover when demonic prophets receive their revelation from the very demons, even then can they at times foretell what is true: sometimes in virtue of their own nature whose author is the Holy Spirit himself; sometimes also from a revelation of good spirits, as Augustine says.[15] Thus even that truth which demons proclaim is from the Holy Spirit.

2. A true prophet is always inspired by the spirit of truth in whom there is no trace of falsehood, and so he never utters untruths. But a prophet of falsehood is not always instructed by a spirit of falsehood, but at times also by the spirit of truth. The spirit of falsehood itself at times proclaims truths, at others falsehood, as we have said above.[16]

3. Proper to demons is what they derive from themselves, namely lies and sins. But what relates to their own proper nature is not from themselves but from God. In virtue of their own proper nature they sometimes foretell what is true, as we have said.[17] God also uses them to bring about the manifestation of truth through them, while divine mysteries are revealed to them by the angels as noted in the same place.

---

their own purposes: pagan oracles were re-shaped to introduce monotheism and Mosaic ordinances. After the Jews, Christians carried on in much the same way but of course introduced the theme of Christ. It is thought that the process went on to the 6th century AD. Some fifteen books were composed, twelve are extant; the second book speaks of Christ as Judge to come, the third book has much about Moses and the Law and Messianic times, the eighth book has an acrostically written passage spelling out Jesus Christ Son of God Saviour Cross. Such passages struck the imagination of the medieval world including St Thomas and Thomas of Celano.

Solvet sæclum in favilla
teste David cum Sibylla.

Quæstio 173. de modo propheticæ cognitionis

Deinde considerandum est de modo propheticæ cognitionis: et circa hoc quæruntur quatuor:

1. utrum prophetæ videant ipsam Dei essentiam;
2. utrum revelatio prophetica fiat per influentiam aliquarum specierum, vel per solam influentiam luminis;
3. utrum prophetica revelatio semper sit cum alienatione a sensibus;
4. utrum prophetia semper sit cum cognitione eorum quæ prophetantur.

articulus 1. *utrum prophetæ videant ipsam Dei essentiam*

AD PRIMUM sic proceditur:[1] 1. Videtur quod prophetæ ipsam Dei essentiam videant. Quia super illud *Isa.*,[2] *Dispone domui tuæ*, etc., dicit *Glossa*,[3] *Prophetæ in ipso libro præscientiæ Dei, in quo omnia scripta sunt, legere possunt.* Sed præscientia Dei est ipsa ejus essentia. Ergo prophetæ vident ipsam Dei essentiam.

2. Præterea, Augustinus dicit[4] quod *in illa æterna veritate, ex qua temporalia facta sunt omnia, formam secundum quam sumus, et secundum quam operamur visu mentis aspicimus.* Sed prophetæ inter omnes homines altissimam habent divinorum cognitionem. Ergo ipso maxime divinam essentiam vident.

3. Præterea, futura contingentia præcognoscuntur a prophetis secundum immobilem veritatem. Sic autem non sunt nisi in ipso Deo. Ergo prophetæ ipsum Deum vident.

SED CONTRA est quod visio divinæ essentiæ non evacuatur in patria. Prophetia autem evacuatur, ut habetur 1 ad *Cor.*[5] Ergo prophetia non fit per visionem divinæ essentiæ.

RESPONSIO: Dicendum quod prophetia importat cognitionem divinam ut procul existentem. Unde et de prophetis dicitur *Heb.*[6] quod *erant a longe aspicientes.* Illi autem qui sunt in patria, in statu beatitudinis existentes non vident ut a remotis, sed magis quasi ex propinquo, secundum illud *Psalm.*,[7]

---

[1]cf *De veritate* XII, 6. *In Isaiam* 1 & 6
[2]*Isaiah* 38, 1
[3]*Glossa ordinaria*
[4]*De Trin.* IX, 7. PL 42, 967

Question 173. the manner of prophetic knowledge

Now we need to consider the manner of prophetic knowledge. Four points of inquiry come to mind:

1. do prophets see God's very essence?
2. does prophetic revelation come about by an infusion of some species or simply by an influx of light?
3. does prophetic revelation always suppose alienation from the senses?
4. is prophecy always accompanied by a knowledge of what is being prophesied?

article 1. do prophets see God's very essence?

THE FIRST POINT:[1] 1. On the text, *Set your house in order,*[2] the *Gloss* says,[3] *Prophets are able to read into the very book of God's foreknowledge in which all is written.* But God's foreknowledge is God's very essence.

2. Augustine writes,[4] *It is in this eternal truth, source of all that is made in time, that we see with our mind's sight the form of our being and of our action.* Now of all men prophets are those who have the highest knowledge of divine realities. So they, above all others, must see the divine essence.

3. Future contingents are known beforehand by prophets in terms of unchanging truth. Such only exist in the divine essence. Therefore prophets see the very essence of God.

ON THE OTHER HAND, vision of the divine essence is unceasing in heaven. But 1 *Corinthians*[5] tells us that *prophecies will disappear.* So prophecy does not connote vision of the divine essence.[a]

REPLY: Prophecy implies a divine knowledge which is, as it were, far from us: hence *Hebrews*[6] says that the prophets *had seen . . . from afar.* But those who are in heaven, in the state of beatitude, do not see as 'from afar', but as it were near at hand, as the psalm says,[7] *The upright shall dwell in thy presence.* So it is clear that prophetic knowledge is not that perfect knowledge which will be in heaven but distinguished from it, as the imperfect is

---

[5]*1 Corinthians* 13, 8
[6]*Hebrews* 11, 13
[7]*Psalms* 139, 14
[a]For this discussion see 1a. 12. Vol. 3 of this series. ed. H. McCabe. Introduction (1–17) by T. Gilby.

Habitabunt recti cum vultu tuo. Unde manifestum est quod cognitio prophetica alia est a cognitione perfecta, quæ erit in patria: unde et distinguitur ab ea sicut imperfectum a perfecto, et ea adveniente evacuatur, ut patet per Apostolum.[8]

Fuerunt autem quidam qui cognitionem propheticam a cognitione beatorum distinguere volentes, dixerunt quod prophetæ vident ipsam divinam essentiam, quam vocant *speculum æternitatis*,* non tamen secundum quod est objectum beatorum, sed secundum quod sunt in ea rationes futurorum eventuum: quod quidem est omnino impossibile. Deus enim est objectum beatitudinis secundum ipsam sui essentiam, secundum illud quod Augustinus dicit,[9] *Beatus est qui te scit, etiam si illas,* idest creaturas, *nesciat.* Non est autem possibile quod aliquis videat rationes creaturarum in ipsa divina essentia, ita quod eam non videat, tum quia ipsa divina essentia est ratio omnium eorum quæ fiunt—ratio autem idealis non addit supra divinam essentiam nisi respectum ad creaturam—tum etiam quia prius est cognoscere aliquid in se, quod est cognoscere Deum, ut est objectum beatitudinis, quam cognoscere illud per comparationem ad alterum, quod est cognoscere Deum secundum rationes rerum in ipso existentes. Et ideo non potest esse quod prophetæ videant Deum secundum rationes creaturarum, et non prout est objectum beatitudinis. Et ideo dicendum est quod visio prophetica non est visio ipsius divinæ essentiæ, neque in ipsa divina essentia vident ea quæ vident, sed in quibusdam similitudinibus, secundum illustrationem divini luminis.

Unde Dionysius dicit,[10] de visionibus propheticis loquens, quod *sapiens theologus visionem illam dicit esse divinam, quæ fit per similitudinem rerum forma corporali carentium ex reductione videntium in divina.* Et hujusmodi similitudines divino lumine illustratæ magis habent rationem speculi quam Dei essentia: nam in speculo resultant species ab aliis rebus; quod non potest dici de Deo. Sed hujusmodi illustratio mentis propheticæ potest dici speculum, inquantum resultat ibi similitudo veritatis divinæ præscientiæ, et propter hoc dicitur *speculum æternitatis*, quasi repræsentans Dei præscientiam, qui in sua æternitate omnia præsentialiter videt, ut dictum est.[11]

1. Ad primum ergo dicendum quod prophetæ dicuntur inspicere in libro præscientiæ Dei, inquantum ex ipsa præscientia Dei resultat veritas in mentem prophetæ.

2. Ad secundum dicendum quod in prima veritate dicitur homo videre propriam formam, qua existit, inquantum primæ veritatis similitudo refulget in mente humana, ex qua anima habet quod seipsam cognoscat.

3. Ad tertium dicendum quod ex hoc ipso quod in Deo futura contingentia sunt secundum immobilem veritatem, potest imprimere menti

---

*Piana, *speculum Trinitatis*, mirror of the Trinity

from the perfect; and, as St Paul says,[8] *when the perfect comes the imperfect will pass away.*

There were some[b] however who, wishing to distinguish prophetic knowledge from that of the blessed, maintained that prophets see the divine essence itself, which they term 'mirror of eternity', not however in so far as that essence is the object of beatitude but in so far as it embraces the why and wherefore of future contingents—which reasoning is wholly untenable. For God is the object of beatitude in his very essence, as Augustine says,[9] *Blessed is he who knows you even if others he knows not.* It is impossible that anyone should see the why and wherefore of creatures in the divine essence itself, without seeing that essence. The first reason being that the divine essence itself is the reason of all that is; and a reason in the mind does not add to the divine essence except relationship to a creature.

The second reason is that knowing an object in itself is prior to knowing it in relationship to other things. So here, we know God as object of beatitude before we know the reason of things as existing in him. That is why prophets cannot see God in terms of the reason for creatures without seeing him as object of beatitude.

So we must hold that prophetic vision is not a vision of the divine essence itself. When the prophets see what they do see, it is not in the divine essence but in certain similitudes lighted up by a God-given light. Thus Dionysius speaking about prophetic visions says,[10] *A wise theologian calls that vision divine which is effected by images of things lacking a bodily form through the seer being rapt in divine things.* It is these similitudes, made light by the divine light, which deserve the name of mirror for more than the divine essence. For in a mirror images are formed from other realities, and this cannot be said of God. Yet the enlightening of the mind in a prophetical mode can be called a mirroring, in so far as is reflected in it an image of the truth of the divine foreknowledge. That is why it is termed 'mirror of eternity', because it represents the foreknowledge of God who in his eternity sees all presentially, as we have established.[11]

Hence: 1. Prophets are said to see into the book of God's foreknowledge in so far as truth issues forth from the divine foreknowledge, and is planted in the prophet's mind.

2. Man is said to see his own form, whereby he exists, in so far as a similitude of that first truth is reflected in the human mind. From which it follows that a soul may know itself.

3. Future contingents are in God in terms of an unchanging truth. And

---

[8] *I Corinthians* 13, 10
[10] *De cœl. hier.* 4. PG 3, 180
[9] *Confessions* v, 4. PL 32, 708
[11] 2a2æ. 172, 1
[b] e.g. William of Auxerre, d. 1231. Author of the *Summa aurea.*

prophetæ similem cognitionem, absque eo quod prophetæ Deum per essentiam videant.

articulus 2. *utrum in prophetica revelatione imprimantur divinitus menti prophetæ novæ rerum species, an solum novum lumen*

AD SECUNDUM sic proceditur:[1] 1. Videtur quod in prophetica revelatione non imprimantur divinitus menti prophetæ novæ rerum species, sed solum novum lumen; quia, sicut dicit *Glossa* Hieronymi,[2] *Prophetæ utuntur similitudinibus rerum in quibus conversati sunt.* Sed si visio prophetica fieret per aliquas species de novo impressas, nihil operaretur ibi præcedens conversatio. Ergo non imprimuntur aliquæ species de novo in animam prophetæ, sed solum propheticum lumen.

2. Præterea, sicut Augustinus dicit,[3] *Visio imaginaria non facit prophetam, sed solum visio intellectualis.* Unde etiam *Dan.*[4] dicitur quod *intelligentia opus est in visione.* Sed visio intellectualis, sicut in eodem lib. dicitur,[5] non fit per aliquas similitudines, sed per ipsam rerum veritatem. Ergo videtur quod prophetica revelatio non fiat per impressionem aliquarum specierum.

3. Præterea, per donum prophetiæ Spiritus Sanctus exhibet homini id quod est supra facultatem naturæ humanæ. Sed formare quascumque rerum species potest homo ex facultate naturali. Ergo videtur quod in prophetica revelatione non infundatur aliqua rerum species, sed solum intelligibile lumen.

SED CONTRA est quod dicitur *Osee,*[6] *Ego visiones multiplicavi eis, et in manibus prophetarum assimilatus sum.* Sed multiplicatio visionum non fit secundum lumen intelligibile, quod est commune in omni prophetica visione, sed solum secundum diversitatem specierum, secundum quas etiam est assimilatio. Ergo videtur quod in prophetica revelatione imprimantur novæ species rerum, et non solum intelligibile lumen.

RESPONSIO: Dicendum quod, sicut Augustinus dicit,[7] *cognitio prophetica maxime ad mentem pertinet.* Circa cognitionem autem humanæ mentis duo oportet considerare, scilicet acceptionem sive repræsentationem rerum, et judicium de rebus repræsentatis. Quando autem repræsentantur menti humanæ res aliquæ secundum aliquas species et secundum naturæ ordinem, primo oportet quod species præsententur sensui, secundo imaginationi, tertio intellectui possibili, qui immutantur a speciebus phantasmatum

---

[1]cf *De veritate* XII, 7. *In Isaiam* 1. *In* 1 *Cor.* 14, *lect.* 1
[2]*Glossa ordinaria.* Jerome on *Amos* 1, 2. PL 25, 1041

so God can impress upon the mind of prophets a similar kind of knowledge, without implying that prophets see God's essence.

article 2. whether in prophetic revelation God infuses new species in the mind of a prophet, or simply grants a new light

THE FIRST POINT:[1] 1. In prophetic revelation God impresses no new species of realities on the prophet's mind, but merely a new light. A note of Jerome on *Amos*[2] says that prophets use images of objects with which they are familiar. But if prophetic revelation was due to infusing new species, any previous experience would be ineffective. So, no new species are impressed on the prophet's mind but merely prophetic light.

2. Augustine says[3] that imaginative vision does not constitute a prophet, but only intellectual vision; and in *Daniel* it is said[4] that there is need of understanding in vision. But intellectual vision, Augustine notices[5] in the same book, does not derive from some sort of similitudes but from the reality of things in themselves. So it seems that prophetic revelation is not effected by an impression of species.

3. By the gift of prophecy the Holy Spirit shows to a man that which surpasses his natural powers. But a man can from his natural powers fashion the species of all manner of things. So we conclude that in prophetic revelation there is no infusion of species but only intellectual light.

ON THE OTHER HAND, *It was I who multiplied visions and through the prophets gave parables.*[6] But the multiplying of visions is not the work of intellectual light, which is common to all prophetic vision, by only according to the diversity of the species, according to which also there comes about an assimilation. Therefore in prophetic revelation there is a new infusion of species and not simply an intellectual light.

REPLY: As Augustine says,[7] *Prophetic knowledge most of all relates to the mind.* Two points arise as regards the knowledge of a human mind. There is first the acceptance or representation of things and then the judgment about what is presented. Now some things are made present to the human mind by certain species; and, according to nature's ordering, species are first presented to the senses, secondly to the imagination, thirdly to the passive intellect which is modified by species derived from the phantasms by the enlightening action of the active intellect. In the imagination, however, are not only the forms of sense objects as they are received by the

---

[3]*Super Gen. ad litt.* XII, 9. PL 34, 461   [4]*Daniel* 10, 1
[5]op cit 6. PL 34, 458   [6]*Hosea* 12, 10   [7]loc cit note 3

secundum illustrationem intellectus agentis. In imaginatione autem non solum sunt formæ rerum sensibilium, secundum quod accipiuntur a sensu, sed transmutantur diversimode, vel propter aliquam transmutationem corporalem (sicut accidit in dormientibus et furiosis), vel etiam secundum imperium rationis disponuntur phantasmata in ordine ad id quod est intelligendum. Sicut enim ex diversa ordinatione earumdem litterarum accipiuntur diversi intellectus; ita etiam secundum diversam dispositionem phantasmatum resultant in intellectu diversæ species intelligibiles.

Judicium autem humanæ mentis fit secundum vim intellectualis luminis. Per donum autem prophetiæ confertur aliquid humanæ menti supra id quod pertinet ad naturalem facultatem quantum ad utrumque, scilicet et quantum ad judicium per influxum luminis intellectualis, et quantum ad acceptionem, seu repræsentationem rerum, quæ fit per aliquas species.

Et quantum ad hoc secundum potest assimilari doctrina humana revelationi propheticæ, non autem quantum ad primum. Homo enim suo discipulo repræsentat aliquas res per signa locutionum; non autem potest interius illuminare, sicut facit Deus.

Horun autem duorum principalius est primum in prophetia, quia judicium est completivum cognitionis.

Et ideo sic cui fiat divinitus repræsentatio aliquarum rerum per similitudines imaginarias (ut Pharaoni et Nabuchodonosor), aut etiam per similitudines corporales (ut Balthasar), non est talis censendus propheta, nisi illuminetur ejus mens ad judicandum: sed talis apparitio est quiddam imperfectum in genere prophetiæ. Unde a quibusdam vocatur extasis prophetiæ, sicut et divinatio somniorum.

Erit autem propheta, si solummodo intellectus ejus illuminetur ad judicandum etiam ea quæ aliis imaginarie visa sunt, ut patet de Joseph, qui exposuit somnium Pharaonis. Sed, sicut Augustinus dicit,[8] *Maxime propheta est qui utroque præcellit, ut scilicet videat in spiritu corporalium rerum significativas similitudines, et eas vivacitate mentis intelligat.*

Repræsentantur autem divinitus menti prophetæ, quandoque quidem mediante sensu exterius quædam formæ sensibiles; sicut Daniel vidit scripturam parietis, ut legitur;[9] quandoque autem per formas imaginarias, sive omnino divinitus impressas, non per sensum acceptas (puta si alicui cæco nato imprimerentur in imaginatione colorum similitudines) vel etiam divinitus ordinatas ex his quæ a sensibus sunt acceptæ; sicut Jeremias *vidit ollam succensam a facie aquilonis,* ut habetur;[10] sive etiam imprimendo species intelligibiles ipsi menti; sicut patet de his qui accipiunt scientiam, vel sapientiam infusam, sicut Salomon et Apostoli.

---

[8]loc cit note 3   [9]*Daniel* 5, 17   [10]*Jeremiah* 1, 13
[a]cf Maimonides. *Guide for the Perplexed* II, 36.

senses, but also these are transformed in various ways: thus by some bodily transformation, as in those who are asleep or out of their minds, and also because images are ordered by the reason in such a way as to make understanding possible. Just as the different ordering of the same letters of the alphabet produces different understandings, so too different dispositions of images bring out different intellectual species in the mind.

However, judgment in the human mind is proportionate to the efficacity of intellectual light. Now by the gift of prophecy something is conferred on the human mind over and above the powers of its natural faculty in both respects, namely in respect of judgment by the infusion of intellectual light, and in respect of the acceptation or representation of realities which is done through certain species.

In this second respect, but not in the first, human teaching can be likened to prophetic revelation, for a man furnishes his pupil with realities through word-symbols, but he cannot illumine from within as God docs.

Of these two aspects of knowledge, the first looms the larger in prophecy: because judgment is the full fruit of cognition.

And so if anyone is favoured by a God-given representation of certain realities through imaginative images, as with Pharaoh and Nebuchadnezzar; or through bodily images, as with Belshazzar—such are not to be considered prophets, unless their minds are enlightened for judging. Such apparitions are something imperfect in the genus prophecy, so that they are sometimes referred to as 'substitute-prophecy',[a] as also is divination of dreams.

But a prophet is he whose mind only is enlightened to pass judgment even on those elements which have been seen by others in imaginative forms. This is clear from the story of Joseph who expounded Pharaoh's dream.[b] However, as Augustine says,[8] *Most of all a prophet is he who excels in both: so that he sees in spirit the significant images of corporeal realities and grasps them by the living quality of his mind.*

God presents some sense-perceptible forms to a prophet's mind, sometimes outwardly through the senses; thus Daniel saw the writing on the wall;[9] sometimes through imaginative forms, either wholly impressed by God and not received from the senses, e.g. as if the likeness of colours were infused in the imagination of a man born blind; or again so disposed by God that the reality is gathered from what is grasped by the senses; thus Jeremiah saw *a boiling pot facing away from the north.*[10] Or again, by an impressing of intellectual images on the mind itself: as is manifest in those who receive infused knowledge or wisdom, as Solomon[c] did or the Apostles.[d]

---

[b]*Genesis* 41.   [c]I *Kings* 3, 5.   [d]*Acts* 2.

Lumen autem intelligibile quandoque quidem imprimitur menti humanæ divinitus ad dijudicandum ea quæ ab aliis visa sunt; sicut dictum est de Joseph, et sicut patet de Apostolis, quibus *Dominus aperuit sensum, ut intelligerent Scripturas*, ut dicitur *Luc*.;[11] et ad hoc pertinet interpretatio sermonum; sive etiam ad dijudicandum secundum divinam veritatem ea quæ cursu naturali homo apprehendit; sive etiam ad dijudicandum veraciter et efficaciter ea quæ agenda sunt, secundum illud *Isa.*,[12] *Spiritus Domini ductor ejus fuit.*

Sic igitur patet quod prophetica revelatio quandoque quidem fit per solam luminis influentiam, quandoque autem etiam per species de novo impressas, vel aliter ordinatas.

1. Ad primum ergo dicendum quod, sicut dictum est, quandoque in prophetica revelatione divinitus ordinantur species imaginariæ præacceptæ a sensu, secundum congruentiam ad veritatem revelandam; et tunc conversatio præcedens aliquid operatur ad ipsas similitudines, non autem quando totaliter ab extrinseco imprimuntur.

2. Ad secundum dicendum quod visio intellectualis non fit secundum aliquas similitudines corporales et individuales; fit tamen secundum aliquam similitudinem intelligibilem. Unde Augustinus dicit[13] quod *habet animus nonnullam speciei notæ similitudinem*, quæ quidem similitudo intelligibilis in revelatione prophetica quandoque immediate a Deo imprimitur, quandoque a formis imaginatis resultat secundum adjutorium prophetici luminis, quia ex eisdem formis imaginatis subtilior conspicitur veritas secundum illustrationem altioris luminis.

3. Ad tertium dicendum quod quascumque formas imaginatas naturali virtute homo potest formare, absolute hujusmodi formas considerando; non tamen ut sint ordinatæ ad repræsentandas intelligibiles veritates quæ hominis intellectum excedunt; sed ad hoc necessarium est auxilium supernaturalis luminis.

articulus 3. utrum visio prophetica semper fiat cum abstractione a sensibus

AD TERTIUM sic proceditur:[1] 1. Videtur quod visio prophetica semper fiat cum abstractione a sensibus. Dicitur enim *Num.*,[2] *Si quis fuerit inter vos propheta Domini, in visione apparebo ei, vel per somnium loquar ad illum.* Sed, sicut *Glossa* dicit in principio Psalterii,[3] *visio quæ est per somnia et visiones, est per ea quæ videntur dici vel fieri:* cum autem aliqua videntur dici vel fieri quæ non dicuntur vel fiunt, est alienatio a sensibus. Ergo prophetia semper fit cum alienatione a sensibus.

2. Præterea, quando una virtus multum intenditur in operatione sua, alia potentia abstrahitur a suo actu; sicut illi qui vehementer intendunt ad

---

[11]*Luke* 24, 45   [12]*Isaiah* 63, 14   [13]*De Trin.* IX, 11. PL 42, 969

God sometimes infuses an intellectual light into the mind of man so as to pass judgment on those realities which have been seen by others as was said of Joseph, and as appears with the Apostles,[11] (*The Lord*) *opened their minds so that they should understand the scriptures.* This is the object of 'interpretation of speeches'. Or for judging in terms of divine truth what a man grasps by his natural faculties. Or again to judge really and efficaciously what has to be done, as in *Isaiah*,[12] *The spirit of the Lord has been his guide.*

Thus it appears that prophetic revelation sometimes takes place by an infusion of light only, sometimes by the infusion of new species or species differently disposed.

Hence: 1. Sometimes, then, in prophetic revelation images previously obtained from the senses are so ordered as to make them apt for the revelation of truth. In that instance antecedent experiences have some effect on the images themselves. Not so when the images are impressed wholly from outside.

2. Intellectual vision is not affected by bodily and individual images, but by an intellectual image. Hence Augustine says,[13] *the mind has some likeness to the form that is known.* Such an intellectual image in prophetic revelation is sometimes immediately impressed by God; sometimes it derives from imaginative forms with the help of prophetic light, because from these same imaginative forms a more delicate truth becomes apparent in the radiance of a higher light.

3. A man can form all manner of images by his natural capacity. Absolutely speaking this is so if we refer to the forms imagined. Yet a man cannot arrange these forms to represent truths which surpass the mind of man. For this the help of a supernatural light is needed.

article 3. does prophetic revelation always suppose alienation from the senses?

THE FIRST POINT:[1] 1. Yes, so it seems, *If there is a prophet among you, I the Lord make myself known to him in a vision, I speak with him in a dream.*[2] But, as the *Gloss* says at the beginning of the Psalter,[3] *A vision granted in dreams and apparitions is through those things which seem to be said or to happen.* Now when things seem to be said or to happen, and are not simply sayings or happenings then there is an abstraction from the senses. Thus prophecy always supposes abstraction from the senses.

2. When one capacity is fully extended in its act another is weakened in its effect—thus people who are trying very hard to hear something fail to

---

[1]cf *De veritate* XII, 9   [2]*Numbers* 12, 6   [3]From Cassiodorus. PL 70, 12

aliquid audiendum non percipiunt visu ea quæ coram ipsis sunt. Sed visione prophetica est maxime intellectus elevatus, et intenditur in suo actu. Ergo videtur quod semper fiat cum abstractione a sensibus.

3. Præterea, impossibile est idem simul ad oppositas partes converti. Sed in visione prophetica mens convertitur ad accipiendum a superiori. Ergo non potest simul converti ad sensibilia. Necessarium ergo videtur quod revelatio prophetica semper fiat cum abstractione a sensibus.

4. Sed contra est quod dicitur ad *Cor.*,[4] *Spiritus prophetarum prophetis subjecti sunt.* Sed hoc esse non posset, si propheta non esset sui compos, a sensibus alienatus existens. Ergo videtur quod prophetica visio non fiat cum alienatione a sensibus.

RESPONSIO: Dicendum quod, sicut dictum est,[5] prophetica revelatio fit secundum quatuor, scilicet secundum influxum intelligibilis luminis, secundum emissionem intelligibilium specierum, secundum impressionem, vel ordinationem imaginabilium formarum, et secundum expressionem formarum sensibilium.

Manifestum est autem quod non fit abstractio a sensibus quando aliquid repræsentatur menti prophetæ per species sensibiles, sive ad hoc specialiter formatas divinitus, sicut rubus ostensus Moysi,[6] et scriptura ostensa Danieli,[7] sive etiam per alias causas productas; ita tamen quod secundum divinam providentiam ad aliquid prophetice significandum ordinetur, sicut per arcam Noë significabatur Ecclesia.

Similiter etiam non est necesse ut fiat alienatio a sensibus exterioribus per hoc quod mens prophetæ illustratur intelligibili lumine, aut formatur intelligibilibus speciebus, quia in nobis perfectum judicium intellectus habetur per conversionem ad sensibilia, quæ sunt prima nostræ cognitionis principia, ut in *Primo* habitum est.[8]

Sed quando fit revelatio prophetica secundum formas imaginarias, necesse est fieri abstractionem a sensibus, ut talis apparitio phantasmatum non referatur ad ea quæ exterius sentiuntur. Sed abstractio a sensibus quandoque fit perfecte, ut scilicet nihil homo sensibus percipiat quandoque autem imperfecte, ut scilicet aliquid percipiat sensibus, non tamen

---

[4]I *Corinthians* 14, 32
[5]above art. 2
[6]*Exodus* 3
[7]*Daniel* 5
[8]1a. 84, 6
ªAn example of the typical sense of Scripture (cf 1a. 1, 10. Vol. 1 of this series). This obtains when some reality, deed or person of the Old Testament is significant of some reality of the New Testament. The significance or link between Old and New is wholly due to divine preordination; and to grasp the relation of type to

see what lies straight in front of them. But in prophetic vision the intellect is supremely elevated and exercised in its act. So we must suppose that this is always with abstraction from the senses.

3. An object cannot possibly go simultaneously in two opposite directions. But in prophetic vision the mind is bent on reception from a power above. Therefore it cannot at the same time be turned towards sense-objects. So prophetic revelation always supposes an abstraction from the senses.

4. On the contrary it is said in 1 *Corinthians*,[4] *The spirits of prophets are subject to prophets*. But this would not be possible were not the prophet master of himself and alienated from his senses. So it seems that prophetic vision does not occur with abstraction from the senses.

REPLY: As we have noticed,[5] prophetic revelation occurs in four ways: by an infusion of intellectual light, by an infusion of intellectual species, by an impression or arrangement of forms in the imagination, by an outward expression of sense-perceptible images.

Now it is clear that there is no abstraction from the senses when anything is made present to the prophet's mind by sense-perceptible species, whether these are specially formed by God, as e.g. the bush shown to Moses,[6] and the handwriting shown to Daniel;[7] or whether they are produced by yet other causes, yet so as to be in line with God's providence, and as ordained to be prophetically significant, e.g. the Ark of Noah as a symbol of the Church.[a]

So too there is no need for abstraction from the external senses because the prophet's mind is enlightened by an intellectual light or endowed with intellectual species; the reason being that with us men, a perfect judgment of the mind obtains through turning to sense-objects which are the first principles of our knowledge, as we have seen.[8]

But when prophetic revelation is conveyed by images in the imagination, then there must be an abstraction from the senses, lest what is seen in imagination be taken for external sense-objects. Yet abstraction from the senses is sometimes complete, so that a man perceives nothing from his senses. At other times the abstraction is incomplete, so that a certain amount

---

antitype most often requires faith. The classic illustration of this principle is in *John* 3, 14, *As Moses lifted up the serpent in the wilderness, so must the Son of Man be lifted up that whoever believes in him may have eternal life*. In this example the divine preordination is made known to us by the word of Christ.

More basically still, the reason for this typical sense in which things, persons, events become significant of other realities, is that God is Lord of all that is and happens; and that then he goes on to teach us by making some realities symbolical or significant of others.

plene discernat ea quæ exterius percipit ab his quæ imaginabiliter videt. Unde Augustinus dicit,[9] *Sic videntur quæ in spiritu fiunt, imagines corporum, quemadmodum corpora ipsa per corpus, ita ut simul cernatur et homo aliquis præsens oculis, et absens alius spiritu, tanquam oculis.*

Talis tamen alienatio a sensibus non fit in prophetis cum aliqua inordinatione naturæ (sicut in arreptitiis vel in furiosis) sed per aliquam causam ordinatam, vel naturalem, sicut per somnium, vel spiritualem,* sicut per contemplationis vehementiam, sicut de Petro legitur[10] quod cum oraret in cœnaculo, factus est in excessu mentis; vel virtute divina rapiente, secundum illud *Ezech.,*[11] *Facta super eum manus Domini.*

1. Ad primum ergo dicendum quod auctoritas illa loquitur de prophetis quibus imprimebantur vel ordinabantur imaginariæ formæ vel in dormiendo, quod significatur per somnium, vel in vigilando, quod significatur per visionem.

2. Ad secundum dicendum quod quando mens intenditur in suo actu circa absentia quæ sunt a sensibus remota, tunc propter vehementiam intentionis sequitur alienatio a sensibus; sed quando mens intenditur in suo actu circa dispositionem, vel judicium sensibilium, non oportet quod a sensibus abstrahatur.

3. Ad tertium dicendum quod motus mentis propheticæ non est secundum virtutem propriam, sed secundum virtutem superioris influxus. Et ideo quando ex superiori influxu mens prophetæ inclinatur ad judicandum, vel disponendum aliquid circa sensibilia, non fit alienatio a sensibus, sed solum quando elevatur mens ad contemplandum aliqua sublimiora.

4. Ad quartum dicendum quod spiritus prophetarum dicuntur esse subjecti prophetis quantum ad propheticam enuntiationem, de qua ibi Apostolus loquitur, quia scilicet ex proprio sensu loquuntur ea quæ viderunt, non mente perturbata sicut arreptitii, ut dixerunt Priscilla et Montanus.[12] Sed in ipsa prophetica revelatione potius ipsi subjiciuntur spiritui prophetiæ, id est dono prophetico.

articulus 4. utrum prophetæ semper cognoscant ea quæ prophetant

AD QUARTUM sic proceditur:[1] 1. Videtur quod prophetæ semper cognoscant ea quæ prophetant. Quia, ut Augustinus dicit,[2] *Quibus signa per aliquas*

---

*Leonine: *animalem,* psychological
[9]*Super Gen. ad litt.* XII, 12. PL 34, 463
[10]*Acts* 10, 9
[11]*Ezekiel* 1, 3
[12]cf Jerome on *Isaiah.* Prol. PL 24, 19
[1]cf *In Joan.* 11, *lect.* 7
[2]*Super Gen. ad litt.* XII, 9. PL 34, 461

is perceived from the senses, but without fully distinguishing what is perceived outwardly from what is seen in imagination. Hence Augustine says,[9] *We see the images of bodies produced in the soul just as we see bodies in real life, so that we no longer distinguish between a man who is present and a man who is absent, whom we behold in our imagination as we would with our eyes.*

Such an alienation from the senses[b] does not take place in prophets with a distortion of nature, as with the possessed or the raving mad; but it is due to some well-ordered cause: natural, as in sleep, or spiritual when there is very great intensity of contemplation, as we read of St Peter that he went on to the house-top to pray and fell into a trance;[10] or as when the divine power lays hold of one, as in *Ezekiel,*[11] *The hand of the Lord was upon him.*

Hence: 1. The authority quoted refers to prophets in whom imaginary pictures were formed or co-ordinated, either while asleep, which is what 'dream' refers to; or awake, which is what 'vision' refers to.

2. When a mind is fully and actually intent upon non-present realities, remote from the senses, there ensues abstraction from the senses. But when the mind is occupied with the disposition of or judgments about sense-objects, there is no need for abstraction from the senses.

3. The motion of a mind in prophecy is not in terms of its own capacity, but in virtue of the infusion of a higher power. And so, when through this higher infusion the mind of a prophet is disposed to judge or co-ordinate some sense-objects, there is no alienation from the senses; but only when the mind is uplifted to the contemplation of some yet more sublime realities.

4. The spirits of the prophets are said to be subject to the prophets in the matter of prophetic utterances, of which St Paul speaks in that text. Because of their own sense-experience, they told of what they had seen without being thrown off their mental balance like madmen, as Priscilla and Montanus asserted.[12] But in prophetic revelation proper, prophets are if anything subject to the spirit of prophecy, that is to the gift of prophecy.

article 4. do prophets always know what they are prophesying?

THE FOURTH POINT:[1] 1. Prophets seemingly always know what they are prophesying. The reason is, as Augustine says,[2] *For those to whom signs*

---

[b]Cajetan refers to this sentence as a golden rule. Alienation from the senses must be wholly orderly, for the well-established reason that grace always enhances nature. Note how St Thomas quietly talks about intensity of contemplation—something he knew about from his own personal experience. But we must allow also for the violent grasp of God as e.g. in Ezekiel (1,3) or St Paul, or Jeremiah (1 & 20). cf *Phil.* 3, 12.

rerum corporalium similitudines demonstrabantur in spiritu, nisi accessisset mentis officium, ut etiam intelligerentur, nondum erat prophetia. Sed ea quæ intelliguntur non possunt esse incognita. Ergo propheta non ignorat ea quæ prophetat.

2. Præterea, majus est lumen prophetiæ quam lumen naturalis rationis. Sed quicumque lumine naturali habet scientiam non ignorat ea quæ scit. Ergo quicumque lumine prophetico aliqua enuntiat, non potest ea ignorare.

3. Præterea, prophetia ordinatur ad hominum illuminationem: unde dicitur,[3] *Habemus propheticum sermonem, cui bene facitis attendentes, quasi lucernæ lucenti in caliginoso loco.* Sed nihil potest alios illuminare, nisi in se sit illuminatum. Ergo videtur quod propheta prius illuminetur ad cognoscendum ea quæ aliis enuntiat.

SED CONTRA est quod dicitur *Joan.,*[4] *Hoc autem a semetipso* (Caiphas) *non dixit, sed cum esset Pontifex anni illius, prophetavit quod Jesus moriturus erat pro gente,* etc. Sed hoc Caiphas non cognovit. Ergo non omnis qui prophetat, cognoscit ea quæ prophetat.

RESPONSIO: Dicendum quod in revelatione prophetica movetur mens prophetæ a Spiritu Sancto, sicut instrumentum deficiens respectu principalis agentis. Movetur autem mens prophetæ non solum ad aliquid apprehendendum, sed etiam ad aliquid loquendum, vel ad aliquid faciendum; et quandoque quidem ad omnia tria simul; quandoque autem ad duo horum; quandoque vero ad unum tantum. Et quodlibet horum contingit esse cum aliquo cognitionis defectu.

Nam cum mens prophetæ movetur ad aliquid æstimandum vel apprehendendum, quandoque quidem inducitur ad hoc quod solum apprehendat rem illam, quandoque autem ulterius ad hoc quod cognoscat hæc sibi esse divinitus revelata.

Similiter etiam quandoque movetur mens prophetæ ad aliquid loquendum, ita quod intelligat id quod per hæc verba Spiritus Sanctus intendit, sicut David, qui dicebat,[5] *Spiritus Domini locutus est per me.* Quandoque autem ille cujus mens movetur ad aliqua verba exprimenda* non intelligit quid Spiritus Sanctus per hæc verba intendat, sicut patet de Caipha.

Similiter etiam cum Spiritus Sanctus movet mentem alicujus ad aliquid faciendum, quandoque quidem intelligit quid hoc significet, sicut patet de Jeremia, qui abscondit lumbare in Euphrate, ut habetur;[6] quandoque vero non intelligit, sicut milites dividentes vestimenta Christi, non intelligebant quid hoc significaret.

---

*Leonine: *depromenda,* bring out
[3]II *Peter* 1, 19

have been shown in spirit through resemblances with bodily things, there was *no question of prophecy—so long as mind had not intervened to understand those signs.* Thus a prophet is not ignorant of what he prophesies.

2. Prophetic light is more perfect than that of reason so he who by his natural light possesses science is not ignorant of what he knows. So too he who announces something by prophetic light cannot be ignorant of that reality.

3. Prophecy's aim is to enlighten men: hence we read,[3] *We have the prophetic word made more sure; you do well to pay attention to this, as to a lamp shining in a dark place.* Now nothing can enlighten others unless it be lightsome in itself. Thus a prophet must first be enlightened in himself so as to know what he proclaims to others.

ON THE OTHER HAND: It is recorded[4] that Caiphas *did not say this of his own accord, but being high priest that year he prophesied that Jesus should die for the nation.* Now Caiphas did not understand what he was saying. Therefore not every prophet knows what he prophesies.

REPLY: In prophetic revelation the prophet's mind is moved by the Holy Spirit as a defective instrument by its principal cause. Now the Holy Spirit moves the prophet's mind to perceive or say or accomplish something; and sometimes all three at once, sometimes two only, sometimes one only. In each instance there can be some measure of defective knowledge.

Let us now suppose that the prophet's mind is moved to judge or apprehend something: sometimes he will be simply led to grasp the truth; at others he is led further and knows that the truths have been revealed by God.

Again, the mind of a prophet may come to making a proclamation, in such wise that he understands what the Holy Spirit intends by these words, as with David who said,[5] *The Spirit of the Lord speaks by me.* On the other hand a mind can be moved to utter certain words without understanding what the Holy Spirit means by these words, as with Caiphas.

So too when the Holy Spirit moves a mind to action, sometimes there will be understanding of its significance, as with Jeremiah[6] who hid his waist-cloth in the Euphrates; sometimes there will be no understanding at all, as with the soldiers who divided the garments of Christ and understood not the meaning of what they did.

---

[4]*John* 11, 51
[5]II *Samuel* 23, 2
[6]*Jeremiah* 13, 5, 9

Cum ergo aliquis cognoscit se moveri a Spiritu Sancto ad aliquid æstimandum vel significandum verbo, vel facto, hoc proprie ad prophetiam pertinet; cum autem movetur, sed non cognoscit, non est perfecta prophetia, sed quidam instinctus propheticus.

Sciendum tamen quod quia mens prophetæ est instrumentum deficiens, ut dictum est in corp. art. etiam veri prophetæ non omnia cognoscunt quæ in eorum visis, aut verbis, aut etiam factis Spiritus Sanctus intendit.

Et per hoc patet responsio ad objecta. Nam primæ rationes loquuntur de veris prophetis, quorum mens divinitus illustratur perfecte.

When someone knows that he is being moved by the Holy Spirit to judge about or to signify something by word or deed, this constitutes prophecy properly so called. When a man is moved but does not know it, this is not perfect prophecy, but a kind of prophetic instinct.

Remember always that, because the prophet's mind is a deficient instrument, as was said, even genuine prophets do not know all that the Holy Spirit intends in visions, words and even deeds.

This clearly answers the objections. The first reasonings refer to true prophets whose minds are perfectly enlightened by God.

Quæstio 174. de divisione prophetiæ

Deinde considerandum est de divisione prophetiæ; et circa hoc quæruntur sex:

1. de divisione prophetiæ in suas species;
2. utrum sit altior prophetia quæ est sine imaginaria visione;
3. de diversitate graduum prophetiæ;
4. utrum Moyses fuerit excellentissimus prophetarum;
5. utrum aliquis comprehensor possit esse propheta;
6. utrum prophetia creverit per temporis processum.

articulus 1. utrum convenienter dividatur prophetia

AD PRIMUM sic proceditur: 1. Videtur quod inconvenienter dividatur prophetia in *Glossa*[1] super[2] *Matt., Ecce virgo in utero habebit,* ubi dicitur quod *prophetia alia est ex prædestinatione Dei, quam necesse est omnibus modis evenire, ut sine nostro impleatur arbitrio; ut hæc de qua hic agitur: alia est ex præscientia Dei, cui nostrum admiscetur arbitrium: alia est quæ comminatio dicitur, quæ fit ob signum divinæ animadversionis.* Illud enim quod consequitur omnem prophetiam non debet poni ut membrum dividens prophetiam. Sed omnis prophetia est secundum præscientiam divinam, quia *prophetæ legunt in libro præscientiæ,* ut dicit *Glossa Isa.*[3] Ergo videtur quod non debeat poni una species prophetiæ quæ est secundum præscientiam.

2. Præterea, sicut aliquid prophetatur secundum comminationem, ita etiam secundum promissionem, et utraque variatur: dicitur enim *Jerem.,*[4] *Repente loquar adversum gentem et adversum regnum, ut eradicem et destruam, et disperdam illud. Si pænitentiam egerit gens illa a malo suo, agam et ego pænitentiam;* et hoc pertinet ad prophetiam comminationis. Et postea subdit de prophetia promissionis: *Subito loquar de gente et regno, ut ædificem, et plantem illud. Si fecerit malum in oculis meis, pænitentiam agam super bono quod locutus sum ut facerem ei.* Ergo sicut ponitur prophetia comminationis: ita debet poni prophetia promissionis.

3. Præterea, Isidorus dicit[5] prophetiæ genera sunt septem. Primum genus est extasis, quod est mentis excessus; sicut vidit Petrus vas submissum de cœlo cum variis animalibus. Secundum genus est visio, sicut apud Isaiam dicentem, *Vidi Dominum sedentem,* etc. Tertium genus est somnium, sicut Jacob scalam dormiens vidit. Quartum genus est per nubem, sicut ad Moysen loquebatur Deus. Quintum genus est vox de

---

[1]*Glossa ordinaria,* cf Jerome. PL 26, 25   [2]*Matthew* 1, 23
[3]*Ordinaria* on *Isaiah* 38, 1   [4]*Jeremiah* 18, 7
[5]*Etymologies* VII, 8. PL 82, 286

Question 174. divisions of prophecy

Six points of inquiry arise about the divisions of prophecy:

1. is prophecy divided into species?
2. whether prophecy without vision in the imagination is of a higher type;
3. the diversity of grades in prophecy;
4. whether Moses was the most outstanding prophet;
5. whether one in beatitude[a] can be a prophet;
6. whether prophecy grew with the passage of time.

article 1. is prophecy divided into species?

THE FIRST POINT: 1. The divisions given in the *Gloss*[1] on *Matthew*,[2] *Behold a virgin shall conceive*, etc, do not seem suitable. We are told that *prophecy is on the one hand from God's predestination, which must of necessity be fulfilled in every possible instance, so that God's providence is fulfilled without our willing, for instance the one in question. Another prophecy derives from God's foreknowledge, with which there is an admixture of our own will. A third form of prophecy is termed denunciation, which is significative of the divine wrath.* Now something which follows on all prophecy should not be presented as an element in the divisions of prophecy. But all prophecy is in accord with the divine foreknowledge, because *prophets read in the book of foreknowledge*, as the *Gloss*[3] on *Isaiah* says. So we cannot lay down one particular species of prophecy as being in accord with God's foreknowledge.

2. If a prophecy is uttered as a denunciation, so too it can be in terms of promise: the two can be mingled, for it is said,[4] *If at any time I declare concerning a nation or a kingdom, that I will pluck up and break down and destroy it . . . if that nation turns from its evil, I will repent of the evil that I intend to do to it*—so we speak about a prophecy of denunciation and so too we need to speak about a prophecy of promise.

3. Isidore says[5] that there are seven forms of prophecy. First comes ecstasy or ravishing of the mind, as in the instance of St Peter when he saw what seemed a great cloth let down from heaven filled with all manner of animals. Second is vision, as when Isaiah says, *I saw the Lord* etc. Third is a dream, thus Jacob while asleep saw a ladder. Fourth is a cloud, as when God spoke to Moses. Fifth is the voice from Heaven which

---

[a]*Comprehensor.* The technical term, which comes from the Vulgate, 1 *Corinthians* 9, 24, for one who has 'laid hold' of the happiness of heaven, cf 1a2æ. 4, 3. Vol. 16 of this series. Used by contrast to *viator*, wayfarer. The terms are found in St Bernard.

69

cœlis, sicut ad Abraham sonuit dicens, *Ne mittas manum in puerum*. Sextum genus accepta parabola, sicut apud Balaam. Septimum genus repletio Spiritus Sancti, sicut pene apud omnes prophetas. Ponit etiam tria genera visionum: unum secundum oculos corporis; alterum secundum spiritum imaginarium; tertium per intuitum mentis. Sed hæc non exprimuntur in prius dicta divisione. Ergo est insufficiens.

SED CONTRA est auctoritas. Hieronymi, cujus dicitur esse *Glossa* inducta in arg. I.

RESPONSIO: Dicendum quod species habituum et actuum in moralibus distinguuntur secundum objecta. Objectum autem prophetiæ est id quod est in cognitione divina supra humanam facultatem existens. Et ideo secundum horum differentiam prophetia distinguitur in diversas species, secundum prius dictam divisionem.

Dictum est autem supra[6] quod futurum est in divina cognitione dupliciter. Uno modo, prout est in sua causa: et sic accipitur prophetia comminationis, quæ non semper impletur, sed per eam prænuntiatur ordo causæ ad effectum, qui quandoque aliis supervenientibus impeditur. Alio modo præcognoscit Deus aliqua in seipsis: vel ut fienda ab ipso; et horum est prophetia prædestinationis, quia, secundum Damascenum,[7] *Deus prædestinat ea quæ non sunt in nobis*. Vel ut fienda per liberum arbitrium hominis; et sic est prophetia præscientiæ, quæ potest esse bonorum et malorum: quod non contingit de prophetia prædestinationis, quæ est bonorum tantum.

Et quia prædestinatio sub præscientia comprehenditur, ideo in *Glossa*,[8] in principio Psalterii, ponitur tantum duplex prophetiæ species, scilicet secundum præscientiam, et secundum comminationem.

1. Ad primum ergo dicendum quod præscientia proprie dicitur præcognitio futurorum eventuum prout in seipsis sunt, et secundum hoc ponitur species prophetiæ; prout autem dicitur respectu futurorum eventuum, sive secundum quod in seipsis sunt, sive secundum quod sunt in suis causis, communiter se habet ad omnem speciem prophetiæ.

2. Ad secundum dicendum quod prophetia promissionis comprehenditur sub prophetia comminationis, quia eadem est ratio veritatis in utraque. Denominatur tamen magis a comminatione, quia Deus pronior est ad relaxandum pœnam quam ad subtrahendum promissa beneficia.

3. Ad tertium dicendum quod Isidorus distinguit prophetiam secundum modum prophetandi: qui quidem potest distingui vel secundum

---

[6]2a2æ. 171, 6 ad 2
[7]*De fide orth.* II, 30. PG 94, 972

sounded in Abraham's ears, *Lay not your hand upon the lad.* Sixth comes from the parable, as in the story of Balaam. Seventh is the filling with the Holy Spirit, as happened with almost all the prophets. Isidore also lays down three types of vision: one according to bodily sight, another in the imagination, a third by grasp of intellect. Now all these forms of prophecy are not expressed in the *Gloss* cited above. So it is inadequate.

ON THE OTHER HAND stands the authority of Jerome to whom the *Gloss* cited at the beginning is attributed.

REPLY: In moral theology the specification of acts and habits is in terms of their objects. Now the object of prophecy is that which is known by God and which surpasses all human capacity. And so prophecy is divided into different species according to their various objects, in line with the division previously given.

We said above[6] that the future is in the divine mind in two ways, first as its cause. Denunciative prophecy is of this sort, and it is not always accomplished: it merely states antecedently a relation of cause and effect, which, at times, when other considerations intervene, come to nothing. Secondly, there is another way in which God knows antecedently some realities in themselves. Either they are things to be accomplished by God himself; and then the term prophecy of predestination is applied, because, as Damascene says,[7] *God predestines those things which are not in us.* Or they are to be accomplished by the free willing of man. In this case we have a prophecy of foreknowing. This can be of good or evil—which is not true of the prophecy of predestination, which is of the good only.

And because predestination is grouped under foreknowledge, the *Gloss*[8] on the opening words of the Psalter gives only two species of prophecy, viz, prophecy of foreknowledge and prophecy of denunciation.

Hence: 1. Foreknowledge strictly speaking is precognition of future events as they are in themselves and in this way is established a species of prophecy. But if we understand foreknowledge in its connection with future events, whether as in themselves or as in their causes, it is a genus in respect of every type of prophecy.

2. Prophecy of promise can be listed under prophecy of denunciation: for the motive of truth is the same in both. It is however denominated in preference from denunciation because God is more inclined to relax a penalty than to withdraw the benefits which he has promised.

3. Isidore distinguishes prophecy according to the various modes of

---

[8]*Ordinaria.* Lombard. PL 191, 59

potentias cognoscitivas in homine; quæ sunt sensus, imaginatio et intellectus: et sic sumitur triplex visio quam ponit tam ipse quam Augustinus.[9]
Vel potest distingui secundum differentiam prophetici influxus; qui quidem quantum ad illustrationem intellectus significatur per repletionem Spiritus Sancti, quam septimo loco ponit.

Quantum vero ad impressionem formarum imaginabilium ponit tria; scilicet somnium, quod ponit tertio loco; et visionem, quæ fit in vigilando respectu quorumcumque communium, quam ponit in secundo loco; et extasim, quæ fit per elevationem mentis in aliqua altiora, quam ponit primo loco.

Quantum vero ad sensibilia signa ponit tria, quia sensibile signum aut est aliqua res corporea exterius apparens visui, sicut nubes, quam ponit quarto loco; aut est vox formata exterius ad auditum hominis delata, quam ponit quinto loco; aut est vox per hominem formata cum similitudine alicujus rei, quod pertinet ad parabolam, quam ponit sexto loco.

articulus 2. utrum excellentior sit prophetia quæ habet visionem intellectualem et imaginariam quam ea quæ habet visionem intellectualem tantum

AD SECUNDUM sic proceditur:[1] 1. Videtur quod excellentior sit prophetia quæ habet visionem intellectualem et imaginariam quam ea quæ habet visionem intellectualem tantum. Dicit enim Augustinus[2] et habetur in *Glossa ordin.* I ad. *Cor.* super illud,[3] *Spiritus autem loquitur mysteria: Minus est propheta qui rerum quæ significantur, sola ipsa signa in spiritu per rerum corporalium imagines videt; et magis est propheta, qui solo earum intellectu est præditus, sed maxime propheta est qui in utroque præcellit.* Hoc autem pertinet ad prophetam qui simul habet intellectualem et imaginariam visionem. Ergo hujusmodi prophetia est altior.

2. Præterea, quanto virtus alicujus rei est major, tanto ad magis distantia se extendit. Sed lumen propheticum principaliter ad mentem pertinet, ut ex dictis patet.[4] Ergo perfectior videtur esse prophetia quæ derivatur usque ad imaginationem quam illa quæ existit in solo intellectu.

3. Præterea, Hieronymus in prol. lib. *Reg.*[5] distinguit prophetas contra hagiographos. Omnes autem illi quos prophetas nominat (puta Isaias, Jeremias, et alii hujusmodi) simul cum intellectuali visione imaginariam habuerunt; non autem illi qui dicuntur hagiographi, sicut ex inspiratione Spiritus Sancti scribente (sicut Job, David, Salomon et hujusmodi). Ergo videtur quod magis proprie dicuntur prophetæ illi qui simul habent visionem imaginariam cum intellectuali, quam illi qui habent intellectualem tantum.

---

[9] *Super Gen. ad litt.* XII, 6. PL 34, 458. cf 459

prophecy. These can be distinguished according to man's knowing faculties—senses, imagination, intellect. That is why Isidore and Augustine[9] recognize three types of vision.

Or you can make a division in terms of degrees of prophetic infusion. The enlightening of the mind is indicated by the filling of the Holy Ghost, which comes seventh in the classification.

As to the imprinting of imaginative forms Isidore mentions three: dreams (third), visions while awake relating to any truth in general (second), and ecstasy, which results from the mind's being raised to higher things (this is placed first).

As regards sense-perceptible signs, he lays down three kinds of prophecy. This sign is either a bodily thing, externally visible to the sight, as was 'the cloud' (fourth), or the 'voice' coming from outside a man's ear (fifth), or finally, words formed by men to indicate a comparison. This makes for parable (the sixth type).

article 2. whether prophecy which has intellective and imaginative vision is more excellent than that which is intellective only

THE SECOND POINT:[1] 1. Prophecy which is intellective and imaginative is seemingly more excellent than that which is intellective only. Augustine says,[2] and he is repeated in the *Gloss* on *the Spirit tells of mysteries*,[3] *Less of a prophet is he who sees in his mind only the images of what has been signified to him; more of a prophet is he who has only the understanding of these; most of all is he prophet who excels in both.* This refers to the prophet who has both intellective and imaginative vision. So this type of prophecy is superior.

2. The greater the effectiveness of anything, the further does its effectiveness extend. But the light of prophecy principally relates to mind, as was said.[4] So seemingly more perfect is that prophecy which extends right down to imagination than that which exists in the intellect alone.

3. Jerome in his Prologue to *Kings*[5] distinguishes 'prophets' from 'hagiographers'. All those whom he terms prophets, e.g. Isaiah, Jeremiah and the like, had imaginative vision together with intellectual grasp; not so those who are termed hagiographers, as men writing under the inspiration of the Holy Spirit, e.g. Job, David, Solomon and others. So it would seem more proper to call prophets those who had intellective together with imaginative vision, than those who had intellective vision alone.

---

[1]3a. 30, 3 ad 1. *De veritate* XII, 12
[2]*Super Gen. ad litt.* XII, 9. PL 34, 461
[3]On 1 *Corinthians* 14, 2   [4]2a2æ. 173, 2   [5]PL 28, 598

4. Præterea, Dionysius dicit[6] quod *impossible est nobis superlucere divinum radium, nisi varietate sacrorum velaminum circumvelatum.* Sed prophetica revelatio fit per immissionem divini radii. Ergo videtur quod non possit esse absque phantasmatum velaminibus.

SED CONTRA est quod *Glossa* dicit,[7] in principio Psalterii, quod *ille modus prophetiæ dignior est cæteris, quando scilicet ex sola Spiritus Sancti inspiratione remoto omni exteriori adminiculo facti, vel dicti, vel visionis, vel somnii, prophetatur.*

RESPONSIO: Dicendum quod dignitas eorum quæ sunt ad finem præcipue consideratur ex fine. Finis autem prophetiæ est manifestatio alicujus veritatis supra hominem existentis. Unde quanto hujusmodi manifestatio est potior, tanto prophetia est dignior.

Manifestum est autem quod manifestatio divinæ veritatis quæ fit per nudam contemplationem ipsius veritatis potior est quam illa quæ fit sub similitudine corporalium rerum: magis enim appropinquat ad visionem patriæ, secundum quam in essentia Dei veritas conspicitur.

Et inde est quod prophetia per quam aliqua supernaturalis veritas conspicitur nude secundum intellectualem visionem est dignior quam illa in qua veritas supernaturalis manifestatur per similitudinem corporalium rerum secundum imaginariam visionem.

Et ex hoc etiam ostenditur mens prophetæ sublimior; sicut in doctrina humana auditor ostenditur esse melioris intellectus, qui veritatem intelligibilem a magistro nude prolatam capere potest, quam ille qui indiget sensibilibus exemplis ad hoc manuduci. Unde in commendationem prophetiæ David dicitur *Reg.*,[8] *Mihi locutus est fortis Israel;* et postea subdit, *Sicut lux auroræ, oriente sole, mane absque nubibus rutilat.*

1. Ad primum ergo dicendum quod quando aliqua supernaturalis veritas revelanda est per similitudines corporales, tunc magis est propheta qui utrumque habet, scilicet lumen intellectuale et imaginariam visionem, quam ille qui habet alterum tantum, quia perfectior est prophetia: et quantum ad hoc loquitur Augustinus ut supra. Sed illa prophetia in qua revelatur nude intelligibilis veritas, est omnibus potior.

2. Ad secundum dicendum quod aliud est judicium de his quæ propter se quæruntur, et de his quæ quæruntur propter aliud. In his enim quæ propter se quæruntur, quanto virtus agentis ad plura et remotiora se extendit, tanto potior est; sicut medicus reputatur melior qui plures potest et magis a sanitate distantes sanare.

─────────

[6]*De cæl. hier.* 1. PG 3, 121
[7]Lombard. PL 191, 58

4. Dionysius says[6] that *it is impossible for the divine ray to shine on us, except as girt around with sacred veils.* But prophetic revelation is conveyed by the infusion of a divine ray. So seemingly it cannot be without the veil of images.

ON THE OTHER HAND: The *Gloss* says,[7] on beginning of the Psalter that *the most excellent manner of prophecy is when a man prophesies wholly by the inspiration of the Holy Ghost, apart from any outward help of deed, word, vision or dream.*

REPLY: The excellence of means is principally assessed from the end. Now the end of prophecy is the manifestation of some truth which surpasses the faculty of man. The more this manifestation is effective, the greater is the prophecy to be esteemed.

Now it is clear that a manifestation of divine truth which derives from a bare contemplation of the truth itself is more effective than that which derives from images of bodily things. Sheer contemplation is in fact nearer to the vision of heaven, according to which truth is gazed upon in the essence of God.

So it follows that a prophecy which enables some supernatural truth to be perceived, starkly, in terms of intellective vision, is more to be prized than that in which supernatural truth is manifested by likenesses of bodily things in terms of imaginative vision.

From this too it can be shown that a prophet's mind is more sublime, even as in human teaching, a pupil is shown to have a better mind when he can grasp an intellectual truth which the master puts out without adornment, than the pupil who needs sense-perceptible examples, to lead him up to that truth. That is why David said in praise of prophecy,[8] *The God of Israel has spoken, the Rock of Israel has said to me . . . like the sun shining forth on a cloudless morning.*

Hence: 1. When some supernatural truth is to be revealed through bodily images, then more of a prophet is he who has both, namely intellectual light and imaginative vision, than he who has one only of the two: because the prophecy is then more perfect. This is what Augustine meant to say. Yet that prophecy in which intellectual truth is revealed without adornment is superior to all.

2. Judgment about what is sought for itself differs from judgment about what is sought for another. In what is sought for itself, the more the agent's power is able to extend to more numerous and more remote objects, the more effective it is. Thus a doctor is deemed better when he can heal more people and more seriously ill people.

---

[8] II *Samuel* 23, 3-4

In his autem quæ non quæruntur nisi propter aliud, quanto agens potest ex paucioribus et propinquioribus ad suum intentum pervenire, tanto videtur esse majoris virtutis; sicut magis laudatur medicus qui per pauciora et leniora potest sanare infirmum. Visio autem imaginaria in cognitione prophetica non requiritur propter se, sed propter manifestationem intelligibilis veritatis. Et ideo tanto potior est prophetia, quanto minus ea indiget.

3. Ad tertium dicendum quod nihil prohibet aliquid esse simpliciter melius, quod tamen minus proprie recipit alicujus prædicationem; sicut cognitio patriæ est nobilior quam cognitio viæ, quæ tamen magis proprie dicitur fides propterea quod nomen fidei importat imperfectionem cognitionis. Similiter autem prophetia importat quamdam obscuritatem et remotionem ab intelligibili veritate.

Et ideo magis proprie dicuntur prophetæ qui vident per imaginariam visionem, quamvis illa prophetia sit nobilior quæ est per intellectualem visionem; dummodo tamen sit eadem veritas utrobique revelata.

Si vero lumen intellectuale alicui divinitus infundatur, non ad cognoscendum aliqua supernaturalia, sed ad judicandum secundum certitudinem veritatis divinæ ea quæ humana ratione cognosci possunt, sic talis prophetia intellectualis est infra illam quæ est cum imaginaria visione ducente in supernaturalem veritatem: cujusmodi prophetiam habuerunt omnes illi qui numerantur in ordine prophetarum; qui etiam ex hoc specialiter dicuntur prophetæ, quia prophetico officio fungebantur. Unde ex persona Domini loquebantur, dicentes ad populum, *Hæc dicit Dominus*, quod non faciebant illi qui hagiographa conscripserunt; quorum plures loquebantur frequentius de his quæ humana ratione cognosci possunt, non quasi ex persona Dei, sed ex persona propria, cum adjutorio tamen divini luminis.

4. Ad quartum dicendum quod illustratio divini radii in vita præsenti non fit sine velaminibus phantasmatum qualiumcumque, quia connaturale est homini secundum statum præsentis vitæ ut non intelligat sine phantasmate. Quandoque tamen sufficiunt phantasmata quæ communi aliquo modo a sensibus abstrahuntur; nec exigitur aliqua visio imaginaria divinitus procurata. Et sic dicitur revelatio prophetica fieri sine imaginaria visione.

articulus 3. utrum gradus prophetiæ possint distingui secundum visionem imaginariam

AD TERTIUM sic proceditur:[1] 1. Videtur quod gradus prophetiæ non possint distingui secundum visionem imaginariam. Gradus enim alicujus rei

---

[1]cf IV *Sent.* 49, 2, 7 ad 2. *De veritate* XII, 13. *In* I *Cor.* 13, *lect.* 4

But in those things which are sought only for another, the more an agent can attain his end with means which are fewer and better to hand, the more appears to be his capability. Thus a doctor is the more praised when he can heal a sick person by fewer and gentler means.

Now imaginative vision in prophetic knowledge is not required for its own sake, but for the manifestation of intellectual truth. So all the more effective is prophecy when it has less need of imaginative vision.

3. That a particular predicate is applicable to one thing and less properly to another does not prevent the latter from being simply better than the former. Thus the knowledge of the blessed is superior to the knowledge of this life, which is more properly called faith, because faith implies an imperfection of knowledge. So too prophecy implies a certain obscurity and remoteness from truth.

That is why we term 'prophets' in the more proper sense, those who see in imaginative visions. Nevertheless that prophecy is to be more esteemed which obtains through intellectual vision: so long as the same truth is revealed either way.

If however God infuses intellectual light in someone, not in order to know supernatural truths, but for judging with the certainty of divine truth, elements which are accessible to human reason—this type of intellectual prophecy is inferior to that which is, with imaginative vision, leading towards supernatural truth. This sort of prophecy is that of all who are listed in the ranks of the prophets. These too are specially called prophets because they exercised a prophetic office: hence they spoke as mouthpieces for God, saying to the people, *Thus says the Lord*. This however was not done by writers of sacred books. Many of these wrote more often of those things which can be known by human reason, not as it were from the mouth of God, but out of their own mouths, and yet with the help of a divine light.[a]

4. Divine rays of light do not enlighten us in this present life without the veils of some or other images—because it is natural to men, in the conditions of this life, only to be able to understand with images. Sometimes, however, images drawn from the senses in the ordinary fashion are enough, nor is an imaginative vision required which is divinely procured. And so we can speak of prophetic revelation taking place without imaginative vision.

article 3. whether grades of prophecy can be distinguished in terms of imaginative vision

THE THIRD POINT:[1] 1. Grades of prophecy cannot seemingly be distinguished in terms of imaginative vision. The grade (or degree) of any reality is not

---

[a]A capital text for biblical inspiration in the modern sense.

non attenditur secundum id quod est propter aliud, sed secundum id quod est propter se. In prophetia autem propter se quæritur visio intellectualis, propter aliud autem visio imaginaria, ut supra dictum est.[2] Ergo videtur quod gradus prophetiæ non distinguantur secundum imaginariam visionem, sed solum secundum intellectualem.

2. Præterea, unius prophetæ videtur esse unus gradus prophetiæ. Sed uni prophetæ fit revelatio secundum diversas imaginarias visiones. Ergo diversitas imaginariæ visionis non diversificat gradus prophetiæ.

3. Præterea, secundum *glossam* in principio Psalterii,[3] prophetia consistit in dictis, et factis, et somnio, et visione. Non ergo debent prophetiæ gradus magis distingui secundum imaginariam visionem, ad quam pertinet visio, et somnium, quam secundum dicta et facta.

SED CONTRA est quod medium diversificat gradus cognitionis, sicut scientia *propter quid* est altior, eo quod est per nobilius medium quam scientia *quia est*, vel etiam quam opinio. Sed visio imaginaria in cognitione prophetica est sicut quoddam medium. Ergo gradus prophetiæ distingui debent secundum imaginariam visionem.

RESPONSIO: Dicendum quod, sicut dictum est,[4] prophetia in qua per lumen intelligibile revelatur aliqua veritas supernaturalis per imaginariam visionem, medium gradum tenet inter illam prophetiam in qua revelatur supernaturalis veritas absque imaginaria visione, et illam in qua per lumen intelligibile absque imaginaria visione dirigitur homo ad ea cognoscenda, vel agenda quæ pertinent ad humanam conversationem.

Magis autem est proprium prophetiæ cognitio quam operatio. Et ideo infimus gradus prophetiæ est cum aliquis ex interiori instinctu movetur ad aliqua exterius facienda; sicut de Samsone dicitur[5] quod *irruit Spiritus Domini in eum: et sicut solent ad ardorem ignis ligna consumi, ita et vincula, quibus ligatus erat, dissipata sunt et soluta.* Secundus autem gradus prophetiæ est cum aliquis ex interiori lumine illustratur ad cognoscendum aliqua, quæ tamen non excedunt limites naturalis cognitionis; sicut dicitur de Salomone[6] quod *locutus est parabolas, et disputavit super lignis a cedro quæ est in Libano usque ad hyssopum quæ egreditur de pariete, et disseruit de jumentis et volucribus et reptilibus et piscibus;* et hoc totum fuit ex divina inspiratione, nam præmittitur, *Dedit Deus sapientiam Salomoni, et prudentiam multam nimis.*

---

[2] above art. 2 ad 2
[3] From Cassiodorus. PL 70, 12
[4] above art. 2
[5] *Judges* 15, 14
[6] I *Kings* 4, 29, 32-3

measured by what is accidental but by what is essential. Now in prophecy intellectual vision is sought for its own sake whereas imaginative vision is ordered to another reality, as we have seen.[2] Thus, seemingly, degrees of prophecy can only be established by intellectual vision and not by imaginative vision.

2. Each single prophet is, it seems, endowed with one grade of prophecy. But the one prophet can have revelation in terms of various imaginative visions. And so diversity of imaginative vision does not diversify grades of prophecy.

3. According to a gloss on the beginning of the Psalter,[3] prophecy consists of sayings, deeds, dreams and visions. Thus grades of prophecy should no more be distinguished in terms of imaginative vision, comprising vision and dream, than in terms of words and deeds.

ON THE OTHER HAND: The medium of knowledge differentiates the degrees of knowledge: thus a science which explains by a cause (*propter quid*) is of a higher order than a science which shows that something is (*quia*), or than opinion, because the medium of knowledge is of a higher order.[a] Now in prophetic knowledge, imaginative vision functions as a means of knowledge. So we should distinguish grades of prophecy in terms of imaginative vision.

REPLY: As was said above,[4] prophecy in which by intellectual light some supernatural truth is revealed through imaginative vision holds a middle place between prophecy in which supernatural truth is revealed without imaginative vision and that in which, through intellectual light, but without imaginative vision, a man is led to know and act in what relates to human conduct.

But knowledge is more appropriate to prophecy than action. So the lowest grade of prophecy is when an inward instinct moves one to some outward action: as is said of Samson,[5] *The Spirit of the Lord came mightily upon him, and the ropes which were on his arms became flax that has caught fire, and his bonds melted off his hands.* A second grade of prophecy is when an inward light heightens a man's knowledge to know truths which however do not exceed the capacities of natural knowledge; as is said of Solomon,[6] who *uttered three thousand proverbs and his songs were one thousand and five, and he spoke of birds and beasts and reptiles and fishes.* And all this was of divine inspiration, for we read, *God gave Solomon wisdom and understanding beyond measure.*

---

[a]Or a proof which shows 'why' and a proof which shows 'that'. cf 1a. 2, 2. Vol. 2 of this series. Ed. T. McDermott.

Hi tamen duo gradus sunt infra prophetiam proprie dictam, quia non attingunt ad supernaturalem veritatem.

Illa autem prophetia in qua manifestatur supernaturalis veritas per imaginariam visionem, diversificatur. Primo secundum differentiam somnii, quod fit in dormiendo, et visionis, quæ fit in vigilando, quæ pertinet ad altiorem gradum prophetiæ, quia major vis prophetici luminis esse videtur quæ aliquem occupatum circa sensibilia in vigilando abstrahit ad supernaturalia, quam illa quæ animam hominis abstractam a sensibilibus invenit in dormiendo.

Secundo autem diversificantur gradus prophetiæ quantum ad expressionem signorum imaginabilium, quibus veritas intelligibilis exprimitur. Et quia signa maxime expressa intelligibilis veritatis sunt verba, ideo altior gradua prophetiæ videtur, quando propheta audit verba exprimentia intelligibilem veritatem sive in vigilando, sive in dormiendo, quam quando videt aliquas res significativas veritatis, sicut septem spicæ plenæ significant septem annos ubertatis.[7] In quibus etiam signis tanto videtur prophetia esse altior, quanto signa sunt magis expressa; sicut quando Jeremias vidit incendium civitatis sub similitudine ollæ succensæ, sicut dicitur.[8]

Tertio autem ostenditur altior esse gradus prophetiæ, quando propheta non solum videt signa verborum vel factorum, sed etiam videt vel in vigilando vel in dormiendo aliquem sibi colloquentem, aut aliquid demonstrantem, quia per hoc ostenditur quod mens prophetæ magis appropinquat ad causam revelantem.

Quarto autem potest attendi altitudo gradus prophetalis ex conditione ejus qui videtur. Nam altior gradus prophetiæ est, si ille qui loquitur vel demonstrat, videatur in vigilando vel in dormiendo; in specie angeli quam si videatur in specie hominis: et adhuc altior, si videatur in dormiendo vel in vigilando in specie Dei, secundum illud *Isa.*,[9] *Vidi Dominum sedentem.*

Super omnes autem hos gradus est tertium genus prophetiæ, in quo intelligibilis veritas et supernaturalis absque imaginaria visione ostenditur; quæ tamen excedit rationem prophetiæ proprie dictæ, ut dictum est.[10] Et ideo consequens est quod gradus prophetiæ proprie dictæ distinguantur secundum imaginariam visionem.

1. Ad primum ergo dicendum quod discretio luminis intelligibilis non potest a nobis cognosci, nisi secundum quod judicatur per aliqua signa imaginaria vel sensibilia. Et ideo ex diversitate imaginatorum perpenditur diversitas intellectualis luminis.

2. Ad secundum dicendum quod, sicut supra dictum est,[11] prophetia non est per modum habitus immanentis, sed magis per modum passionis

---

[7]*Genesis* 41, 26   [8]*Jeremiah* 1, 13
[9]*Isaiah* 6, 1   [10]above art. 2 ad 3

These two grades are below prophecy properly so-called, for the reason that they do not arrive at supernatural truth.

However, that prophecy in which supernatural truth is shown by imaginative vision is diversified, first by dreams which occur during sleep and by vision which occur when awake. This latter is a higher grade of prophecy: for the prophetic light must seemingly be more effective in detaching a soul occupied, when awake, with sense-perceptible realities and then drawing it towards supernatural truths, than that required to instruct a man already abstracted from sense-objects in sleep.

Secondly, grades of prophecy are diversified by diversity of imaginative symbols which serve for the expressions of intellectual truths. And because the symbols which are most expressive of intellectual truths are words, so a higher grade of prophecy seems to come about when a prophet hears words expressing intelligible truths, whether while awake or while asleep—higher indeed than when he sees objects which tell of a truth, as *seven full ears of corn* signifying *seven years of plenty*.[7] Again, with these signs, a prophecy is the more lofty the more the signs are expressive: as when Jeremiah saw the burning of the city under the similitude of a *boiling pot*.[8]

Thirdly, a yet higher grade of prophecy obtains when the prophet not only sees symbols, words, or deed but also perceives, while awake or asleep, someone speaking with him or showing him something—because in this way it is shown that the prophet's mind is nearer to the cause of revelation.

Fourthly, the height of a prophet's grade can be assessed from the condition of the one who is seen. Thus we get a higher grade of prophecy if he who speaks or shows something, appears, while awake or sleeping, in the guise of an angel rather than that of a man. Still higher is that grade of prophecy when, awake or asleep, there appears the very guise of God himself, as in *Isaiah*,[9] *I saw the Lord sitting upon a throne*.

Yet above all these grades is a third type of prophecy, in which intelligible and supernatural truth is shown without imaginative vision. But this kind surpasses the notion of prophecy properly speaking, as we have seen.[10] Consequently grades of prophecy in the strict sense are distinguished in terms of imaginative vision.

Hence: 1. Intellectual light can only be distinguished by us by means of certain imaginative or sense-perceptible signs. Hence the diversification of intellectual light is assessed from the diversity of imaginative objects.

2. As we have seen,[11] prophecy is not given as a lasting inward form, but rather as a passing passion. So it is quite possible for one and the same

---

[11]2a2æ. 171, 2

transeuntis. Unde non est inconveniens quod uni et eidem prophetæ fiat revelatio prophetica diversis vicibus secundum diversos gradus.

3. Ad tertium dicendum quod dicta et facta de quibus ibi fit mentio, non pertinent ad revelationem prophetiæ, sed ad denuntiationem quæ fit secundum dispositionem eorum quibus denuntiatur id quod prophetæ revelatum est: et hoc fit quandoque per dicta, quandoque per facta. Denuntiatio autem et operatio miraculorum consequenter se habent ad prophetiam, ut supra dictum est.[12]

articulus 4. utrum Moyses fuerit excellentior omnibus prophetis

AD QUARTUM sic proceditur:[1] 1. Videtur quod Moyses non fuerit excellentior omnibus prophetis. Dicit enim *Glossa*[2] in principio Psalt. quod *David dicitur propheta per excellentiam*. Non ergo Moyses fuit excellentissimus omnium.

2. Præterea, majora miracula facta sunt per Josue, qui fecit stare solem et lunam, ut habetur *Jos.*,[3] et per Isaiam, qui fecit retrocedere solem, ut habetur *Isa.*,[4] quam per Moysen, qui divisit mare Rubrum; similiter etiam per Eliam, de quo dicitur *Eccl.*,[5] *Quis poterit tibi militer gloriari, qui sustulisti mortuum ab inferis?* Non ergo Moyses fuit excellentissimus prophetarum.

3. Præterea, *Matt.*[6] dicitur quod *inter natos mulierum non surrexit major Joanne Baptista*. Non ergo Moyses fuit excellentior omnibus prophetis.

SED CONTRA est quod dicitur *Deut.*,[7] *Non surrexit propheta ultra in Israel, sicut Moyses.*

RESPONSIO: Dicendum quod, licet quantum ad aliquid aliquis alius prophetarum fuerit major Moyse, simpliciter tamen Moyses fuit omnibus aliis major. In prophetia enim sicut ex dictis patet,[8] consideratur et cognitio tam secundum visionem intellectualem quam secundum visionem imaginariam, et denuntiatio et confirmatio per miracula. Moyses ergo fuit aliis excellentior.

Primo quidem quantum ad visionem intellectualem, eo quod vidit ipsam Dei essentiam, sicut Paulus in raptu, sicut Augustinus dicit.[9] Unde dicitur[10] quod *palam, non per ænigmata Deum vidit.*

Secundo quantum ad imaginariam visionem, quam quasi ad nutum habebat, non solum audiens verba, sed etiam videns loquentem etiam in specie Dei, non solum in dormiendo, sed etiam in vigilando. Unde dicitur

[12]2a2æ. 171, 1
[1]cf *De veritate* XII, 9 ad 1. *In Isaiam 6*

prophet to receive prophetic revelations in different degrees and at different times.

3. The words and actions spoken of here do not refer to the revelation of prophecy, but to its proclamation. This latter is proportionate to the one who receives the revelation; and he uses sometimes words, sometimes deeds. But the proclamation, and the effecting of miracles, are only secondary effects of prophecy, as we have seen above.[12]

article 4. was Moses greater than all the prophets?

THE FOURTH POINT:[1] 1. The *Gloss* says[2] at the beginning of the Psalter that *David is the prophet par excellence*. Therefore Moses was not more excellent than all.

2. Greater miracles were done by Joshua who caused sun and moon to stop,[3] and by Isaiah who made the sun go back,[4] than by Moses who parted the Red Sea. Greater miracles were done by Elijah too, of whom it is said,[5] *Who has the right to boast as you have? you have raised a corpse from death.* So Moses was not the greatest of the prophets.

3. Our Lord says,[6] *Among those born of women there has arisen no one greater than John the Baptist.* So Moses was not greater than all the prophets.

ON THE OTHER HAND, *Deuteronomy* says,[7] *There has not arisen a prophet since in Israel like Moses.*

REPLY: In a number of particulars some other prophets were greater than Moses, nevertheless, absolutely speaking he surpasses them all.

In prophecy, as we saw above,[8] we must consider first the knowledge, both by intellectual and by imaginative vision, secondly the proclamation, and thirdly the confirmation by miracles. Moses excelled others first in intellectual vision, seeing that he gazed upon God's very essence, as St Paul did in ecstasy, according to Augustine.[9] Hence he beholds the form of the Lord.[10]

Secondly, as regards imaginative vision. This was his, as it were at his command, not only hearing words but seeing the speaker, even in the form of God—and this not only while asleep but also while awake. Hence

[2]*Ordinaria*
[4]*Isaiah* 38, 8
[6]*Matthew* 11, 11
[8]above art. 3, 2a2æ. 171, 1
[9]*Super Gen. ad litt.* XII, 27 & 28. PL 34, 477 & 478
[10]*Numbers* 12, 8

[3]*Joshua* 10, 12
[5]*Ecclesiasticus* 48, 4
[7]*Deuteronomy* 34, 10

Exod.[11] quod *loquebatur ei Dominus facie ad faciem, sicut solet loqui homo ad amicum suum.*

Tertio, quantum ad denuntiationem, quia loquebatur toti populo fidelium ex persona Dei, quasi de novo legem proponens; alii vero prophetæ loquebantur ad populum in persona Dei, quasi inducentes ad observantiam legis Moysi, secundum illud *Malach.,*[12] *Mementote legis Moysi servi mei.*

Quarto quantum ad operationem miraculorum, quæ fecit toti populo infidelium. Unde dicitur *Deut.,*[13] *Non surrexit ultra propheta in Israel, sicut Moyses, quem nosset Dominus facie ad faciem in omnibus signis atque portentis, quæ misit per eum ut faceret in terra Ægypti Pharaoni, et omnibus servis ejus, universæque terræ illius.*

1. Ad primum ergo dicendum quod prophetia David ex propinquo attingit visionem Moysis quantum ad visionem intellectualem, quia uterque accepit revelationem intelligibilis et supernaturalis veritatis absque imaginaria visione; visio tamen Moysis fuit excellentior quantum ad cognitionem divinitatis, sed David plenius cognovit, et expressit mysteria incarnationis Christi.

2. Ad secundum dicendum quod illa signa illorum prophetarum fuerunt majora secundum substantiam facti, sed tamen miracula Moysis fuerunt majora secundum modum faciendi, quia sunt facta toti populo.

3. Ad tertium dicendum quod Joannes pertinet ad novum Testamentum; cujus ministri præferuntur etiam ipsi Moysi, quasi magis revelate speculantes, ut habetur.[14]

articulus 5. utrum aliquis gradus prophetiæ sit etiam in beatis

AD QUINTUM sic proceditur:[1] 1. Videtur quod aliquis gradus prophetiæ est etiam in beatis. Moyses enim, ut dictum est,[2] vidit divinam essentiam; qui tamen propheta dicitur. Ergo pari ratione beati possunt dici prophetæ.

2. Præterea, prophetia est divina revelatio. Sed divinæ revelationes fiunt etiam angelis beatis. Ergo etiam angeli beati possunt dici prophetæ.

3. Præterea, Christus ab instanti conceptionis fuit comprehensor; et tamen ipse prophetam se nominat *Matt.,*[3] ubi dicit, *non est propheta sine honore, nisi in patria sua.* Ergo etiam comprehensores et beati possunt dici prophetæ.

4. Præterea, de Samuele dicitur *Eccl.,*[4] *Exaltavit vocem suam de terra in*

---

[11]*Exodus* 33, 11
[12]*Malachi* 4, 4
[13]*Deuteronomy* 34, 10
[14]II *Corinthians* 3, 18

Exodus,[11] *Thus the Lord used to speak to Moses face to face, as a man speaks to his friend.*

Thirdly, in the matter of proclamation: because his it was to speak to the whole body of believers as God's mouthpiece, as it were newly propounding the law. But other prophets spoke to the people on God's behalf, as it were urging them to observe the law of Moses: *Remember the law of my servant Moses.*[12]

Fourthly, as for working miracles, he wrought these on a whole people of unbelievers. Hence *Deuteronomy*,[13] *There has not arisen a prophet since in Israel, like Moses, whom the Lord knew face to face, none like him for all the signs and wonders which the Lord sent him to do in the land of Egypt to Pharaoh and to all his servants and to all his land.*

Hence: 1. David's prophecy comes near to that of Moses as regards the intellectual vision: both in fact received a revelation of intellectual and supernatural truth without imaginative vision. But Moses' vision was more outstanding as regards knowledge of the divinity: David however more fully knew and expressed the mysteries of the Incarnation of Christ.

2. The miracles of those other prophets were greater in the substance of what was done: yet Moses' miracles were greater because of the way in which they were wrought on a whole people.

3. John belongs to the New Testament whose ministers are preferred even to Moses himself, in so far as they are the more *with unveiled face beholding the Lord.*[14]

article 5. is there a degree of prophecy in the blessed?

THE FIFTH POINT:[1] 1. Seemingly even among the blessed there is a degree of prophecy. Moses, as we have seen,[2] saw the divine essence, and he is called a prophet. For a like reason the blessed can be called prophets.

2. Prophecy is a divine revelation. But divine revelations are made even to angels in beatitude. Therefore even the angels in blessedness can be called prophets.

3. From the moment of his conception Christ had the beatific vision. And yet he called himself a prophet, saying,[3] *a prophet is not without honour except in his own country and in his own house.* So both those who have beatific vision on earth and the blessed can thus be called prophets.

4. Moreover it is said[4] of Samuel, *He lifted up his voice out of the earth*

---

[1]cf 2a2æ. 173, 1. 3a, 7, 8. *In* II *Cor.* 23, *lect.* 3
[2]above art. 4
[3]*Matthew* 13, 57
[4]*Ecclesiasticus* 46, 23

prophetia delere impietatem gentis. Ergo eadem ratione alii sancti post mortem possunt prophetæ dici.

SED CONTRA est quod II *Pet.*[5] sermo propheticus comparatur *lucernæ lucenti in caliginoso loco.* Sed in beatis nulla est caligo. Ergo non possunt dici prophetæ.

RESPONSIO: Dicendum quod prophetia importat visionem quamdam alicujus supernaturalis veritatis, ut procul existentis. Quod quidem contingit esse dupliciter. Uno modo ex parte ipsius cognitionis, quia videlicet veritas supernaturalis non cognoscitur in seipsa, sed in aliquibus suis effectibus, et adhuc erit magis procul, si hoc fit per figuras corporalium rerum quam per intelligibiles effectus: et talis maxime est visio prophetica, quæ fit per figuras et similitudines corporalium rerum.

Alio modo visio est procul ex parte ipsius videntis, quia scilicet non est totaliter in ultimam perfectionem adductus, secundum illud,[6] *Quamdiu in corpore sumus, peregrinamur a Domino.* Neutro autem modo beati sunt procul: unde non possunt dici prophetæ.

1. Ad primum ergo dicendum quod visio illa Moysis fuit raptim per modum passionis, non autem permanens per modum beatitudinis, unde adhuc erat videns procul: et propter hoc non totaliter talis visio amittit rationem prophetiæ.

2. Ad secundum dicendum quod angelis fit revelatio divina, non sicut procul existentibus, sed sicut jam totaliter Deo conjunctis. Unde talis revelatio non habet rationem prophetiæ.

3. Ad tertium dicendum quod Christus simul erat comprehensor et viator. In quantum ergo erat comprehensor, non competit ipsi ratio prophetiæ, sed solum in quantum erat viator.

4. Ad quartum dicendum quod etiam Samuel nondum pervenerat ad statum beatitudinis. Unde etsi voluntate Dei ipsa anima Samuelis Sauli eventum belli prænuntiavit, Deo sibi hoc revelante, pertinet ad rationem prophetiæ. Non autem est eadem ratio de sanctis qui sunt modo in patria. Nec obstat quod arte dæmonum hoc dicitur factum quia, etsi dæmones animam alicujus sancti evocare non possint, neque cogere ad aliquid agendum, potest tamen hoc fieri divina virtute, ut dum dæmon consulitur, ipse Deus per suum nuntium veritatem enuntiet; sicet per Eliam veritatem respondit nuntiis regis, qui mittebantur ad consulendum Deum Accaron, ut habetur.[7]

Quamvis etiam dici possit quod non fuerit anima Samuelis, sed dæmon ex persona ejus loquens; quem Sapiens Samuelem nominat, et ejus

---

[5] II *Peter* I, 19

in prophecy to blot out the wickedness of the people. So, for the same reason, other saints, after their death, could be called prophets.

ON THE OTHER HAND in II *Peter* the 'prophetic word' is compared to *a light shining in a dark place.*[5] But for the blessed there is no dark place. So they cannot be called prophets.

REPLY: Prophecy implies a certain vision of some supernatural truth beyond our reach. This can be in two ways. First, on the part of the knowledge itself, because indeed the supernatural truth is not known in itself but in some of its effects. And it would be even more remote if that knowledge was effected by symbols drawn from bodily rather than intellectual effects. Such most properly is prophetic vision which is conveyed by symbols of bodily things.

Secondly, the vision is remote because the seer has not arrived wholly at ultimate perfection as is said in II *Corinthians,*[6] *While we are at home in the body we are away from the Lord.* In neither of these ways are the blessed remote. So they cannot be called prophets.

Hence: 1. The vision of the divine essence which Moses had was in an ecstasy and transitorily, and not a permanent state as with the blessed. So he still contemplates from afar. For this reason the vision does not wholly lose the character of prophecy.

2. Revelation to angels is not made to beings who are far from but fully united to God. So this revelation has not the character of prophecy.

3. Christ had at once beatific vision and experimental knowledge. In so far as he had beatific vision, the element of prophecy had no place; it could only exist in his human (experimental) knowledge.

4. Even Samuel had not reached the state of beatitude. So, if, by God's willing, the soul of Samuel foretold the outcome of Saul's war—God having revealed this to him—this pertains to prophecy. But the same does not hold of saints now in heaven. Nor is there any objection in saying that it was done by demonic arts. Because even if demons cannot call up the soul of a saint, and cannot compel it to do anything, yet by divine power it can come about that while a demon is consulted, God himself by his own messenger announces the truth: just as Elijah answered truth to the king's messengers who were sent to consult the god of Accaron.[7]

Yet we can also say that it was not the soul of Samuel, but a demon speaking in his name. The Wisdom writer calls him Samuel and his

---

[6] II *Corinthians* 5, 6
[7] II *Kings* 2, 1

87

prænuntiationem propheticam, secundum opinionem Saulis et adstantium, qui ita opinabantur.

articulus 6. utrum gradus prophetiæ varientur secundum temporis processum

AD SEXTUM sic proceditur:[1] 1. Videtur quod gradus prophetiæ varientur secundum temporis processum. Prophetia enim ordinatur ad cognitionem divinorum, ut ex dictis patet.[2] Sed, sicut dicit Gregorius,[3] *Per succesiones temporum crevit divinæ cognitionis augmentum.* Ergo et gradus prophetiæ secundum processum temporis debent distingui.

2. Præterea, revelatio prophetica fit per modum divinæ allocutionis ad hominem. A prophetis autem ea quæ sunt eis revelata, denuntiantur et verbo et scripto; dicitur[4] enim, quod *ante Samuelem sermo Domini erat pretiosus,* idest, rarus, qui tamen postea ad multos factus est: similiter etiam non inveniuntur libri prophetarum esse conscripti ante tempus Isaiæ, cui dictum est, *Sume tibi librum grandem, et scribe in eo stylo hominis,* ut patet *Isa.,*[5] post quod tempus plures prophetæ suas prophetias conscripserunt. Ergo videtur quod secundum processum temporum profecerit prophetiæ gradus.

3. Præterea, Dominus dicit, *Matt.,*[6] *Lex et prophetæ usque ad Joannem prophetaverunt.* Postmodum autem fuit donum prophetiæ in discipulis Christi multo excellentius quam fuerit in antiquis prophetis, secundum illud ad *Eph.,*[7] *Aliis generationibus non est agnitum filiis hominum,* scilicet mysterium Christi, *sicut nunc revelatum est sanctis Apostolis ejus et Prophetis in spiritu.* Ergo videtur quod secundum processum temporis creverit prophetiæ gradus.

SED CONTRA est quia Moyses fuit excellentissimus prophetarum, ut dictum est,[8] qui tamen alios prophetas præcessit. Ergo gradus prophetiæ non profecit secundum temporis processum.

RESPONSIO: Dicendum quod, sicut dictum est,[9] prophetia ordinatur ad cognitionem divinæ veritatis; per cujus contemplationem non solum in fide instruimur, sed etiam in nostris operibus gubernamur, secundum illud,[10] *Emitte lucem tuam et veritatem tuam: ipsa me deduxerunt.* Fides autem

---

[1]cf 1a. 57, 4 ad 3. *De veritate* XII, 14 ad 1
[2]above art. 2
[3]*On Ezekiel* II, 4. PL 76, 980
[4]*I Samuel* 3, 1   [5]*Isaiah* 8, 1
[6]*Matthew* 11, 13   [7]*Ephesians* 3, 5
[8]above art. 4   [9]above art. 2
[10]*Psalms* 42, 3

utterance a prophecy, in line with the opinion of Saul and bystanders who thought thus.[a]

article 6. whether grades of prophecy vary with the passage of time

THE SIXTH POINT:[1] 1. Grades of prophecy vary with the passage of time. For prophecy is ordered to knowledge of divine truths, as was said.[2] But St Gregory says,[3] *With the passage of times, there grew a knowledge of God.* So grades of knowledge should be distinguished according to the process of time.

2. Prophetic revelation takes the form of God speaking to man. But what is revealed to prophets is by them announced in word and writing. However it is said[4] that before Samuel *the word of the Lord was rare in those days;* yet this same word was afterwards conveyed to many. So too no books of the prophets seem to have been written before the time of Isaiah, who was told,[5] *Take a large tablet and write in it in common characters.* After this time several prophets wrote their prophecies. So seemingly grades of prophecy grew with the passage of time.

3. Our Lord says,[6] *All the prophets and the law prophesied until John.* Subsequently the gift of prophecy among the disciples of Christ was far more excellent than that of the ancient prophets, as is said,[7] *The mystery of Christ was not made known to the sons of men in other generations as it has now been revealed to his holy apostles and prophets by the Spirit.* Thus degrees of prophecy seem to have progressed with the passage of time.

ON THE OTHER HAND, Moses, as we saw,[8] was the most outstanding of prophets, yet he came before other prophets. Therefore grades of prophecy did not progress with the passage of time.

REPLY: As was said,[9] prophecy is ordered to the knowledge of divine truth. By contemplation of this truth we are not only instructed in faith but also governed in our works: *Send out thy light and thy truth, let them lead me.*[10] Our faith however is mainly compounded of two truths, first,

---

[a]In this reference to the story of the Witch of Endor (1 *Sam.* 28) St Thomas, as often with scriptural texts, proposes two explanations without committing himself to one more than another. Here (*a*) following Augustine, the calling up of Samuel really took place because God saw fit to instruct Saul about his fate in that way. This would explain the witch's panic (1 *Sam.* 28, 12); for once something had happened which transcended her witchcraft.

(*b*) it was a diabolical illusion in which the real Samuel had no part.

(*a*) fits in with *Ecclesiasticus* 46, 20. (*b*) requires a laboured explanation: a devil spoke, impersonating Samuel and called Samuel by the author, expressing the thoughts of Saul and other bystanders.

nostra in duobus principaliter consistit: primo quidem in vera Dei cognitione secundum illud,[11] *Accedentem ad Deum oportet credere, quia est.* Secundo in mysterio incarnationis Christi, secundum illud,[12] *Creditis in Deum, et in me credite.* Si ergo de prophetia loquamur, inquantum ordinatur ad fidem Deitatis, sic quidem crevit secundum tres temporum distinctiones; scilicet ante legem, sub lege et sub gratia. Nam ante legem, Abraham et alii patres prophetice sunt instructi de his quæ pertinent ad fidem Deitatis. Unde et prophetæ nominantur, secundum illud,[13] *In prophetis meis nolite malignari,* quod specialiter dicitur propter Abraham et Isaac.

Sub lege autem facta est revelatio prophetica de his quæ pertinent ad fidem Deitatis, excellentius quam ante, quia jam oportebat circa hoc institui non solum speciales personas, aut quasdam familias, sed totum populum. Unde dicit Moysi,[14] *Ego Dominus, qui apparui Abraham, Isaac et Jacob, in Deo omnipotente; et nomen meum Adonai non indicavi eis,* quia scilicet præcedentes patres fuerant instructi in fide communi de omnipotentia unius Dei; sed Moyses postea plenius fuit instructus de simplicitate divinæ essentiæ, cum dictum est ei,[15] *Ego sum qui sum,* quod quidem nomen significatur a Judæis per hoc nomen *Adonai,* propter venerationem illius ineffabilis nominis.

Postmodum vero tempore gratiæ ab ipso Filio Dei revelatum est mysterium Trinitatis, secundum illud *Matt.,*[16] *Euntes, docete omnes gentes, baptizantes eos in nomine Patris, et Filii, et Spiritus Sancti.*

In singulis tamen statibus prima revelatio excellentior fuit. Prima autem revelatio ante legem facta est Abrahæ, cujus tempore cœpessrunt homines a fide unius Dei deviare ad idololatriam declinando; ante autem non erat necessaria talis revelatio omnibus in cultu unius Dei persistentibus. Isaac vero facta est inferior revelatio, quasi fundata super revelatione facta Abrahæ: unde dictum est ei,[17] *Ego sum Deus Abraham, patris tui*; et similiter ad Jacob dictum est,[18] *Ego sum Deus Abraham, patris tui, et Deus Isaac.* Et similiter in statu legis prima revelatio facta Moysi excellentior fuit; supra quam fundatur omnis alia prophetarum revelatio. Ita etiam in tempore gratiæ super revelatione facta Apostolis de fide Unitatis et Trinitatis fundatur tota fides Ecclesiæ, secundum illud,[19] *Super hanc petram,* scilicet confessionis tuæ, *ædificabo Ecclesiam meam.*

---

[11]*Hebrews* 11, 6
[12]*John* 14, 1
[13]*Psalms* 104, 15
[14]*Exodus* 6, 2
[15]ibid 3, 14
[16]*Matthew* 28, 19
[17]*Genesis* 26, 24

a true knowledge of God, as in *Hebrews*,[11] *Whoever would draw near to God must believe that he exists*, and secondly, the mystery of the Incarnation of Christ: *Believe in God, believe in me also.*[12]

Now if we speak of prophecy as ordered to faith in God, in this sense it grew with the passage of time in three stages, viz before the law, under the law, and under grace. In fact, before the law, Abraham and the other patriarchs were prophetically taught about what relates to faith in God. Hence they are named prophets: *touch not my anointed ones, do my prophets no harm.*[13] These words are especially said on account of Abraham and Isaac.

Under the law, however, prophetic revelation was about common faith in God, yet more excellently than before, because then instruction about this became necessary not only for special persons or certain families, but for a whole people. Hence the Lord said to Moses,[14] *I am the Lord: I appeared to Abraham, to Isaac, and to Jacob, as God Almighty. But by my name Yahweh (the Lord) I did not make myself known to them.* The older Patriarchs were instructed in general about the omnipotence of the One God, but Moses after them was more fully taught about the simplicity of the divine essence when he was told,[15] *I am who I am.* This name was represented by the Jews by the term Adonai, out of respect for God's ineffable name.

Finally, at the time of grace, the mystery of the Trinity was revealed by the Son of God himself, as is said,[16] *Go therefore and make disciples of all nations, baptizing them in the name of the Father and of the Son and of the Holy Spirit.*

Nevertheless, taking each state singly, the first was the more excellent. For the first revelation, before the law, was made to Abraham, in whose time men began to fall aside from faith in the One God, by declining into idolatry. Before that no such revelation was needed since all persisted in the worship of the One God.

A lesser revelation was made to Isaac, one as it were founded on the revelation made to Abraham; hence we read,[17] *I am the God of Abraham your father.* So too to Jacob was said,[18] *I am the God of Abraham your father and the God of Isaac.*

So too, under the law, the first revelation made to Moses was the more excellent, and on it was founded the revelation made to all the prophets.

Then again, in the time of grace, the whole faith of the Church is founded on the revelation made to the Apostles about belief in the Unity and the Trinity. It is founded, in the words of *Matthew*,[19] *Upon this rock*, that is of your confession, *I will build my Church.*

---

[18]Genesis 28, 13   [19]*Matthew* 16, 18

Quantum vero ad fidem incarnationis Christi, manifestum est quod quanto fuerunt Christo propinquiores, sive ante, sive post, ut plurimum plenius de hoc instructi fuerunt; post tamen plenius quam ante, ut Apostolus dicit.[20]

Quantum vero ad directionem humanorum actuum, prophetica revelatio diversificata est non secundum temporis processum, sed secundum conditionem negotiorum, quia ut dicitur,[21] *Cum defecerit prophetia, dissipabitur populus.* Et ideo quolibet tempore instructi sunt homines divinitus de agendis, secundum quod erat expediens ad salutem electorum.

1. Ad primum ergo dicendum quod dictum Gregorii intelligendum est de tempore ante Christi incarnationem, quantum ad cognitionem hujus mysterii.

2. Ad secundum dicendum quod, sicut Augustinus dicit,[22] *Quemadmodum regni Assyriorum primo tempore extitit Abraham, cui promissiones apertissime fierent; ita in occidentalis Babylonis, idest Romanæ urbis, exordio, qua imperante fuerat Christus venturus, in quo implerentur illa promissa oracula prophetarum, non solum loquentium, verum etiam scribentium in tantæ rei futuræ testimonium solverentur, scilicet promissiones Abrahæ factæ. Cum enim prophetæ nunquam fere defuissent populo Israel, ex quo ibi reges esse cœperunt, in usum tantummodo eorum fuere, non gentium. Quando autem ea scriptura prophetica manifestius condebatur quæ gentibus quandoque prodesset, tunc oportebat incipere quando condebatur hæc civitas, scilicet Romana, quæ gentibus imperaret.* Ideo autem maxime tempore regum oportuit prophetis in illo populo abundare, quia tunc populus non opprimebatur ab alienigenis, sed proprium regem habebat: et ideo oportebat per prophetas eum instrui de agendis, quasi libertatem habentem.

3. Ad tertium dicendum quod prophetæ prænuntiantes Christi adventum non potuerunt durare nisi usque ad Joannem, qui præsentialiter Christum digito demonstravit: et tamen, ut Hieronymus ibidem dicit,[23] *Non hoc dicitur, ut post Joannem excludat prophetas. Legimus enim in Actibus Apostolorum, et Agabum prophetasse, et quatuor virgines filias Philippi.* Joannes etiam librum propheticum conscripsit de fine Ecclesiæ: et singulis temporibus non defuerunt aliqui prophetiæ spiritum habentes, non quidem ad novam doctrinam fidei depromendam, sed ad humanorum atuum directionem, sicut Augustinus refert,[24] quod *Theodosius Augustus ad Joannem in Ægypti eremo constitutum, quem prophetandi spiritu præditum fama crebrescente didicerat, misit, et ab eo nuntium victoriæ certissimum accepit.*

---

[20]*Ephesians* 3, 5
[21]*Proverbs* 29, 18
[22]*De civit. Dei* XVIII, 27. PL 41, 584

As regards faith in the Incarnation of Christ, it is clear that those who were near to Christ, whether before or after him, were, generally speaking, more fully instructed. Yet after him more than before him, as St Paul says in *Ephesians*.[20]

As regards the direction of human acts, prophetic revelation was diversified not according to the progress of time but according to the needs of circumstances; because, as is said in *Proverbs*,[21] *where there is no prophecy, the people cast off restraint.* That is why at every period men were instructed by God about what they were to do, according as was expedient for the salvation of the elect.

Hence: 1. Gregory's words are to be understood of the time before the Incarnation of Christ as regards knowledge of this mystery.

2. We read in Augustine[22] that *just as at the time of the Assyrian domination, Abraham arose, and to him the most clear promises were made; so too in the beginning of that western Babylon, the city of Rome, under whose rule Christ was to come, to fulfil those promises, it was only right that the Oracles of the prophets, spoken or written, and recalling the promises made to Abraham, should bear witness to so great a happening which was soon to be. Prophets hardly ever ceased to be in Israel, from the day when they began to have kings, but they had served their kings only and had not profited the nations. But when the era of Scripture dawned, the content of which was more manifestly prophetic, and was one day to profit the nations—then it was that Rome was founded, the Rome which was to rule over nations.* Why specially in the period of the kings prophets were numerous in Israel is because the people were not oppressed by foreigners and had their own kings. They had then, being as it were free, to be instructed by prophets about their conduct.

3. Prophets who announced the coming of Christ could only last up to the time of John Baptist who with his finger pointed to Christ actually present. But Jerome says,[23] *This is not said to exclude prophets after John Baptist, for we read in the Acts of Agabus who prophesied, as did the four virgin daughters of Philip.* And St John wrote a prophetical book about the end of the Church. At each period there were always some who had the spirit of prophecy, not for the purpose of setting out new doctrine to be believed, but for the governance of human activities. And, as Augustine says,[24] *Theodosius Augustus sent a delegation to a monk called John who lived in the desert of Egypt. He had heard about his growing reputation as a prophet, and he received from him the announcement of a victory which would most certainly be his.*

---

[23]*On Matthew* 11, 13. PL 26, 74
[24]*De civit. Dei* v, 26. PL 41, 172

Quæstio 175. de raptu

Deinde considerandum est de raptu; et circa hoc quæruntur sex:

1. utrum anima hominis rapiatur ad divina;
2. utrum raptus pertineat ad vim cognoscitivam vel appetitivam;
3. utrum Paulus in raptu viderit Dei essentiam;
4. utrum fuerit alienatus a sensibus;
5. utrum fuerit totaliter anima a corpore separata in statu illo;
6. quid circa hoc sciverit et quid ignoraverit.

articulus 1. *utrum anima hominis rapiatur ad divina*

AD PRIMUM sic proceditur:[1] 1. Videtur quod anima hominis non rapiatur ad divina. Definitur enim a quibusdam raptus, ab eo quod est secundum naturam, in id quod est supra naturam, vi superioris naturæ elevatio. Est autem secundum naturam hominis ut ad divina elevetur: dicit enim Augustinus,[2] *Fecisti nos, Domine, ad te; et inquietum est cor nostrum donec requiescat in te.* Non ergo hominis anima rapitur ad divina.

2. Præterea, Dionysius dicit[3] quod justitia Dei in hoc attenditur quod omnibus rebus distribuit secundum suum modum et dignitatem. Sed quod aliquis elevetur supra id quod est secundum naturam, non pertinet ad modum hominis vel dignitatem. Ergo videtur quod non rapiatur mens hominis a Deo in divina.

3. Præterea, raptus quamdam violentiam importat. Sed Deus non regit nos per violentiam et coacte, ut Damascenus dicit.[4] Non ergo mens hominis rapitur ad divina.

SED CONTRA est quod dicit Apostolus,[5] *Scio hominem in Christo . . . raptum usque ad tertium cœlum:* ubi dicit *Glossa,*[6] *raptum, idest contra naturam elevatum.*

RESPONSIO: Dicendum quod raptus violentiam quandam importat, ut dictum est.[7] *Violentum* autem *dicitur cujus principium est extra, nil conferente eo quod vim patitur,* ut dicitur in *Ethic.*[8] Confert autem unumquodque ad id

---

[1]cf *De Veritate* XIII, 1 & 2. *In* II *Cor.* 12, *lect.* 1
[2]*Confessions* 1, 1. PL 32, 661
[3]*De div. nom.* 8. PG 3, 893
[4]*De fide orth.* II, 30. PG 94, 972
[5]II *Corinthians* 12, 2
[6]*Glossa Lombardi* PL 192, 80
[7]3rd argument   [8]*Ethics* III, 1. 1110a1, b15

Question 175. ecstasy

We must now consider ecstasy. There are six points of inquiry:

1. whether a man's soul is carried away to divine realities;
2. whether ecstasy relates to a faculty of knowledge or an appetitive power;
3. whether Paul when 'rapt to heaven' saw God's essence;
4. whether then he was abstracted from his senses;
5. whether in that state his soul was wholly apart from the body;
6. what, in that state, he knew and did not know;

article 1. whether a man's soul is carried away to divine realities

THE FIRST POINT:[1] 1. Ecstasy is defined by some as an elevation from a state in accordance with nature towards that which is above nature, by the power of a superior nature.[a] But it is in line with a man's nature that he should be raised to divine realities, as Augustine says,[2] *You have made us, O Lord, for you, and our heart is unquiet until it rests in you.* Thus man's soul is not carried away to divine realities.

2. Dionysius says[3] that *the justice of God is realized in this that he distributed to every single being according to his mode and worth.* But to be raised above nature's level bears no relationship to a man's mode and worth. So seemingly man's mind is not carried away to divine realities.

3. Ecstasy connotes a certain violence. But God does not rule us by violence and compulsion, as Damascene says.[4] Therefore man's mind is not carried away to God.

ON THE OTHER HAND, St Paul says,[5] *I know a man in Christ who was caught up to the third heaven,* and the *Gloss* adds,[6] *Caught up, that is to say raised against his nature.*

REPLY: Ecstasy does imply a certain violence, as was said.[7b] Violence however is done *when the principle is external and the sufferer confers nothing to it.*[8] Every being contributes something in the direction of its

---

[a] A definition attributed to Peter Lombard.
[b] *Raptus* has been translated 'ecstasy', but this needs to be understood in the sense of *Philippians* 3, 12, of being taken up or grasped by Christ Jesus.
St Thomas here speaks of extrinsic causes of ecstasy, and particularly of God who is most properly the cause of ecstasy. There is another cause of ecstasy which is interior to the subject, treated of in *De veritate* XII, 9 and XIII, 3. This is born of an intensity of contemplation and love which rises to such a pitch that the lover is drawn out of his senses, 2a2æ. 173, 3 & ad 2; 1a2æ. 28, 3.

in quod tendit secundum propriam inclinationem vel voluntariam vel naturalem. Et ideo oportet quod ille qui rapitur ab aliquo exteriori rapiatur in aliquid quod est diversum ab eo in quod ejus inclinatio tendit. Quæ quidem diversitas attenditur dupliciter: uno quidem modo quantum ad finem inclinationis; puta si lapis, qui naturaliter inclinatur ad hoc quod feratur deorsum, projiciatur sursum; alio modo quantum ad modum tendendi, puta si lapis velocius projiciatur deorsum quam sit motus ejus naturalis.

Sic igitur et anima hominis dupliciter dicitur rapi in id quod est præter naturam: uno modo quantum ad terminum raptus, puta quando rapitur ad pœnas, secundum illud Psal.,[9] Ne quando rapiat, et non sit qui eripiat; alio modo quantum ad modum homini connaturalem, qui est ut per sensibilia intelligat veritatem. Et ideo quando abstrahitur a sensibilium apprehensione dicitur rapi, etiamsi elevetur ad ea ad quæ naturaliter ordinatur, dum tamen hoc non fiat ex propria intentione; sicut accidit in somno, qui est secundum naturam, unde non potest proprie raptus dici.

Hujusmodi autem abstractio, ad quæcumque fiat, potest ex triplici causa contingere. Uno modo ex causa corporali, sicut patet* in his qui propter aliquam infirmitatem alienationem patiuntur. Secundo modo ex virtute dæmonum, sicut patet in arreptitiis. Tertio modo ex virtute divina, et sic loquimur nunc de raptu, prout scilicet aliquis spiritu divino elevatur ad aliqua supernaturalia cum abstractione a sensibus, secundum illud Ezech.,[10] Spiritus elevavit me inter cœlum et terram et adduxit me in Jerusalem in visione Dei.

Sciendum tamen quod rapi quandoque dicitur aliquis non solum propter alienationem a sensibus, sed etiam propter alienationem ab his quibus intendebat; sicut cum aliquis patitur evagationem mentis præter propositum. Sed hoc non ita proprie dicitur.

1. Ad primum ergo dicendum quod naturale est homini ut in divina tendat per sensibilium apprehensionem, secundum illud Rom.,[11] Invisibilia Dei per ea quæ facta sunt, intellecta conspiciuntur. Sed iste modus, quod aliquis elevetur ad divina cum abstractione a sensibus, non est homini naturalis.

2. Ad secundum dicendum quod ad modum et dignitatem hominis pertinet quod ad divina elevetur, ex hoc ipso quod homo factus est ad imaginem Dei. Et quia bonum divinum in infinitum excedit humanam facultatem, indiget homo ut supernaturaliter ad illud bonum capessendum adjuvetur: quod fit per quodcumque beneficium gratiæ. Unde quod sic elevetur mens a Deo per raptum, non est contra naturam, sed supra facultatem naturæ.

---

*Piana: accidit, happens

own proper inclinations, whether voluntary or natural. But for him who is carried away by some external force it must be in a direction other than that taken by his natural inclination. It differs in two ways; first as regards the term of the inclination; as when a stone, which naturally tends to fall, is projected upwards; and secondly as regards the way it tends, as when a stone is hurled downwards at a greater speed than that caused by gravity's pull.

So then the soul of man is said to be carried away beyond nature, first, as regards the term of that carrying away, as when carried away for punishment: thus the *Psalm*,[9] *Lest I rend you and there be none to deliver you*. Secondly, as regards the mode which is connatural to man, namely, understanding truths through the medium of sense-objects. So when he is abstracted from the apprehension of sense-objects, he is said to be carried away, even if uplifted to those truths to which he is naturally ordered: provided this is not done intentionally, as when a man takes to sleep which is in accordance with nature and which therefore cannot properly be called ecstasy.

Now abstraction of this sort, in whatever direction it tends, can happen for three reasons; first, from a bodily cause, as is clear from those who by reason of some infirmity have lost their reason. Secondly, from the power of demons, as with those who are possessed. Thirdly, from the divine power. It is in this sense that we now speak of ecstasy, in so far, namely, as one by the Spirit of God is uplifted to a supernatural level, with abstraction from the senses, as is said,[10] *The Spirit lifted me up between heaven and earth and brought me in visions of God to Jerusalem*.

We should realize however that ecstasy is sometimes spoken of not only when a person is abstracted from his senses, but also withdrawn from what he was attending to, as when a man's mind wanders contrary to his purpose. But this is to use ecstasy in a less proper sense.

Hence: 1. It is natural for a man to tend towards the divine by an apprehension of sense-objects. Thus *Romans*,[11] *His invisible nature has been clearly perceived by the things that have been made*. But that condition in which a person is uplifted to the divine with an abstraction from the senses is not natural to man.

2. It belongs to the mode and worth of a man to be uplifted to the divine because man was created in the image of God. But as the divine goodness infinitely surpasses human capacities, man needs to be supernaturally helped to attain this good—and this takes place in any bestowal of grace. That a mind should so be uplifted by God is not against nature but above the capacities of nature.

---

[9] *Psalms* 49, 22   [10] *Ezekiel* 8, 3   [11] *Romans* 1, 20

97

3. Ad tertium dicendum quod verbum Damasceni est intelligendum quantum ad ea quæ sunt per hominem facienda; quantum vero ad ea quæ excedunt liberi arbitrii facultatem, necesse est quod homo quadam fortiori operatione elevetur: quæ quidem quantum ad aliquid potest dici coactio, si scilicet attendatur modus operationis, non autem si attendatur terminus operationis, in quem natura hominis et ejus intentio ordinatur.

articulus 2. *utrum raptus magis pertineat ad vim cognoscitivam quam ad vim appetitivam*

AD SECUNDUM sic proceditur:[1] 1. Videtur quod raptus magis pertineat ad vim appetitivam quam ad vim cognoscitivam. Dicit enim Dionysius,[2] *Est autem extasim faciens divinus amor.* Sed amor pertinet ad vim appetitivam. Ergo et extasis sive raptus.

2. Præterea, Gregorius dicit[3] quod *ille qui porcos pavit, vagatione mentis et immunditiæ sub semetipso cecidit; Petrus vero, quem angelus solvit ejusque mentem in extasi rapuit, extra se quidem, sed supra semetipsum fuit.* Sed ille filius prodigus per affectum in inferiora dilapsus est. Ergo etiam illi qui rapiuntur in superiora per affectum hoc patiuntur.

3. Præterea, super illud *Psal.,*[4] *In te, Domine, speravi, non confundar in æternum,* dicit *Glossa,*[5] *Extasis græce, latine dicitur excessus mentis qui fit duobus modis, vel pavore terrenorum, vel mente rapta ad superna, et inferiorum oblita.* Sed pavor terrenorum ad affectum pertinet. Ergo etiam raptus mentis ad superna, qui ex opposito ponitur, pertinet ad affectum.

SED CONTRA est quod super illud *Psal.,*[6] *Ego dixi in excessu meo, Omnis homo mendax,* dicit *Glossa,*[7] *Dicitur extasis, cum mens non pavore alienatur, sed aliqua inspiratione revelationis sursum assumitur.* Sed revelatio pertinet ad vim intellectivam. Ergo et extasis sive raptus.

RESPONSIO: Dicendum quod de raptu dupliciter loqui possumus. Uno modo quantum ad id in quod aliquis rapitur, et sic proprie loquendo, raptus non potest pertinere ad vim appetitivam, sed solum ad cognoscitivam. Dictum est enim,[8] quod raptus est præter propriam inclinationem ejus quod rapitur: ipse autem motus appetitivæ virtutis est quædam inclinatio ad bonum appetibile. Unde, proprie loquendo, ex hoc quod homo appetit aliquid, non rapitur, sed per se movetur. Alio modo potest considerari raptus quantum ad suam causam: et sic potest habere causam ex parte

---

[1]cf 1a2æ. 28, 3. *In* II *Cor.* 12, *lect.* I [2]*De div. nom.* 4, PG 3, 712
[3]*Dialog.* II, 3. PL 66, 138 [4]*Psalms* 30, 2
[5]*Ordinaria,* from Augustine. PL 36, 230 [6]*Psalms* 115, 2

3. The words of Damascene must be understood with respect to what a man must do. However, for what exceeds the capacities of free-will, a man needs to be uplifted by a more powerful source of action. This source might be termed coercive if we consider the mode of action, not so however if we consider the term of the action, namely the end to which man's nature and tendency is ordered.

article 2. whether ecstasy relates to a cognitive or to an affective power

THE SECOND POINT:[1] 1. Ecstasy seems more related to an affective power than to a faculty of knowledge. Dionysius says,[2] *Divine love is the cause of ecstasy*. But love is an affective power. So too, then, is ecstasy or rapture.

2. Gregory tells us[3] that *he who fed the swine, because of his uncontrolled mind and uncleanness, fell beneath himself. St Peter, however, who was released by an angel and whose spirit was caught up in ecstasy, was in truth beside himself yet above himself.* The prodigal son surely fell so low because of his affective powers. So too those who are rapt up to higher things do this through their affective powers.

3. On *Psalm* 29,[4] *In thee O Lord do I seek refuge let me never be put to shame*, the *Gloss* says,[5] *Ekstasis in Greek becomes in Latin, 'carrying away of the mind'. This takes place in two ways: either one is afraid of earthly realities, or the mind is caught up to higher things and forgets the earthly.* Fear of earthly realities concerns the affective powers. So too must it concern the opposite process when the mind is rapt to heavenly realities.

ON THE OTHER HAND on the verse,[6] *I said in my consternation, Men are all a vain hope*, the *Gloss* says,[7] *Ecstasy is meant here, when the mind is not moved by fear, but by some inspiration of revelation is drawn upward.* But revelation relates to intellectual processes. Therefore ecstasy or rapture does so too.

REPLY: We can speak of ecstasy in two ways. First as regards its object or term to which a man is drawn. In this respect, strictly speaking, ecstasy cannot relate to appetitive powers but only to the intellective. As was said,[8] ecstasy is outside the inclination of him who is rapt. Now the movement of an appetitive power is a sort of inclination towards desirable good. It follows that, properly speaking, a man who desires some good is not in ecstasy but simply moving himself. Secondly, ecstasy can be considered in terms of its cause. In this respect, ecstasy can have its cause in the

---

[7]*Ordinaria*, from Augustine. PL 37, 1492
[8]above art. 1

appetitivæ virtutis. Ex hoc enim ipso quod appetitus ad aliquid vehementer afficitur, potest contingere quod ex violentia affectus homo ab omnibus aliis alienetur.

Habet etiam affectum in appetitiva virtute, cum scilicet aliquis delectatur in his ad quæ rapitur. Unde et Apostolus dixit se raptum non solum ad tertium cœlum, quod pertinet ad contemplationem intellectus, sed etiam in paradisum, quod pertinet ad affectum.

1. Ad primum ergo dicendum quod raptus addit aliquid supra extasim. Nam extasis importat simpliciter excessum a seipso, secundum quem scilicet aliquis extra suam ordinationem ponitur; sed raptus super hoc addit violentiam quandam. Potest igitur extasis ad vim appetitivam pertinere, puta cum alicujus appetitus tendit in ea quæ extra ipsum sunt: et secundum hoc Dionysius dicit quod *divinus amor facit extasim,* inquantum scilicet facit appetitum hominis tendere in res amatas: unde postea subdit quod *etiam ipse Deus, qui est omnium causa, per abundantiam amatoriæ bonitatis extra seipsum fit per providentiam ad omnia existentia.*[9] Quamvis etiam si expresse hoc diceretur de raptu, non designaretur, nisi quod amor esset causa raptus.

2. Ad secundum dicendum quod in homine est duplex appetitus; scilicet intellectivus, qui dicitur voluntas, et sensitivus, qui dicitur sensualitas. Est autem proprium homini ut appetitus inferior subdatur appetitui superiori, et superior moveat inferiorem. Dupliciter ergo homo secundum appetitum potest fieri extra seipsum. Uno modo quando appetitus intellectivus totaliter in divina tendit, prætermissis his ad quæ inclinat appetitus sensitivus; et sic Dionysius dicit[10] quod *Paulus ex virtute divini amoris extasim faciente dixit, Vivo ego, jam non ego, vivit vero in me Christus.*[11]

Alio modo quando prætermisso appetitu superiori, homo totaliter fertur in ea quæ pertinent ad appetitum inferiorem, et sic *ille qui porcos pavit, sub semetipso cecidit.*[12] Et iste excessus vel extasis plus appropinquat ad rationem raptus quam primus, quia scilicet appetitus superior est magis homini proprius. Unde quando homo ex violentia appetitus inferioris abstrahitur a motu appetitus superioris, magis abstrahitur ab eo quod est sibi proprium. Quia tamen non est ibi violentia, eo quod voluntas potest resistere passioni, deficit a vera ratione raptus; nisi forte tam vehemens passio sit quod usum rationis totaliter tollat, sicut contingit in his qui propter vehementiam iræ vel amoris insaniunt.

Considerandum tamen quod uterque excessus secundum appetitum existens potest causare excessum cognoscitivæ virtutis: vel quia mens ad

---

[9]loc cit
[10]loc cit

affective powers. In fact, should one's desire cleave very strongly to something, it can be that the great intensity of that love causes a man to become a stranger to all else.

Ecstasy also has an effect on the appetitive powers: a person can delight in the object of his ecstasy. That is why St Paul said that he was caught up not only to the 'third heaven', which relates to intellectual contemplation, but also to 'Paradise' which relates to the affective powers.

Hence: 1. Rapture adds something to ecstasy. For ecstasy implies simply 'standing outside oneself' as when a person is placed outside his usual disposition. But rapture ('being caught up') adds a note of violence to this. Accordingly Dionysius says that *divine love causes ecstasy*—in so far as it causes a man's inclination to tend towards the objects of his love. Hence he goes on,[9] *even God himself, who is cause of all, because of the immensity of his loving goodness, goes outside himself by his providence towards all existing beings.* If these words were applied expressly to ecstasy, they would say no more than that love is the cause of ecstasy.

2. In man the appetitive is twofold: first the intellective appetite which is termed will, and the sense appetite which is termed 'sensitive'. Now it is proper to man's nature that the lower appetite should be subject to the higher and directed by it. In two ways then can a man be 'outside himself' as regards his appetitive powers. One is when his intellective appetite wholly inclines to divine realities, and all the inclinations of his sense appetite are left behind. And in this way, Dionysius,[10] *St Paul by virtue of the divine love which put him into ecstasy said, 'I live now, not I, but Christ lives in me.'*[11]

The second is when the higher appetite is left behind and a man is wholly carried away by what relates to his lower appetite. Thus *he who fed the swine fell into a state beneath himself.*[12] And this kind of excess or going out of oneself comes nearer to the reality of ecstasy than the former. Because the higher appetite is more characteristic of man, when a man is torn away by the violence of a lower appetite from the influence of a higher appetite, he is being drawn away from that which is more characteristically his. Since however there is no violence in this situation, seeing that the will can resist passion, there is no real ecstasy here: unless perhaps the passion is so intense that it makes away with all use of reason, as happens in those who are mad because of the intensity of their wrath or of their love.

Note however that both these excesses in the appetitive can cause an excess in the intellective power, either because the mind is caught

[11]*Galatians* 2, 20
[12]Gregory, loc cit

quædam intelligibilia rapiatur, alienata a sensibus; vel quia rapiatur ad aliquam imaginariam visionem, seu phantasticam apparitionem.

3. Ad tertium dicendum quod sicut amor est motus appetitus respectu boni, ita timor est motus appetitus respectu mali. Unde eadem ratione ex utroque potest causari excessus mentis; præsertim cum *timor ex amore causetur*, sicut Augustinus dicit.[13]

articulus 3. utrum Paulus in raptu viderit Dei essentiam

AD TERTIUM sic proceditur:[1] 1. Videtur quod Paulus in raptu non viderit Dei essentiam. Sicut enim de Paulo legitur[2] quod est raptus *usque ad tertium cœlum*; ita et de Petro legitur[3] quod *cecidit super eum mentis excessus*. Sed Petrus in suo excessu non vidit Dei essentiam, sed quamdam imaginariam visionem. Ergo videtur quod nec Paulus Dei essentiam viderit.

2. Præterea, visio Dei facit hominem beatum. Sed Paulus in illo raptu non fuit beatus, alioquin nunquam ad vitæ hujus miseriam rediisset; sed corpus ejus fuisset per redundantiam ab anima glorificatum, sicut erit in sanctis post resurrectionem: quod patet esse falsum. Ergo Paulus in raptu non vidit Dei essentiam.

3. Præterea, fides et spes esse non possunt simul cum visione divinæ essentiæ, ut habetur 1 ad *Cor.*[4] Sed Paulus in statu illo habuit fidem et spem. Ergo non vidit Dei essentiam.

4. Præterea, sicut Augustinus dicit,[5] *Secundum visionem imaginariam quædam similitudines corporum videntur.* Sed Paulus in raptu dicitur quasdam similitudines vidisse, puta tertii cœli et paradisi, ut habetur II ad *Cor.*[6] Ergo videtur esse raptus ad imaginariam visionem magis quam ad visionem divinæ essentiæ.

SED CONTRA est quod Augustinus determinat,[7] quod *ipsa Dei substantia a quibusdam videri potuit in hac vita positis; sicut a Moyse et Paulo, qui raptus audivit ineffabilia verba, quæ non licet homini loqui.*

RESPONSIO: Dicendum quod quidam dixerunt Paulum in raptu non vidisse ipsam Dei essentiam, sed quamdam refulgentiam claritatis ipsius. Sed contrarium manifeste Augustinus determinat, non solum in libro de videndo Deum, loc. cit., sed etiam *Super Genes. ad litt.*[8] et habetur in *Glossa* ord. sup. illud, *Usque ad tertium cœlum.*[9] Et hoc etiam ipsa verba

---

[13]*De civit. Dei* XIV, 7. PL 41, 410
[1]cf 1a. 12, 13. IV *Sent.* 49, 2, 7 ad 5. *De veritate* XIII, 2. *In* II *Cor.* 12, *lect.* 1 & 2
[2]II *Corinthians* 12, 2
[3]*Acts* 10, 10
[4]I *Corinthians* 13, 8

up by certain intellectual truths which are remote from the senses or because he is drawn to some vision of the imagination or some imaginative apparition.

3. Love is a movement of the affective appetite in relation to a good; fear is this movement when related to evil. Either of these can cause, in the same way, a carrying away of the mind; especially, as Augustine says,[13] *fear itself is caused by love.*

article 3. *whether Paul, rapt to heaven, saw God's essence*

THE THIRD POINT:[1] 1. It seems that Paul did not see God's essence. Just as it is written of Paul that he was rapt to the third heaven,[2] so of St Peter it is said,[3] *He fell into a trance.* But Peter in this state did not see the essence of God but some vision in the imagination. So too we would argue that Paul did not see the divine essence.

2. The vision of God makes a man blessed. But Paul in that vision was not blessed: otherwise he would never have returned to the wretchedness of this life, and his body would have been glorified by the radiance of his soul, as it will be with the saints after the general resurrection. This is manifestly false. Therefore Paul in his ecstasy did not see the divine essence.

3. Faith and hope cannot co-exist with a vision of the divine essence: thus 1 *Corinthians.*[4] But Paul in that state had faith and hope. Therefore he did not see the divine essence.

4. Augustine says[5] that *in imaginative vision certain bodily forms are seen.* But Paul in ecstasy seems to have seen certain forms or likenesses namely, the third heaven and Paradise.[6] So it seems that he was rapt up to some imaginative vision not to that of the divine essence.

ON THE OTHER HAND Augustine lays down[7] that *God's own substance could be seen by some in a this-life state, as it was by Moses and Paul who was rapt up to hear ineffable words which no man can utter.*

REPLY: Some have said that Paul did not see the divine essence itself, but simply a reflection of its gleaming clarity. But Augustine clearly lays down the opposite, not only in his book on the Vision of God we have quoted, but also on *Genesis*[8] used in the *Gloss.*[9] This too is conveyed by the very

---

[5] *Super Gen. ad litt.* XII, 24, 26, 28. PL 34, 474, 476, 478. cf PL 33, 610
[6] II *Corinthians* 12, 2 & 4
[7] *De videndo Deum ad Paulinam.* Ep. 147, 13. PL 33, 610
[8] *Super Gen. ad litt.* XII, 28. PL 34, 478
[9] *Ordinaria.* cf Lombard PL 192, 80

Apostoli designant: dicit[10] enim se audivisse *ineffabilia verba, quæ non licet homini loqui*. Hujusmodi autem videntur ea quæ pertinet ad visionem beatorum, quæ excedit statum viæ, secundum illud *Isa.*,[11] *Oculus non vidit, Deus, absque te, quæ præparasti diligentibus te.* Et ideo convenientius dicitur quod Deum per essentiam vidit.

1. Ad primum ergo dicendum quod mens humana divinitus rapitur ad contemplandam veritatem divinam tripliciter. Uno modo ut contempletur eam per similitudines quasdam imaginarias, et talis fuit excessus mentis qui cecidit supra Petrum. Alio modo ut contempletur veritatem divinam per intelligibiles effectus; sicut fuit excessus David dicentis,[12] *Ego dixi in excessu meo: Omnis homo mendax.* Tertio modo ut contempletur eam in sua essentia; et talis fuit raptus Pauli, et etiam Moysis: et satis congruenter, nam sicut Moyses fuit primus doctor Judæorum, ita Paulus fuit primus doctor Gentium.

2. Ad secundum dicendum quod divina essentia videri ab intellectu creato non potest nisi per lumen gloriæ, de quo dicitur in *Psal.*,[13] *In lumine tuo videbimus lumen.* Quod tamen dupliciter participari potest. Uno modo per modum formæ immanentis: et sic beatos facit sanctos in patria. Alio modo per modum cujusdam passionis transeuntis, sicut dictum est de lumine prophetiæ;[14] et hoc modo lumen illud fuit in Paulo quando raptus fuit. Et ideo ex tali visione non fuit simpliciter beatus ut fieret redundantia ad corpus, sed solum secundum quid. Et ideo talis raptus aliquo modo ad prophetiam pertinet.

3. Ad tertium dicendum quod quia Paulus in raptu non fuit beatus habitualiter, sed solum habuit actum beatorum, consequens est ut simul tunc in eo non fuerit actus fidei; fuit tamen simul tunc in eo fidei habitus.

4. Ad quartum dicendum quod nomine tertii cœli potest uno modo intelligi aliquid corporeum, et sic tertium cœlum dicitur cœlum empyreum, quod dicitur tertium respectu cœli aerei, et cœli siderei, vel potius respectu cœli siderei, et respectu cœli aquei sive chrystallini. Et dicitur raptus ad tertium cœlum, non quia raptus sit ad videndum similitudinem alicujus rei corporeæ, sed propter hoc quod locus ille est contemplationis beatorum. Unde *Glossa* dicit,[15] quod *cœlum tertium est spirituale cœlum, ubi angeli et*

---

[10]II *Corinthians* 12, 4   [11]*Isaiah* 64, 4
[12]*Psalms* 115, 2   [13]*Psalms* 35, 10
[14]2a2æ. 171, 2
[15]*Ordinaria*. On II *Corinthians* 12, 2
[a]The guarded conclusion is based on the authority of Augustine and on St Paul's own words as read by St Thomas. Scripture however does not compel us to believe that St Paul saw the divine essence. 'Third heaven', 'paradise', 'things that cannot be told' can all be understood of some profound mystical experience which yet falls far short of that vision of heaven. The authority of Augustine carried much

words of the Apostle: for he says (v. 4) that *he heard things which cannot be told, which man may not utter.*[10] Words of this sort refer to the vision of the blessed which exceeds the state of this life, as Isaiah says,[11] *No one has heard or perceived by the ear, no eye has seen a God besides thee, what he works for those who wait for him.* So it is better to say that he did see God in his essence.[a]

Hence: 1. The human mind is rapt up by God to contemplate divine truth in three ways. First, to contemplate it by certain imaginative comparisons. This was the sort of trance that came upon Peter. Second, to contemplate it by its effects upon the intellect. This was the ecstasy of David who said,[12] *I said in my consternation, All men are a vain hope.* Third, to contemplate the divine truth in its essence. Such was the ecstasy of Paul and even of Moses. Fittingly enough, for as Moses was the first Doctor of the Jews, so Paul was first Doctor of the Gentiles.

2. The divine essence cannot be seen by created intellect except through the light of glory, of which the psalm speaks,[13] *in thy light we shall see light.* There are two ways in which a man can participate in this light. First, by an immanent form. Thus with saints made blessed in heaven. Secondly, by a sort of transient affection, as was said of the light of prophecy.[14] In this way was the light in St Paul when he was rapt up. And so from such a vision he was not simply blessed (so that the blessedness would redound upon his body), but only in a degree. Being rapt up in this way relates in some sense to prophecy.

3. Because Paul in ecstasy was not in a permanent state of blessedness, but simply had a momentary actualization of that blessedness. It follows that he did not have the act of faith at the same time, but the ingrained habit of faith.

4. 'Third heaven' can be understood of something bodily. In this sense the third heaven is the empyrean.[b] It is called 'third' in relation to the aerial and starry heavens, or better still in relation to the aqueous and crystalline heavens. And Paul speaks about being 'rapt to the third heaven', not to gaze upon the likeness of any earthly reality but because this place is that of the contemplation of the blessed. Hence the *Gloss* says[15] that *the third is a spiritual heaven where angels and holy souls enjoy the*

---

weight for medieval theologians generally; they all felt bound to teach as he did. But other Fathers have nothing to say on the question, or, like St John Chrysostom and Theodoret, are of another opinion. Modern theologians generally do not admit that Moses and St Paul saw the divine essence.

[b]The 'heavens' for St Thomas belong of course to the cosmology of his period. He seems to have had a geocentric view of the universe (cf. 1a, 68, 4 ad 1) and to have accepted the possibility of many 'heavens' as so many circumferences round one point.

sanctæ animæ fruuntur Dei contemplatione; ad quod cum dicit se raptum, signat quod Deus ostendit ei vitam, in qua videndus est in æternum.

Alio modo per tertium cœlum potest intelligi aliqua visio supermundana: quæ potest dici tertium cœlum triplici ratione. Una modo secundum ordinem potentiarum cognoscitivarum; ut primum cœlum dicatur visio supermundana corporalis, quæ fit per sensum, sicut visa est manus scribentis in pariete, *Dan.*,[16] secundum autem cœlum sit visio imaginaria, puta quam vidit Isaias et Joannes in *Apocalypsi*; tertium vero cœlum dicatur visio intellectualis, ut Augustinus exponit.[17]

Secundo modo potest dici tertium cœlum secundum ordinem cognoscibilium; ut primum cœlum dicatur cognitio cœlestium corporum; secundum cognitio cœlestium spirituum; tertium cognitio ipsius Dei.

Tertio modo potest dici tertium cœlum contemplatio Dei secundum gradus cognitionis qua Deus videtur: quorum primus pertinet ad angelos infimæ hierarchiæ; secundus ad angelos mediæ; tertius ad angelos supremæ, ut dicit *Glossa.*[18] Et quia visio Dei non potest esse sine delectatione, propterea non solum se dicit raptum ad tertium cœlum ratione contemplationis, sed etiam in paradisum ratione delectationis consequentis.

articulus 4. utrum Paulus in raptu fuerit alienatus a sensibus

AD QUARTUM sic proceditur:[1] 1. Videtur quod Paulus in raptu non fuerit alienatus a sensibus. Dicit enim Augustinus,[2] *Cur non credamus quod tanto Apostolo doctori gentium rapto usque ad istam excellentissimam visionem voluerit Deus demonstrare vitam, in qua post hanc vitam vivendum est in æternum?* Sed in illa vita futura sancti post resurrectionem videbunt Dei essentiam absque hoc quod fiat abstractio a sensibus corporeis. Ergo nec in Paulo fuit hujusmodi abstractio facta.

2. Præterea, Christus vere viator fuit, et continue visione divinæ essentiæ fruebatur; nec tamen fiebat abstractio a sensibus. Ergo nec fuit necessarium quod in Paulo fieret abstractio a sensibus, ad hoc quod essentiam Dei videret.

3. Præterea, Paulus, postquam Deum per essentiam viderat, memor fuit illorum quæ in illa visione conspexerat; unde dicebat,[3] *Audivi arcana verba, quæ non licet homini loqui.* Sed memoria ad partem sensitivam pertinet, ut patet per Philosophum.[4] Ergo videtur quod etiam Paulus videndo Dei essentiam non fuerit alienatus a sensibus.

---

[16]*Daniel* 5, 5
[17]*Super Gen. ad litt.* XII, 26. PL 34, 476
[18]loc cit note 15
[1]2a2æ. 180, 5. IV *Sent.* 49, 2, 7 ad 4. *De veritate* X, 10; XIII, 3. *In* II *Cor.* 12, *lect* I. *In Joan.* I, *lect.* II. *Quodl.* I, I

contemplation of God. When he is said to be 'rapt up' to, this means that God has shown him the life in which He will be contemplated in eternity.

By 'third heaven' we can also mean a vision which surpasses that of this world, and it does so in three ways: first, according to the ordering of cognitive powers, so that 'first heaven' refers to a vision which is above this world and conveyed through the senses, e.g. in *Daniel*,[16] when a hand was seen to be writing on the wall. 'Second heaven' then refers to a vision in the imagination, as Isaiah saw or St John in the *Apocalypse*. Finally 'third heaven' is an intellectual vision, as St Augustine explains.[17]

Secondly, 'third heaven' can be taken in an order of knowable realities, so that 'first heaven' means knowledge of heavenly bodies, the 'second' of spiritual bodies, and the 'third'—a knowledge of God's very self.

'Third heaven' can also be used of the degree of contemplation making God to be seen. The first grade then is that of the angels of the lowest hierarchy, the second, that of angels of an intermediate hierarchy, and the third, that of angels of the supreme hierarchy. So we read in the *Gloss*.[18] And because this vision of God entails utter joy, St Paul said he was 'rapt up' not only to the third heaven by reason of his contemplation, but also to 'Paradise' because of the supreme joy that ensued.

article 4. whether St Paul in ecstasy was abstracted from his senses

THE FOURTH POINT:[1] I Augustine says,[2] *Why not believe that God wanted to reveal to this very great Apostle and Doctor of the Gentiles, who was rapt up to that most wonderful vision of himself, that life which, after this life, is to be lived eternally?* Now in that life to come, after the resurrection, the saints will see God's essence without any abstraction from the senses of the body. So too in St Paul there was none of this sort of abstraction.

2. Christ was truly a pilgrim on earth and ceaselessly enjoyed the vision of the divine essence, without, however, abstraction from the senses. So too there was no need for St Paul to be abstracted from the senses to see God's essence.

3. St Paul, after seeing God's essence, remembered what he had seen in that vision: hence his words,[3] *He heard things that cannot be told, which man may not utter.* But memory is one of the senses, as Aristotle shows.[4] Therefore Paul too, while seeing the divine essence, was not abstracted from his senses.

---

[2]*Super Gen. ad litt.* XII, 28. PL 34, 478
[3]II *Corinthians* 12, 4
[4]*De mem. et remin.* 1. 450a12

SED CONTRA est quod Augustinus dicit,[5] *Nisi ab hac vita quisque quodammodo moriatur, sive omnino exiens de corpore, sive ita aversus et alienatus a carnalibus sensibus, ut merito nesciat, sicut Apostolus ait, utrum in corpore an extra corpus sit, cum in illam rapitur et subvehitur visionem.*

RESPONSIO: Dicendum quod divina essentia non potest ab homine videri per aliam vim cognoscitivam quam per intellectum. Intellectus autem humanus non convertitur ad sensibilia* nisi mediantibus phantasmatibus, quæ per species intelligibiles a sensibus accipit, et in quibus considerans de sensibilibus judicat et ea disponit. Et ideo in omni operatione qua intellectus noster abstrahitur a phantasmatibus, necesse est quod abstrahatur a sensibus.

Intellectus autem hominis in statu viæ necesse est quod a phantasmatibus abstrahatur, si videat Dei essentiam. Non enim per aliquod phantasma potest Dei essentia videri, quinimo nec per aliquam speciem intelligibilem creatam; quia essentia Dei in infinitum excedit non solum omnia corpora, quorum sunt phantasmata, sed etiam omnem intelligibilem creaturam.

Oportet autem, cum intellectus hominis elevatur ad altissimam Dei essentiæ visionem, ut tota mentis intentio illuc advocetur, ita scilicet quod nihil intelligat aliud ex phantasmatibus, sed totaliter feratur in Deum. Unde impossibile est quod homo in statu viæ videat Deum per essentiam sine abstractione a sensibus.

1. Ad primum ergo dicendum quod, sicut dictum est,[6] post resurrectionem in beatis Dei essentiam videntibus fiet redundantia ab intellectu ad inferiores vires, et usque ad corpus: unde secundum ipsam regulam divinæ visionis anima intendet phantasmatibus et sensibilibus. Talis autem redundantia non fit in his qui rapiuntur, sicut dictum est.[7] Et ideo non est similis ratio.

2. Ad secundum dicendum quod intellectus animæ Christi erat glorificatus per habituale lumen gloriæ, quo divinam essentiam videbat multo amplius quam aliquis angelus vel homo. Erat autem viator propter corporis passibilitatem, secundum quam paulo minus ab angelis minorabatur, ut dicitur ad *Heb.*,[8] dispensative, et non propter aliquem defectum ex parte intellectus. Unde non est similis ratio de eo et de aliis viatoribus.

3. Ad tertium dicendum quod Paulus, postquam cessavit videre Dei essentiam, memor fuit illorum quæ in illa visione cognoverat per aliquas species intelligibiles habitualiter ex hoc in ejus intellectu relictas; sicut

---

*Piana: *intelligibilia*, mind-objects
[5] *Super Gen. ad litt.* XII, 27. PL 34, 477
[6] above art. 3 arg. 2
[7] above art 3 ad 2
[8] *Hebrews* 11, 7

ON THE OTHER HAND Augustine writes,[5] *Unless one dies in some way to this life, either completely leaving the body, or turned away and abstracted from bodily senses, one cannot be raised to that vision.*

REPLY: The divine essence cannot be seen by any knowing faculty of man other than the intellect. And the human intellect only turns to sense-objects through the medium of images. From these images he arrives at ideas of sense-objects, and while considering these ideas, judges of the realities and disposes of them. So in every operation in which our intellect abstracts from images, it needs also to abstract from the senses.

Now the intellect of man, in its this-life state, must be abstracted from the senses if it is to see the divine essence. For by no image can the essence of God be seen; it cannot even be seen by any created intellectual idea, because the essence of God infinitely exceeds not only all bodily realities (images are among these), but also all spiritual creatures.

When the intellect of man is raised to the supreme vision of God's essence, it must be that the whole of a mind's intent is borne that way—to the extent that he grasps no other reality from images but is wholly borne to God. Hence it is impossible for a man, in this life, to see God in his essence without abstraction from the senses.

Hence: 1. We have showed[6] that after the Resurrection, among the blessed who see God's essence, there is a sort of overflow from the intellect to the lower powers, and so to the body. Hence, according to the very norms of divine vision, the soul will tend towards images and sense-objects. But this 'overflow' does not occur in those who are 'rapt up'.[7] So the case is not the same.[a]

2. Christ's intellect was glorified by an abiding light of glory which enabled him to see the divine essence much more fully than any angel or man. Yet he was a this-life pilgrim because of the passivity of his body, according as he was *a little lower than the angels*[8] by the dispensation of God, and not because of any defect in the matter of intellect. So the case is not the same for him as for other this-life pilgrims.

3. St Paul, after he had ceased seeing God in his essence, bore in mind what he had known in that vision, by means of some ideas which had remained in their usual state; so too when sense-realities vanish, some

---

[a]In the vision of heaven, which the blessed will enjoy, the body will be wholly cleansed and wholly dominated by the soul. Far from being an obstacle to contemplation, the body will be associated in the vision of God by a certain overflowing of the glorified soul. Not that the senses can grasp the divine essence which is wholly non-material; but the senses will seize upon the reflections of the divine essence which will be in all glorified creation. For this doctrine cf *De Veritate* XIII, 3 ad 1. 1a2æ. 3, 3; 4, 5 & 6. 1a. 12, 3. *Suppl.* 92, 2.

etiam, abeunte sensibili, remanent aliquæ impressiones in anima quas postea conferens ad phantasmata memoratur. Unde nec totam illam cognitionem aut cogitare poterat aut verbis exprimere.

articulus 5. *utrum anima Pauli in statu illo fuerit totaliter a corpore separata*

AD QUINTUM sibi proceditur:[1] 1. Videtur quod anima Pauli in statu illo fuerit totaliter a corpore separata. Dicit enim Apostolus,[2] *Quamdiu sumus in corpore, peregrinamur a Domino; per fidem enim ambulamus, et non per speciem.* Sed Paulus in statu illo non peregrinabatur a Domino, quia videbat Deum per speciem, ut dictum est.[3] Ergo non erat in corpore.

2. Præterea, potentia animæ non potest elevari super ejus essentiam, in qua radicatur. Sed intellectus, qui est potentia animæ, in raptu fuit a corporalibus abstractus per elevationem ad divinam contemplationem. Ergo multo magis essentia animæ fuit separata a corpore.

3. Præterea, vires animæ vegetabilis sunt magis materiales quam vires animæ sensitivæ. Sed oportebat intellectum abstrahi a viribus animæ sensetivæ, ut dictum est,[4] ad hoc ut raperetur ad videndum divinam essentiam. Ergo multo magis oportebat quod abstraheretur a viribus animæ vegetabilis, quarum operatione cessante, jam nullo modo remanet anima corpori conjuncta. Ergo videtur quod oportuit in raptu Pauli animam totaliter a corpore esse separatam.

SED CONTRA est quod Augustinus dicit,[5] *Non incredibile est, etiam quibusdam sanctis nondum ita defunctis, ut sepelienda eorum cadavera remanerent, eis istam excellentiam revelationis fuisse concessam,* ut scilicet viderent Deum per essentiam. Non ergo fuit necessarium ut in raptu Pauli anima ejus totaliter separaretur a corpore.

RESPONSIO: Dicendum quod, sicut supra dictum est,[6] in raptu, de quo nunc loquimur, virtute divina elevatur homo ab eo quod est secundum naturam in id quod est supra naturam. Et ideo duo considerare oportet: primo quidem quid sit homini secundum naturam; secundo, quid divina virtute in homine sit fiendum supra naturam.

Ex hoc autem quod anima corpori unitur tanquam naturalis forma ipsius, convenit animæ naturalis habitudo ad hoc quod per conversionem ad phantasmata intelligat: quod quidem ab ea non aufertur divina virtute in

---

[1]cf 1a. 12, 11. 1a2æ. 180, 5. *De veritate* X, 11; XIII, 4. *In* II *Cor.* 12, *lect.* 1. *In Joan.* 1, *lect.* 11. *Quodl.* 1, 1
[2]II *Corinthians* 5, 6   [3]above art. 3   [4]above art. 4

impressions remain in the soul. Subsequently turning back to such images he recalled the ideas. That is why he could not think of or express in words all the knowledge he had.

article 5. whether in that state St Paul's soul was wholly separate from his body

THE FIFTH POINT:[1] 1. It seems that St Paul's soul in that state was wholly separated from his body. For St Paul[2] writes *while we are at home in the body we are away from the Lord, for we walk by faith and not by sight.* But Paul in that state was not away from the Lord, because he saw God clearly.[3] Therefore he was not in his body.

2. A power of soul cannot be raised above the essence in which it is rooted. But the intellect, which is a power of mind, was in ecstasy abstracted from bodily realities by being raised to the contemplation of divine truths. And so, with all the more reason, the essence of the soul was separated from the body.

3. Powers of a vegetative soul are much more material than those of a sensitive soul, as was said.[4] But the intellect had to be abstracted from the powers of the sensitive soul to enable it to be rapt up to a vision of the divine essence. All the more had it to be abstracted from the powers of the vegetative soul. When the operation of these ceases, then in no sense does the soul remain in the body. Therefore in ecstasy it was needful that St Paul's soul should be wholly separate from his body.

ON THE OTHER HAND: St Augustine says,[5] in his Epistle to Paulinus, *we must believe that certain saints, not so wholly dead that only their bodies remained to be buried, had granted to them this most excellent form of revelation.* Thus it was not necessary that in ecstasy Paul's soul should be wholly separated from his body.

REPLY: As was said above,[6] in the ecstasy of mind of which we are now speaking, by the power of God a man is raised from that which is according to nature to that which is above nature. Because of this, two considerations arise. First, what is, for a man, according to nature. Secondly, what God's power is to accomplish in a man above his nature.

Because the soul is united to the body as its own natural form, it is in keeping for the soul to have a natural aptitude for understanding by turning to images. This natural aptitude is not taken away by the divine power in

[5]*Epist.* 147, 13. PL 33, 610
[6]above art. 1

raptu, quia non mutatur status ejus, ut dictum est.[7] Manente autem hoc statu, aufertur ab anima actualis conversio ad phantasmata et sensibilia, ne impediatur ejus elevatio in id quod excedit omnia phantasmata, ut dictum est.[8] Et ideo in raptu non fuit necessarium quod anima sic separaretur a corpore ut ei non uniretur quasi forma; fuit autem necessarium intellectum ejus abstrahi a phantasmatibus et sensibilium perceptione.

1. Ad primum ergo dicendum quod Paulus in raptu illo peregrinabatur a Domino quantum ad statum, quia adhuc erat in statu viatoris; non autem quoad actum quo videbat Deum per speciem, ut ex prædictis patet.[9]

2. Ad secundum dicendum quod potentia animæ virtute naturali non elevatur super modum convenientem essentiæ ejus; virtute tamen divina potest in aliquid altius elevari, sicut corpus per violentiam fortioris virtutis elevatur supra locum convenientem sibi secundum speciem suæ naturæ.

3. Ad tertium dicendum quod vires animæ vegetabilis non operantur ex intentione animæ, sicut vires sensitivæ, sed per modum naturæ: et ideo non requiritur ad raptum ab eis abstractio, sicut a potentiis sensitivis, per quarum operationes minueretur intentio animæ circa intellectivam cognitionem.

articulus 6. utrum Paulus ignoraverit an anima ejus fuerit a corpore separata

AD SEXTUM sic proceditur:[1] 1. Videtur quod Paulus non ignoraverit an ejus anima fuerit a corpore separata. Dicit enim ipse,[2] *Scio hominem in Christo raptum usque ad tertium cœlum.* Sed homo nominat compositum ex anima et corpore: raptus etiam differt a morte. Videtur ergo quod ipse sciverit animam non fuisse per mortem a corpore separatam, præsertim quia hoc communiter a doctoribus ponitur.

2. Præterea, ex eisdem Apostoli verbis patet quod ipse scivit quo raptus fuerit, quia *in tertium cœlum.* Sed ex hoc sequitur quod sciverit utrum in corpore fuerit vel non, quia si scivit tertium cœlum esse aliquid corporeum, consequens est quod sciverit animam suam non esse a corpore separatam, quia visio rei corporeæ non potest fieri nisi per corpus. Ergo videtur quod non omnino ignoraverit an anima fuerit a corpore separata.

3. Præterea, sicut Augustinus dicit,[3] *Ipse in raptu vidit illa visione Deum qua vident sancti in patria.* Sed sancti ex hoc ipso quod vident Deum, sciunt an animæ eorum sint a corporibus separatæ. Ergo et Paulus hoc scivit.

---

[7]above art. 3 ad 2 & 3
[8]above art. 4
[9]loc cit note 7

ecstasy, because the state of the man is not altered, as was said.[7] As long as the state of ecstasy endures, an actual turning to images and sense-objects is removed from the soul, lest it should impede its elevation to that which excels all images, as was said.[8] And so in ecstasy there was no need for the soul to be so separated from the body as not to be united to it as a kind of form. It was needful however that St Paul's intellect should be abstracted from images and the perception of sense-objects.

Hence: 1. Paul in that ecstasy was away from God as regards his state, for he was still in the state of a pilgrim upon earth: but not as regards the act, whereby he saw God clearly, as was shown above.[9]

2. No natural power can raise a power of the soul to a condition above that which is in keeping with its nature. But the power of God can raise it to something higher—just as a body by the violence of a greater force can be raised to a level above that which is consonant with its nature.

3. The powers of the vegetative soul do not act in response to the soul's intent, as do the sense powers. They act as nature ordains. And so in ecstasy there is no need for an abstraction from these vegetative powers. But there must be abstraction from sense powers, because their activities can lessen the soul's application to intellective knowledge.

article 6. whether St Paul did not know whether or not his soul was separated from his body

THE SIXTH POINT:[1] I : St Paul himself says,[2] *I know a man in Christ who was caught up to the third heaven.* But 'man' means one compounded of soul and body, and 'caught up' differs from death. It seems then that he himself knew that his soul was not separated from the body by death. All the more so because this is the opinion commonly advocated by theologians.

2. From the same words of the Apostle it is clear that he himself knew where he had been caught up to, namely the 'third heaven'. It follows from this that he knew whether he was in the body or not. Because if he knew that the third heaven was something corporeal, it follows that he knew that his body was not separated from his soul: because a corporeal thing can only be seen through the body. So it seems that he was not unaware whether his soul was separated from his body.

3. Augustine says[3] that St Paul in ecstasy saw God by the same vision as that of the saints in heaven. But the saints, from the very fact that they see God, know whether their souls are separated from their bodies. So, too, St Paul must have known.

---

[1]cf *De veritate* XIII, 5. *In* II *Cor.* 12, *lect.* I   [2]II *Corinthians* 12, 2
[3]*Super Gen. ad litt.* XII, 28. PL 34, 478

SED CONTRA est quod dicitur, II *Cor.*,[4] *Sive in corpore, sive extra corpus nescio, Deus scit.*

RESPONSIO: Dicendum quod hujusmodi quæstionis veritatem accipere oportet ex ipsis Apostoli verbis, quibus dicit se aliquid scire, scilicet se raptum esse *usque ad tertium cœlum*; et aliquid nescire, scilicet *utrum in corpore, an extra corpus.* Quod quidem potest intelligi dupliciter. Uno modo ut hoc quod dicitur, *Sive incorpore, sive extra corpus,* non referatur ad ipsum esse hominis rapti, quasi ignoraverit an anima ejus tesse in corpore an non; sed ad modum raptus, ut scilicet ignoraverit an corpus ejus fuerit simul raptum cum anima in tertium cœlum vel non, sed solum anima; sicut *Ezech.*[5] dicitur quod adductus est in visionibus Dei in Jerusalem.

Et hunc intellectum fuisse cujusdam Judæi exprimit Hieronymus in prologo super *Daniel*,[6] ubi dicit, *Denique et Apostolum nostrum* (scilicet dicebat Judæus) *no fuisse ausum affirmare se in corpore raptum, sed dixisse, Sive in corpore, sive extra corpus, nescio.*

Sed hunc sensum reprobat Augustinus[7] per hoc quod Apostolus dicit scivisse se esse raptum usque ad tertium cœlum. Sciebat ergo verum esse tertium cœlum id in quod raptus fuit, et non similitudinem imaginariam tertii cœli: alioquin si tertium cœlum nominavit phantasma tertii cœli, pari ratione dicere potuit se in corpore raptum, nominans corpus proprii corporis phantasma, quale apparet in somniis. Si autem sciebat esse vere tertium cœlum, sciebat ergo aut esse aliquid spirituale et incorporeum; et sic non poterat corpus ejus illuc rapi; aut esse aliquid corporeum, et sic anima non potest illuc sine corpore rapi, nisi separaretur a corpore.

Et ideo oportet secundum alium sensum intelligere, ut scilicet Apostolus sciverit quod fuerit raptus secundum animam et non secundum corpus, nesciverit tamen qualiter se haberet anima ad corpus, utrum scilicet fuerit sine corpore vel non.

Sed circa hoc diversimode aliqui loquuntur. Quidam enim dicunt quod Apostolus scivit quod anima sua erat corpori unita ut forma, sed nescivit utrum esset passus alienationem a sensibus, vel etiam utrum esset facta abstractio ab operibus animæ vegetabilis. Sed quod fuerit facta abstractio a sensibus, hoc non potuit ignorare, ex quo scivit se raptum; quod autem fuerit facta abstractio ab operibus animæ vegetabilis, non erat tantum

---

[4]II *Corinthians* 12, 3
[5]*Ezekiel* 8, 3
[6]PL 28, 1360

ON THE OTHER HAND, St Paul writes,[4] *Whether in the body or out of the body, I do not know: God knows.*

REPLY: We must glean the truth of this question from the Apostle's own words in which he says he knows something, namely that he was caught *up to the third heaven*; and that he was ignorant of something, namely '*whether in the body or out of the body*'. We can understand this last in two ways. When he says, *Whether in the body or out of it,* this does not refer to the being of the man 'caught up', as if not knowing whether his soul was in the body or not, but to the manner in which he was 'caught up'—so that he knew not whether or not his body was simultaneously 'caught up' with the soul to the third heaven, or simply the soul alone, as *Ezekiel*[5] has it the Spirit *brought me in visions of God to Jerusalem.*

According to Jerome's *Prologue to Daniel*[6] this last exegesis was proposed by a certain Jew. When recording the opinion of this Jew he wrote, *Finally, not even our Apostle was bold enough to say that he had been rapt away from his body; he simply said, 'Whether in the body or out of the body, I know not'.*

Nevertheless Augustine rejects this interpretation,[7] precisely because the Apostle says that he knew he had been rapt to the third heaven. Thus he knew that this third heaven, to which he had been rapt, was a real heaven, and not an imagined likeness of the third heaven. Otherwise, if he had referred to the third heaven as a likeness of that third heaven, then he could have said the same of being rapt with his body referring to the likeness of his body as it would appear in a dream. But then, if he realized that the third heaven was really meant, he knew that it was something spiritual and non-bodily; and in that case his body could not be rapt there; or, if it was something bodily, then his soul could not be rapt up thereto without the body—unless it was separated from the body.

So we must give another sense to the Apostle's words, namely, that St Paul knew that he was rapt up as regards his soul and not as regards his body, but was in ignorance how his soul was related to his body, i.e. whether it was or was not with a body during the course of his ecstasy.

But here again there are various interpretations. Some say in effect: the Apostle knew that his soul was united to his body as its form, but did not know whether it had undergone abstraction from the senses, or even abstraction from operations of the vegetative soul. And yet, there must have been an abstraction from the senses, and St Paul must have known this, seeing that he was aware of his ecstasy. As for abstraction from the operation of the vegetative soul, that was not a matter of importance

---

[7]*Super Gen. ad litt.* XII, 3. PL 34, 456

aliquid ut de hoc oporteret tam sollicitam fieri mentionem. Unde relinquitur quod nescivit Apostolus utrum anima ejus fuerit conjuncta corpori ut forma, vel a corpore separata per mortem.

Quidam autem hoc concedentes dicunt quod Apostolus tunc non perpendit quando rapiebatur, quia tota ejus intentio conversa erat in Deum; sed postmodum percepit, considerans ea quæ viderat. Sed hoc etiam contrariatur verbis Apostoli, qui distinguit in verbis suis præteritum a futuro; dicit enim in præsenti se scire quod fuit raptus ante annos quatuordecim, et se in præsenti nescire utrum in corpore fuerit vel extra corpus.

Et ideo dicendum est quod et prius, et postea nescivit utrum ejus anima fuerit a corpore separata. Unde Augustinus dicit,[8] post longam inquisitionem concludens, *Restat ergo fortasse, ut hoc ipsum eum ignorasse intelligamus, utrum quando in tertium cœlum raptus est, in corpore fuerit anima, quomodo est anima in corpore, cum corpus vivere dicitur sive vigilantis, sive dormientis, sive in extasi a sensibus corporis alienati, an omnino de corpore exierit, ut mortuum corpus jaceret.*

1. Ad primum ergo dicendum quod per synecdochen quandoque pars hominis homo nominatur; et præcipue anima, quæ est pars hominis eminentior. Quamvis etiam possit intelligi eum quem raptum dicit, non tunc fuisse hominem quando raptus fuit, sed post annos quatuordecim. Unde dicit, *Scio hominem,* non dicit, *Scio raptum hominem.* Nihil etiam prohiberet mortem divinitus procuratam raptum dici; et sic Augustinus dicit,[9] *Dubitante inde Apostolo, quis nostrum inde certus esse audeat?* Unde qui super hoc loquuntur, magis conjecturaliter quam per certitudinem loquuntur.

2. Ad secundum dicendum quod Apostolus scivit vel illud cœlum esse quid incorporeum,* vel aliquid incorporeum a se visum in illo cœlo; cum hoc potuerit fieri per intellectum ejus, etiamsi anima ejus non esset a corpore separata.

3. Ad tertium dicendum quod visio Pauli in raptu quantum ad aliquid fuit similis visioni beatorum, scilicet quantum ad id quod videbatur; et quantum ad aliquid dissimilis, scilicet quantum ad modum videndi, quia non ita perfecte vidit sicut sancti qui sunt in patria. Unde Augustinus dicit,[10] *Quamvis Apostolo arrepto a carnis sensibus in tertium cœlum hoc defuit ad plenam perfectamque cognitionem rerum, quæ angelis inest, quod sive in corpore, sive extra corpus esset, nesciebat: hoc utique non deerit receptis corporibus in resurrectione mortuorum, cum corruptibile hoc induetur incorruptione.*

---

*Piana: *corporeum,* something bodily
[8]*Super Gen. ad litt.* XII, 5. PL 34, 458
[9]ibid 3. PL 34, 456

deserving explicit mention. So we are left to understand that the Apostle did not know whether his soul had remained united to his body as its form or was separated from it by death.

Others, however, while admitting this explanation, say that the Apostle could not realize what his state was at the time of his ecstasy, for his whole attention was focused on God; he did however, understand later, when reflecting on what he had seen. This opinion also contradicts the Apostle's words, which carefully distinguish past and future. In effect he says in the present tense that he *knows* he was rapt fourteen years ago, and, still in the present, that he *knows not* whether it was with or without his body.

That is why we must say that, before and after, he did not know whether his soul had been separated from his body. Hence Augustine writes,[8] after a long discussion, *It remains that we should understand that the Apostle himself did not know, when rapt to the third heaven, whether his soul was in his body, in the way we say it is when the body is alive, whether awake or sleeping, whether in ecstasy or abstracted from bodily senses; and did not know whether his soul had so completely left the body that this body lay like a corpse.*

Hence: 1. By synecdoche part of a man can be termed 'man', and principally the soul which is the more outstanding part of a man. One can take this to mean that he whom he states to have been rapt was not the man at the time of his ecstasy, but fourteen years later. Hence he says, 'I know a man', not 'I know a rapt man'. There is no objection to calling ecstasy a death produced by the special intervention of God. And Augustine writes,[9] *If the Apostle remained in doubt, who among us can have any certainty?* Those who propound an opinion on this subject speak more from conjecture than from certitude.

2. The Apostle knew, either that the third heaven was something unbodily, or that he had seen an incorporeal reality in heaven. However, this knowledge could have been obtained from his intelligence even if his soul was not separated from his body.

3. St Paul's vision in his ecstasy was in some respects like that of the blessed, namely, as regards the object of the vision. In other respects it differed, namely, as regards the mode of vision, for he did not contemplate as perfectly as the saints who are in heaven. Hence Augustine writes,[10] *St Paul was raised to the third heaven from bodily senses. Yet he lacked something of the full and perfect knowledge which is the lot of angels. He did not know whether his ecstasy had taken place in or out of his body. This surely will not be wanting when our bodies will be recovered at the resurrection of the dead, when this corruptible will have put on incorruption.*

---

[10]ibid 36. PL 34, 484

DEINDE CONSIDERANDUM est de gratiis gratis datis quæ pertinent ad locutionem:

et primo, de gratia linguarum;
secundo, de gratia sermonis sapientiæ seu scientiæ.

Quæstio 176. de gratia linguarum

Circa primum quæruntur duo:

1. utrum per gratiam linguarum homo adipiscatur scientiam omnium linguarum;
2. de comparatione hujus doni ad gratiam prophetiæ.

articulus 1. utrum illi qui consequebantur donum linguarum loquebuantur omnibus linguis

AD PRIMUM sic proceditur:[1] 1. Videtur quod illi qui consequebantur donum linguarum non loquebantur omnibus linguis. Illud enim quod divina virtute aliquibus conceditur, optimum est in suo genere; sicut Dominus aquam convertit in vinum bonum, sicut dicitur *Joan.*[2] Sed illi qui habuerunt donum linguarum melius loquebantur in propria lingua; dicit enim *Glossa* ad *Heb.*,[3] *Non esse mirandum quod Epistola ad Hebræos majore elucet facundia quam aliæ, cum naturale sit unicuique plus in sua quam aliena lingua valere: cæteras enim epistolas Apostolus peregrino, idest Græco sermone composuit; hanc autem scripsit Hebraica lingua.* Non ergo per gratiam gratis datam Apostoli acceperunt scientiam omnium linguarum.

2. Præterea, natura non facit per multa quod potest fieri per unum; et multo minus Deus, qui ordinatius quam natura operatur. Sed poterat Deus facere ut unam linguam loquentes ejus discipuli ab omnibus intelligerentur; unde super illud *Act.*,[4] *Audiebat unquisque lingua sua illos loquentes*, dicit *Glossa*[5] quod *linguis omnibus loquebantur vel sua* (idest Hebraica lingua) *loquentes ab omnibus intelligebantur, ac si propriis singulorum loquerentur.* Ergo videtur quod non habuerunt scientiam loquendi omnibus linguis.

3. Præterea, omnes gratiæ derivantur a Christo in corpus ejus, quod est Ecclesia, secundum illud *Joan.*,[6] *De plenitudine ejus omnes accepimus.* Sed Christus non legitur fuisse locutus nisi una lingua, nec etiam nunc fideles

---

[1]cf *CG* III, 154. *In* I *Cor.* 14, *lect.* 1
[2]*John* 2, 10

WE MUST NOW CONSIDER the charisms of speech.

First, the gift of tongues,
and then the grace of sapiential or learned speech (177).

Question 176. the gift of tongues

Two points of inquiry arise here:

1. whether by the gift of tongues is acquired a knowledge of all tongues, and
2. a comparison of this gift with the grace of prophecy.

article 1. whether those who received the grace of tongues spoke with all tongues

THE FIRST POINT:[1] 1. Those who received the grace of tongues did not, it seems, speak with all tongues. Now that which is bestowed on some by God's power is the best in its own genus. Thus our Lord at Cana changed water into good wine.[2] Yet those who had received the grace of tongues expressed themselves better in their own tongue. The *Gloss* says on *Hebrews*,[3] *It is not surprising that this Epistle is more eloquent than others: it is indeed natural for one to speak better in his own tongue than in a foreign tongue. Now the other Epistles were composed by the Apostle in a foreign tongue, i.e. in Greek, but this one he wrote in Hebrew.* Thus by the gift of tongues the Apostle did not receive a knowledge of all tongues.

2. Nature does not use many instruments when one will do; still less God who acts with more order than nature. But God could have arranged that his disciples speaking one tongue should be understood of all. Hence on *Acts*,[4] *Each one heard them speaking in his own tongue,* the *Gloss* says,[5] *because either they were speaking with all tongues: or speaking their own Hebrew they were understood of all, just as if they were speaking the proper tongue of each of them.* So it seems that they did not have the gift of speaking all tongues.

3. All graces flow from Christ in his Body which is the Church, and *John* says,[6] *We have all received of his fullness.* But Christ is not said to have used more than one language, nor do faithful people today use more than

---

[3]*Ordinaria,* on *Hebrews* 1, 1
[4]*Acts* 2, 6
[5]*Ordinaria.* cf Bede. PL 92, 947
[6]*John* 1, 16

singuli nisi una lingua loquuntur. Ergo videtur quod discipuli Christi non acceperunt ad hoc gratiam ut omnibus linguis loquerentur.

SED CONTRA est quod dicitur *Act.*,[7] quod *repleti sunt omnes Spiritu Sancto, et cœperunt loqui variis linguis, prout Spiritus Sanctus dabat eloqui illis;* ubi dicit *Glossa* Gregorii,[8] quod *Spiritus Sanctus super discipulos in igneis linguis apparuit, et eis omnium linguarum scientiam dedit.*

RESPONSIO: Dicendum quod primi discipuli Christi ad hoc fuerunt ab ipso electi ut per universum orbem discurrentes, fidem ejus ubique prædicarent, secundum illud *Matt.*,[9] *Euntes docete omnes gentes.* Non autem erat conveniens ut qui mittebantur ad alios instruendos, indigerent ab aliis instrui, qualiter aliis loquerentur, vel qualiter quæ alii loquerentur, intelligerent: præsertim quia isti qui mittebantur, erant unius gentis, scilicet Judææ, secundum illud *Isa.*,[10] *Qui egrediuntur impetu a Jacob, implebunt faciem orbis semine.* Illi etiam qui mittebantur, pauperes et impotentes erant; nec de facili a principio reperissent qui eorum verba aliis fideliter interpretarentur, vel verba aliorum eis exponerent, maxime quia ad infideles mittebantur. Et ideo necessarium fuit ut super hoc eis divinitus provideretur per donum linguarum; ut sicut gentibus ad idololatriam declinantibus, introducta est diversitas linguarum, sicut dicitur *Gen.*,[11] ita etiam quando erant gentes ad cultum unius Dei revocandæ, contra hujusmodi diversitatem remedium adhiberetur per donum linguarum.

1. Ad primum ergo dicendum quod, sicut dicitur I ad *Cor.*,[12] *Manifestatio spiritus datur ad utilitatem.* Et ideo sufficienter et Paulus, et alii Apostoli fuerunt instructi divinitus in linguis omnium gentium, quantum requirebatur ad fidei doctrinam. Sed quantum ad quædam quæ superadduntur humana arte ad ornatum et elegantiam locutionis, Apostolus instructus erat in propria lingua, non autem in aliena: sicut etiam in sapientia et scientia fuerunt sufficienter instructi, quantum requirebat doctrina fidei, non autem quantum ad omnia quæ per scientiam acquisitam cognoscuntur, puta de conclusionibus arithmeticæ vel geometriæ.

2. Ad secundum dicendum quod, quamvis utrumque fieri potuisset, scilicet quod per unam linguam loquentes ab omnibus intelligerentur, aut quod omnibus linguis loquerentur, tamen convenientius fuit quod ipsi omnibus linguis loquerentur, quia hoc pertinebat ad perfectionem scientiæ ipsorum, per quam non solum loqui, sed intelligere poterant quæ ab aliis dicebantur. Si autem omnes unam eorum linguam intellexissent, hoc vel

[7]*Acts* 2, 4
[8]*Ordinaria.* Gregory. *In Evang.* II, 30. PL 76, 1222
[9]*Matthew* 28, 19

THE GIFT OF TONGUES

one tongue. So it seems that the disciples of Christ did not receive the grace of speaking with all tongues.

ON THE OTHER HAND, in the *Acts* it is said[7] that *they were all filled with the Holy Spirit and began to speak in other tongues, as the Holy Spirit gave them the power.* The *Gloss* from Gregory says that[8] *the Holy Spirit appeared to the disciples in fiery tongues and gave them the knowledge of all tongues.*

REPLY: The first disciples of Christ were chosen by him to go through the whole world and preach faith in him everywhere: *Go, teach all nations.*[9] Now it was not fitting that those who were sent to instruct others should need to be instructed by others how they should speak to others or how they should understand what others were saying. The more so as those who were sent were of one nation, namely Jews; thus *Isaiah*,[10] *In days to come Jacob shall take root, Israel shall blossom and put forth shoots and fill the whole world with fruit.* Those sent were poor and weak and, from the beginning, would not easily find people who would faithfully interpret their words to others or explain the words of others to them, especially as they were being sent to unbelievers. So it was necessary that God should provide by the gift of tongues. Thus when people were falling into idolatry, diversity of speech ensued:[11] so now, when peoples were being called back to the worship of one God, the gift of tongues was the remedy to be applied to the diversity of tongues.

Hence: 1. *To each is given the manifestation of the Spirit for the common good.*[12] So Paul and other Apostles were instructed by God in the tongues of all peoples as much as was needful for the teaching of the faith. But as regards certain embellishments of human art and eloquence in speech the Apostles were instructed in their own language, not in another. Again, they were sufficiently instructed in wisdom and knowledge, as far as was needed for teaching of the faith. They were not however equipped with all that can be known by acquired sciences, as e.g. conclusions in arithmetic or geometry.

2. Though both could have happened, i.e. speak with one tongue and be understood of all, or speak to all, yet it was more appropriate that the Apostles should speak all tongues, because this relates to a perfection in their own knowledge, that they could not only speak but also understand what others were saying. If, however, all others had understood their own speech, this would flow from the knowledge of those who heard them

[10]*Isaiah* 27, 6
[11]*Genesis* 11, 7
[12]I *Corinthians* 12, 7

fuisset per scientiam illorum qui eos loquentes intelligerent, vel fuisset quasi quædam illusio, dum aliorum verba aliter ad eorum aures perferrentur quam ipsi ea proferrent: et ideo *Glossa* dicit, *Act.*,[13] quod *majori miraculo factum est quod ipsi omnium linguarum generibus loquerentur;* et Paulus dicit,[14] *Gratias ago Deo meo, quod omnium vestrum lingua loquor.*

3. Ad tertium dicendum quod Christus in propria persona uni soli genti prædicaturus erat, scilicet Judæis. Et ideo quamvis ipse absque dubio haberet perfectissime scientiam omnium linguarum, non tamen oportuit quod omnibus linguis loqueretur. Ideo autem, ut Augustinus dicit,[15] *Cum et modo Spiritus Sanctus accipiatur, nemo loquitur linguis omnium gentium, quia jam ipsa Ecclesia linguis omnium gentium loquitur; in qua qui non est, non accipit Spiritum Sanctum.*

articulus 2. utrum donum linguarum sit excellentius quam gratia prophetiæ

AD SECUNDUM sic proceditur:[1] 1. Videtur quod donum linguarum sit excellentius quam gratia prophetiæ. Quæ enim sunt melioribus propria, videntur esse meliora, secundum Philosophum.[2] Sed donum linguarum est proprium Novi Testamenti; unde cantatur in Sequentia Pentecostes, *Ipse hodie Apostolos Christi donans munere insolito et cunctis inaudito seculis.*[3] Prophetia autem magis competit veteri Testamento, secundum illud ad *Heb.*,[4] *Multifariam multisque modis olim Deus loquens patribus in prophetis.* Ergo videtur quod donum linguarum sit excellentius quam donum prophetiæ.

2. Præterea, illud per quod ordinamur ad Deum videtur excellentius esse eo per quod ordinamur ad homines. Sed per donum linguarum homo ordinatur ad Deum, per prophetiam autem ad homines: dicitur enim 1 ad *Cor.*,[5] *Qui loquitur lingua, non hominibus loquitur, sed Deo . . . qui* autem *prophetat, hominibus loquitur ad ædificationem.* Ergo videtur quod donum linguarum sit excellentius quam donum prophetiæ.

3. Præterea, donum linguarum habitualiter permanet in habente ipsum, et homo habet in potestate uti eo cum voluerit: unde dicitur 1 ad *Cor.*,[6] *Gratias ago Deo meo, quod omnium vestrum lingua loquor.* Non autem sic est de dono prophetiæ, ut supra dictum est.[7] Ergo donum linguarum videtur esse excellentius quam donum prophetiæ.

4. Præterea, interpretatio sermonum videtur contineri sub prophetia, quia Scripturæ eodem spiritu exponuntur quo sunt editæ. Sed interpretatio

[13]loc cit note 5 (*Acts* 2, 4)
[14]1 *Corinthians* 14, 18
[15]*Super Joan.* (7, 39) XXXII. PL 35, 1645

speaking and understood, or from a kind of illusion, the words reaching the ears of hearers other than they had been pronounced. So the *Gloss* says,[13] *By a greater miracle it came about that they themselves should speak with all manner of tongues.* And Paul says,[14] *I thank God that I speak in tongues more than you all.*

3. Christ himself was to speak to one people alone, the Jews. So though having the most perfect knowledge of all languages he had no need to speak them all. So Augustine says,[15] *If in fact none who receive the Holy Spirit speak all languages, it is because the Church herself speaks them all. And no one receives the Holy Spirit other than in that Church.*

article 2. does the gift of tongues surpass the gift of prophecy?

THE SECOND POINT:[1] 1. The gift of tongues appears to surpass the gift of prophecy. Seemingly better things are proper to better persons, as Aristotle says.[2] Now the gift of tongues is proper to the New Testament, thus we sing in the sequence of Pentecost,[3] *On this day thou gavest Christ's Apostles an unwonted gift, a marvel to all time.* Prophecy, however, more properly belongs to the Old Testament, as *Hebrews* has it,[4] *In many and various ways God spoke of old to our fathers by the prophets.* Therefore the gift of tongues seems to surpass that of prophecy.

2. That which orders us unto God is seemingly more excellent than that which orders us unto men. But by the gift of tongues, a man is ordered unto God, and by prophecy to men: thus 1 *Corinthians*,[5] *One who speaks in a tongue speaks not to men but to God,* he who *prophesies speaks to men for their upbuilding and encouragement.* Therefore the gift of tongues seems more excellent than prophecy.

3. The gift of tongues constantly remains with him who has it, and the man has it in his power to use when he wishes: thus 1 *Corinthians*,[6] *I thank God that I speak in tongues more than you all.* It is not the same in prophecy, as has been said.[7] Therefore the gift of tongues surpasses that of prophecy.

4. The 'interpretation of speeches' seems to be listed under prophecy, because the Scriptures are expounded by the same Spirit as that which brought them into being. But interpretation of speeches is placed after

---

[1]cf *In* 1 *Cor.* 14, lect. 1–6
[2]*Topics* III, 1. 116b12
[3]Medieval missals. cf PL 141, 943
[4]*Hebrews* 1, 1
[5]1 *Corinthians* 14, 2–3
[6]ibid 18
[7]2a2æ. 171, 2

sermonum, ponitur[8] post genera linguarum. Ergo videtur quod donum linguarum sit excellentius quam donum prophetiæ, maxime quantum ad aliquam ejus partem.

SED CONTRA est quod Apostolus dicit,[9] *Major est qui prophetat quam qui loquitur linguis.*

RESPONSIO: Dicendum quod donum prophetiæ excedit donum linguarum tripliciter.

Primo quidem, quia donum linguarum refertur ad diversas voces proferendas, quæ sunt signa alicujus intelligibilis veritatis, cujus etiam signa sunt quædam ipsa phantasmata, quæ secundum imaginariam visionem apparent. Unde et Augustinus comparat[10] donum linguarum visioni imaginariæ. Dictum est autem supra,[11] quod donum prophetiæ consistit in ipsa illuminatione mentis ad cognoscendam intelligibilem veritatem. Unde sicut prophetica illuminatio excellentior est quam imaginaria visio, ut supra habitum est,[12] ita etiam excellentior est prophetia quam donum linguarum, secundum se consideratum.

Secundo, quia donum prophetiæ pertinet ad rerum notitiam quæ est nobilior quam notitia vocum, ad quam pertinet donum linguarum.

Tertio, quia donum prophetiæ est utilius: et hoc quidem probat Apostolus, 1 ad *Cor.*,[13] tripliciter: Primo quidem, quia prophetia est utilior ad ædificationem Ecclesiæ, ad quam qui loquitur linguis nihil prodest, nisi expositio subsequatur. Secundo, quantum ad ipsum loquentem, qui si acciperet ut loqueretur diversis linguis, sine hoc quod intelligeret, quod pertinet ad propheticum donum, mens ejus non ædificaretur. Tertio, quantum ad infideles, propter quos præcipue esse videtur datum donum linguarum: qui quidem forte eos qui loquerentur linguis, reputarent insanos; sicut et Judæi reputaverunt ebrios Apostolos linguis loquentes, ut dicitur *Act.*[14] Per prophetias autem infideles convincuntur, manifestatis absconditis cordis sui.

1. Ad primum ergo dicendum quod, sicut supra dictum est,[15] ad excellentiam prophetiæ pertinet quod aliquis non solum illuminetur intelligibili lumine, sed etiam percipiat imaginariam visionem. Ita etiam ad perfectionem operationis Spiritus Sancti pertinet quod non solum impleat mentem lumine prophetico, et phantasiam imaginaria visione, sicut erat in Veteri Testamento; sed etiam exterius linguam erudiat ad varia signa

---

[8] *1 Corinthians* 12, 28
[9] *1 Corinthians* 14, 5
[10] *Super Gen. ad litt.* XII, 8. PL 34, 460

'kinds of tongues'.[8] So it seems that the gift of tongues is more excellent than that of prophecy, particularly as regards a part of the latter.

ON THE OTHER HAND St Paul says, *He who prophesies is greater than he who speaks in tongues.*[9]

REPLY: the gift of prophecy surpasses that of tongues in three ways.

First, because the gift of tongues regards utterance of certain words which are symbols of intellectual truth, and this again is signified by certain images which appear in imaginative vision. Hence Augustine compares[10] the gift of tongues to imaginative vision. On the other hand, as said above,[11] the gift of prophecy consists of an enlightening of the mind to know intelligible truth. So, just as prophetic enlightening is more excellent than imaginary vision, as seen above,[12] so too prophecy is more excellent than the gift of tongues considered in itself.

Secondly, the gift of prophecy relates to knowledge of the realities themselves. This is more excellent than the knowledge of words which is the domain of the gift of tongues.

Thirdly, the gift of prophecy is more useful. This is shown by the Apostle[13] in three ways: First, because prophecy is more useful for the edification of the Church. He who speaks with tongues contributes nothing to that unless some explanation follows. Secondly, as regards the speaker; if he received the gift of speaking various tongues without understanding what related to the prophetic gift, his mind would not be edified. Thirdly, as regards unbelievers, on whose behalf the gift of tongues seems principally to have been given, people who might look upon speakers with tongues as mad—just as the Jews thought that the Apostles speaking with tongues were drunk.[14] By prophecies however an unbeliever would be brought to conviction with a manifestation of the secrets of his heart.

Hence: 1. As we have said,[15] it is part of prophecy's excellence that a person is not only enlightened with intellectual light but also has a grasp of imaginative vision. So too it belongs to the perfection of the Holy Spirit's action that he not only fills the mind with prophetic light and the fancy with imaginative vision, as was the case in the Old Testament, but also trains the tongue outwardly to utter various signs of language. The

---

[11]2a2æ. 173, 2
[12]2a2æ. 174, 2
[13]1 *Corinthians* 12
[14]*Acts* 11, 13
[15]2a2æ. 174, 2 ad 1

locutionum proferenda. Quod totum fit in Novo Testamento, secundum illud,[16] *Unusquisque vestrum psalmum habet, doctrinam habet, linguam habet, apocalypsim,* idest propheticam revelationem, *habet.*

2. Ad secundum dicendum quod per donum prophetiæ homo ordinatur ad Deum secundum mentem: quod est nobilius quam ordinari ad eum secundum linguam. Dicitur autem quod ille qui loquitur lingua non loquitur hominibus, idest, ad intellectum hominum, vel utilitatem eorum, sed ad intellectum solius Dei et ad laudem ejus. Sed per prophetiam ordinatur aliquis et ad Deum et ad proximum: unde est perfectius donum.

3. Ad tertium dicendum quod revelatio prophetica se extendit ad omnia supernaturalia cognoscenda: unde ex ejus perfectione contingit quod in statu imperfectionis hujus vitæ non potest haberi perfecte per modum habitus, sed imperfecte per modum cujusdam passionis. Sed donum linguarum se extendit ad cognitionem quamdam particularem, scilicet vocum humanarum: et ideo non repugnat imperfectioni hujus vitæ quod perfecte et habitualiter habeatur.

4. Ad quartum dicendum quod interpretatio sermonum potest reduci ad donum prophetiæ, inquantum scilicet mens illuminatur ad intelligendum et exponendum quæcumque sunt in sermonibus obscura, sive propter difficultatem rerum significatarun, sive etiam propter ipsas voces ignotas, quæ proferuntur, sive etiam propter similitudines rerum adhibitas, secundum illud *Dan.,*[17] *Audivi de te, quod possis obscura interpretari et ligata dissolvere.* Unde interpretatio sermonum est potior quam donum linguarum, ut patet per illud quod Apostolus dicit I ad *Cor.,*[18] *Major est qui prophetat, quam qui loquitur linguis, nisi forte interpretetur.* Postponitur autem interpretatio sermonum dono linguarum, quia etiam ad interpretandum diversa linguarum genera interpretatio sermonum se extendit.

---

[16]I *Corinthians* 14, 20   [17]*Daniel* 5, 16

whole of this takes place in the New Testament, *Each one has a hymn, a lesson, a revelation,*[16] that is his prophetic revelation.

2. The man who is ordered to God by the gift of prophecy is ordered according to the Spirit. This is higher than being ordered according to his tongue. Further, he who speaks in tongues does not speak to men, because he does not address himself to their intelligences and says nothing for their profit: he simply gives himself to the understanding and praise of God. But by prophecy a man is ordered both to God and to his neighbour. Therefore it is the better gift.

3. Prophetic revelation ranges out to a knowledge of all supernatural truth. Hence from its very perfection it happens that in the state of imperfection of this life it cannot be possessed perfectly as a lasting condition but imperfectly as a kind of transitory impression. But the gift of tongues extends to a particular knowledge, namely the words of men. Thus there is nothing to prevent it being possessed perfectly and lastingly in the imperfections of this life.

4. The interpretation of speeches can be reduced to the gift of prophecy—in so far as the mind is enlightened to understand and expound whatever is obscure in speeches, whether because of the difficulty of the matters referred to, or because of the very words uttered, or because of the examples given: thus *Daniel,*[17] *I have heard that you can interpret and solve problems.* Hence interpretation of speeches is superior to the gift of tongues, as appears from what St Paul says,[18] *He who prophesies is greater than he who speaks in tongues, unless some one interprets.* If the interpretation of speeches is however placed *after* the gift of tongues in this Epistle, it is precisely because it also extends to the explanation of different kinds of tongues.

---

[18]I *Corinthians* 14, 5

Quæstio 177. de gratia quæ consistit in sermone

Deinde considerandum est de gratia gratis data, quæ consistit in sermone, de qua dicit Apostolus,[1] *Alii datur per Spiritum sermo sapientiæ, alii sermo scientiæ*: et circa hoc quæruntur duo:

1. utrum in sermone consistat aliqua gratia gratis data;
2. quibus hæc gratia competat.

articulus I. *utrum in sermone consistat aliqua gratia gratis data*

AD PRIMUM sic proceditur:[2] I. Videtur quod in sermone non consistit aliqua gratia gratis data. Gratia enim datur ad id quod excedit facultatem naturæ. Sed ex naturali ratione adinventa est ars rhetorica, per quam aliquis potest *sic dicere ut doceat, ut delectet, ut flectat*, sicut Augustinus dicit.[3] Hoc autem pertinet ad gratiam sermonis. Ergo videtur quod gratia sermonis non sit gratia gratis data.

2. Præterea, omnis gratia ad regnum Dei pertinet. Sed Apostolus dicit,[4] *Non in sermone est regnum Dei, sed in virtute*. Ergo in sermone non consistit aliqua gratia gratis data.

3. Præterea, nulla gratia datur ex meritis, quia *si ex operibus, jam non est gratia*, ut dicitur ad *Rom.*[5] Sed sermo datur alicui ex meritis: dicit enim Gregorius, ponens illud *Psal.*,[6] *Ne auferas de ore meo verbum veritatis*, quod *verbum veritatis est quod omnipotens Deus facientibus tribuit, et non facientibus tollit*.[7] Ergo videtur quod donum sermonis non sit gratia gratis data.

4. Præterea, sicut necesse est quod homo per sermonem pronuntiet ea quæ pertinent ad donum sapientiæ vel scientiæ; ita etiam ea quæ pertinent ad virtutem fidei. Ergo si ponitur sermo sapientiæ, et sermo scientiæ gratia gratis data, pari ratione deberet poni sermo fidei inter gratias gratis datas.

SED IN CONTRARIUM est quod dicitur *Eccl.*,[8] *Lingua eucharis*, idest gratiosa, *in bono homine abundabit*. Sed bonitas hominis est ex gratia. Ergo etiam gratiositas sermonis.

RESPONSIO: Dicendum quod gratiæ gratis datæ dantur ad utilitatem aliorum, ut supra dictum est.[9] Cognitio autem quam aliquis a Deo accipit

---

[1] *I Corinthians* 12, 8
[2] cf *CG* III, 154. *In* I *Cor.* 12, *lect.* 2
[3] *De doctr. Christ.* IV, 12. PL 34, 101
[4] *I Corinthians* 4, 20

Question 177. the grace which is in speech

We are next to consider the charisms which attach to speech or utterance, to which St Paul refers,[1] *to one is given through the Spirit the utterance of wisdom, and to another the utterance of knowledge.* There are two points of inquiry:

1. whether some charism attaches to speech
2. who are the fitting recipients of this gift

article 1. whether some charism attaches to speech

THE FIRST POINT:[2] 1. It seems that in speech there is no place for a charism. Grace is given for that which exceeds the capacity of a man. But it was from natural reason that the art of rhetoric was evolved. By it a person can *so speak as to teach, to delight, and to move*, according to Augustine.[3] Is not all this the object of ordinary grace in speech? So the grace of speech does not suppose any charism.

2. Every grace relates to the kingdom of God. But St Paul says,[4] *The kingdom of God does not consist in talk but in power.* So in speech there is no charism.

3. No grace is given by reason of merits, because *if it is by grace, it is no longer on the basis of works.*[5] Yet speech is given to a person on his merits: in his exposition of *Psalm* 118,[6] *Take not the word of truth utterly out of my mouth*, Gregory says,[7] *God Almighty grants the utterance of truth to those who put it into practice, and takes it away from those who do not.* Thus the gift of speech is not a charism.

4. A man should declare in speech what relates to the virtue of faith, as also what relates to the gifts of wisdom and knowledge. So if 'utterance of wisdom,' and 'utterance of knowledge' are reckoned charisms, so too should 'utterance of faith' be a charism.

ON THE OTHER HAND it is said,[8] *A gracious tongue multiplies courtesies.* But a man's goodness derives from grace; so too should his speech.

REPLY: Charisms are given for the profit of others, as said above.[9] But the knowledge which a man receives from God could not be turned to the

---

[5]*Romans* 11, 6
[6]*Psalms* 118, 43
[7]*Moral.* XI, 15. PL 75, 964
[8]*Ecclesiasticus* 6, 5
[9]1a2æ. 111, 1 & 4

in utilitatem alterius converti non posset, nisi mediante locutione. Et quia Spiritus Sanctus non deficit in aliquo quod pertinet ad Ecclesiæ utilitatem, etiam providet membris Ecclesiæ in locutione: non solum ut aliquis sic loquatur ut a diversis possit intelligi, quod pertinet ad donum linguarum, sed etiam quod efficaciter loquatur, quod pertinet ad gratiam sermonis.

Et hoc tripliciter. Primo quidem ad instruendum intellectum, quod fit dum aliquis sic loquitur quod doceat. Secundo ad movendum affectum, ut scilicet libenter audiat verbum Dei, quod fit dum aliquis sic loquitur quod auditores delectet: quod non debet aliquis quærere propter favorem suum, sed ut homines alliciantur ad audiendum verbum Dei. Tertio ad hoc quod aliquis amet ea quæ verbis significantur, et velit ea implere, quod fit dum aliquis sic loquitur quod auditorem flectat. Ad quod quidem efficiendum Spiritus Sanctus utitur lingua hominis quasi quodam instrumento: ipse autem est qui perficit operationem interius. Unde Gregorius dicit,[10] *Nisi corda auditorum Spiritus Sanctus repleat, ad aures corporis vox docentium incassum sonat.*

1. Ad primum ergo dicendum quod sicut miraculose Deus quandoque operatur quodam excellentiori modo etiam ea quæ natura potest operari; ita etiam Spiritus Sanctus excellentius operatur per gratiam sermonis id quod potest ars operari inferiori modo.

2. Ad secundum dicendum quod Apostolus ibi loquitur de sermone qui innititur humanæ eloquentiæ absque virtute Spiritus Sancti: unde præmisit,[11] *Cognoscam non sermonem eorum qui inflati sunt, sed virtutem*; et de seipso præmiserat,[12] *Sermo meus et prædicatio mea non fuit in persuasibilibus humanæ sapientiæ verbis, sed in ostensione spiritus et virtutis.*

3. Ad tertium dicendum quod, sicut dictum est,[13] gratia sermonis datur alicui ad utilitatem aliorum. Unde quandoque subtrahitur propter auditoris culpam, quandoque autem propter culpam ipsius loquentis. Bona autem opera utriusque non merentur directe hanc gratiam, sed solum impediunt hujus gratiæ impedimenta. Nam etiam gratia gratum faciens subtrahitur propter culpam; non tamen eam meretur aliquis per bona opera, per quæ tollitur tantum gratiæ impedimentum.

4. Ad quartum dicendum quod, sicut dictum est,[14] gratia sermonis ordinatur ad utilitatem aliorum. Quoe autem aliquis fidem suam aliis communicet, fit per sermonem scientiæ sive sapientiæ. Unde Augustinus dicit[15] quod *scire, quemadmodum fides et piis opituletur, et contra impios defendatur, videtur Apostolus scientiam appellare.* Et ideo non oportuit quod poneret sermonem fidei; sed sufficit ponere sermonem scientiæ et sapientiæ.

---

[10]*In Evang*, II, 30. PL 76, 1222
[11]I *Corinthians* 4, 19
[12]ibid 2, 4

profit of others except through the medium of speech. Not only must a person so speak as to be understood by different people—this is a matter of the gift of tongues—but he must also speak effectively, and this pertains to the grace of speech.

This happens in three ways. First, to instruct the intellect, as happens when one so speaks as to *teach*. Secondly, to move the affection, so that a person willingly hears the Word of God. This happens when a person so speaks as to *delight* his audience. No one should seek this for his own personal favour, but rather that men should be drawn to hearing the Word of God. Thirdly, so that men may love what is signified by the words, and want to fulfil what is urged. This happens when a man so speaks as to *move* his hearers. To bring this about the Holy Spirit uses the tongue of a man as a sort of instrument; and it is the same spirit which completes the work inwardly. Hence Gregory says in a homily for Pentecost,[10] *Unless the Holy Spirit fills the hearts of the hearers, the voice of those teaching sounds in vain upon the ears of the body.*

Hence: 1. God sometimes works miraculously in a certain more excellent way even those things which nature can do. So too the Holy Spirit can operate more excellently by the grace of speech that which art could achieve in a lesser way.

2. The Apostle speaks then of utterance which leans on human eloquence, without the power of the Holy Spirit. Hence he says,[11] *I will find out not the talk of these arrogant people but their power.* And about himself he had previously written, *My speech and my message were not in plausible words of wisdom but in demonstration of the Spirit and in power.*[12]

3. As was said,[13] the grace of speech is given to a person for the profit of others. Hence it is sometimes withdrawn because of the hearer's sin, and sometimes because of the sin of the speaker himself. The good works of either party do not directly merit the grace; they simply remove obstacles to grace. For even sanctifying grace is withdrawn because of sin. No one merits this grace by good works; yet the good works remove the obstacles to grace.

4. As said before,[14] the grace of speech is ordered to the utility of others. If anyone communicates his faith to others, this is done through the word of knowledge or wisdom. Hence Augustine says,[15] *To know how faith may profit the godly and be defended against the ungodly is apparently what the Apostle means by knowledge.* So he did not need to talk about the word of faith; it was enough to speak of the word of knowledge and wisdom.

---

[13]in corp
[14]loc cit
[15]*De Trin.* XIV, 1. PL 42, 1037

articulus 2. *utrum gratia sermonis, sapientiæ et scientiæ pertineat
etiam ad mulieres*

AD SECUNDUM sic proceditur:[1] 1. Videtur quod gratia sermonis, sapientiæ et scientiæ pertineat etiam ad mulieres. Ad hujusmodi enim gratiam pertinet doctrina, sicut dictum est.[2] Sed docere competit mulieri: dicitur enim *Prov.*,[3] *Unigenitus fui coram matre mea, et docebat me.* Ergo hæc gratia competit mulieribus.

2. Præterea, major est gratia prophetiæ quam gratia sermonis, sicut major est contemplatio veritatis quam ejus enuntiatio. Sed prophetia conceditur mulieribus, sicut legitur *Jud.*[4] de Debora; et *Reg.*[5] de Olda prophetissa, uxore Sellum; et *Act.*,[6] de quatuor filiabus Philippi Apostolus etiam dicit I ad *Cor.*,[7] *Omnis mulier orans, aut prophetans,* etc. Ergo videtur quod multo magis gratia sermonis competat mulieri.

3. Præterea, I *Pet.* dicitur,[8] *Unusquisque sicut accipit gratiam, in alterutrum illam administrantes.* Sed quædam mulieres accipiunt gratiam sapientiæ et scientiæ, quam non possunt aliis administrare nisi per gratiam sermonis. Ergo gratia sermonis competit mulieribus.

SED CONTRA est quod Apostolus dicit I ad *Cor.*,[9] *Mulieres in Ecclesiis taceant;* et I ad *Tim.*,[10] *Docere mulieri non permitto.* Hoc autem præcipue pertinet ad gratiam sermonis. Ergo gratia sermonis non competit mulieribus.

RESPONSIO: Dicendum quod sermone potest aliquis uti dupliciter. Uno modo privatim ad unum vel paucos, familiariter colloquendo, et quantum ad hoc gratia sermonis potest competere mulieribus. Alio modo publice alloquendo totam Ecclesiam, et hoc mulieri non conceditur. Primo quidem et principaliter propter conditionem fœminei sexus, qui debet esse subditus viro, ut patet *Gen.*[11] Docere autem et persuadere publice in Ecclesia non pertinet ad subditos, sed ad prælatos; magis tamen viri subditi ex commissione possunt exequi, quia non habent hujusmodi subjectionem ex naturali sexu, sicut mulieres, sed ex aliquo accidentaliter superveniente.

Secundo, ne animi hominum alliciantur ad libidinem: dicitur enim *Eccl.*,[12] *Colloquium illius quasi ignis exardescit.*

Tertio, quia communiter mulieres non sunt in sapientia perfectæ, ut eis possit convenienter publica doctrina committi.

---

[1]cf 3a. 55, 1 ad 1. *In* I *Cor.* 14, lect. 7. *In* I *Tim.* 2, lect. 3. *In Tit.* 2, lect. 1
[2]above art. 1
[3]*Proverbs* 4, 3
[4]*Judges* 4, 4
[5]*II Kings* 22, 14
[6]*Acts* 21, 9
[7]*I Corinthians* 11, 5
[8]*I Peter* 4, 10
[9]*I Corinthians* 14, 34

*article 2. whether the charism of wisdom in speech and knowledge
pertains to women also*

THE SECOND POINT:[1] 1. It seems that this grace belongs to women too.
Teaching, as we have seen is attached to this grace.[2] And a woman can
teach: thus *Proverbs*,[3] *I was an only-begotten in the sight of my mother; she
taught me.*

2. The grace of prophecy is greater than that of speech just as contemplation of truth is greater than its enunciation. But prophecy is
granted to women, as we read of Deborah,[4] of Hulda the prophetess, wife
of Sellnor,[5] and of the four daughters of Philip.[6] Even St Paul speaks o
every woman prophesying or praying.[7] All the more then must, it seems, the
grace of speech befit a woman.

3. It is said in 1 *Peter*,[8] *As each has received a gift, employ it for one
another.* But certain women receive the grace of wisdom and knowledge,
which they cannot administer to others except by the grace of speech.
So the grace of speech befits a woman.

ON THE OTHER HAND St Paul says that *women should keep silence in the
Churches*,[9] and, *I permit no woman to teach or to have authority over men.*[10]
But this especially touches the grace of speech. Accordingly that grace does
not pertain to women.

REPLY: Speech can be used in two ways. In one way privately, to one or
a few, in familiar conversation. In this way the grace of speech becomes a
woman. The other way publicly, addressing oneself to the whole Church.
This is not conceded to women. First and principally, because of the
condition of the female sex, which must be subject to man, according to
Genesis[11]. But to teach and persuade publicly in Church is not the task of
subjects but of prelates. Men, when commissioned, can far better do this
work, because their subjection is not from nature and sex as with women,
but from something supervening by accident.

Secondly, lest men's minds be enticed to lust. Thus *Ecclesiasticus*,[12]
*Many have been misled by a woman's beauty. By it passion is kindled like a
fire.*

Thirdly, because generally speaking women are not perfected in
wisdom so as to be fit to be entrusted with public teaching.[a]

---

[10]1 *Timothy* 2, 12
[11]*Genesis* 3, 16
[12]*Ecclesiasticus* 9, 11
[a]The argument was the language of an age in which feminism was unknown;
St Paul's edict, *I permit not a woman to speak in church*, was taken very literally.

1. Ad primum ergo dicendum quod illa auctoritas loquitur de doctrina privata qua mater filium erudit.

2. Ad secundum dicendum quod gratia prophetiæ attenditur secundum mentem illuminatam a Deo; ex qua parte non est in hominibus sexuum differentia, secundum illud ad *Coloss.*,[13] *Induentes novum hominem, qui renovatur . . . secundum imaginem ejus, qui creavit eum, ubi non est masculus neque fœmina.* Sed gratias sermonis pertinet ad instructionem hominum, inter quos differentia sexuum invenitur. Unde non est similis ratio de utroque.

3. Ad tertium dicendum quod gratiam divinitus acceptam diversimode aliqui administrant, secundum diversitatem conditionis ipsorum. Unde mulieres, si gratiam sapientiæ aut scientiæ habeant, possunt eam administrare secundum privatam doctrinam, non autem secundum publicam.

---

[13]*Colossians* 3, 10

Hence: 1. Scripture speaks here of private instruction whereby a woman instructs her son.[b]

2. In the grace of prophecy, it is the mind which is enlightened by God. However, as regards spirit there is no difference of sex; thus *Colossians*,[13] *You have put on the new nature which is being renewed in knowledge after the image of his creator*. But the grace of speech pertains to the instruction of mankind in which is found the difference of the sexes. So the case is different.

3. The recipients of grace conferred by God administer it in different ways according to their various conditions. Hence women, if they have the grace of wisdom or of knowledge, can impart these by teaching privately but not publicly.

---

[b]Well illustrated by the Jews' strong sense of a mother's rôle in the education of children.

Quæstio 178. de gratia miraculorum

Deinde considerandum est de gratia miraculorum: et circa hoc quæruntur duo:

1. utrum sit aliqua gratia gratis data faciendi miracula;
2. quibus conveniat.

articulus 1. *utrum sit aliqua gratia gratis data ad miracula facienda*

AS PRIMUM sic proceditur:[1] 1. Videtur quod nulla gratia gratis data ordinetur ad miracula facienda. Omnis enim gratia ponit aliquid in eo cui datur. Sed operatio miraculorum non ponit aliquid in anima hominis cui datur, quia etiam ad tactum corporis mortui miracula fiunt, sicut legitur *Reg.*,[2] quod *quidam projecerunt cadaver in sepulcro Elisæi, quod cum tetigisset ossa Elisæi, revixit homo, et stetit super pedes suos.* Ergo operatio miraculorum non pertinet ad gratiam gratis datam.

2. Præterea, gratiæ gratis datæ sunt a Spiritu Sancto, secundum illud I *ad Cor.*,[3] *Divisiones gratiarum sunt, idem autem Spiritus.* Sed operatio miraculorum fit etiam a spiritu immundo, secundum illud *Matt.*,[4] *Surgent pseudochristi, et pseudoprophetæ, et dabunt signa, et prodigia magna.* Ergo videtur quod operatio miraculorum non pertineat ad gratiam gratis datam.

3. Præterea, miracula distinguuntur per signa et prodigia, sive portenta, et per virtutes. Inconvenienter ergo ponitur operatio virtutum potius gratia gratis data quam operatio prodigiorum sive signorum.

4. Præterea, miraculosa reparatio sanitatis per divinam virtutem fit. Ergo non debet distingui gratia sanitatum ab operatione virtutum.

5. Præterea, operatio miraculorum consequitur fidem vel facientis, secundum illud I ad *Cor.*,[5] *Si habuero omnem fidem ita ut montes transferam;* sive etiam aliorum, propter quos miracula fiunt: unde dicitur *Matt.*,[6] *Et non fecit ibi virtutes multas propter incredulitatem illorum.* Si ergo fides ponitur gratia gratis data, superfluum est præter hoc ponere aliam gratiam gratis datam operationem signorum.

SED CONTRA est quod Apostolus inter alias gratias gratis datas dicit,[7] *Alii datur gratia sanitatum . . . alii operatio virtutum.*

RESPONSIO: Dicendum quod, sicut supra dictum est,[8] Spiritus Sanctus

---

[1] *CG* III, 154. Ia2æ. 111, 4. *De potentia* VI, 4 & 9 ad 1   [2] II *Kings* 13, 21
[3] I *Corinthians* 12, 4   [4] *Matthew* 24, 24
[5] I *Corinthians* 13, 2   [6] *Matthew* 13, 58
[7] I *Corinthians* 12, 9   [8] 2a2æ. 177, 1

Question 178. the grace of working miracles

We need now to consider the grace of working miracles. Two points arise:

1. whether there is given a charism of miracle-working;
2. who should work miracles

article 1. whether there is given a charism of miracle-working

THE FIRST POINT:[1] 1. It would seem that no charism is directed to the working of miracles.[a] Every grace lays down something in him to whom it is granted. But the working of miracles does not bring about anything in the soul of him to whom the grace is given: indeed even the touching of a dead body is a cause of miracles, as we read in *Kings*,[2] a man was being buried and *they cast the body into the grave of Elisha: and as soon as the body touched the bones of Elisha the man revived.* Thus the power of working miracles is not a charism.

2. Charisms are from the Holy Spirit: *There are varieties of gifts, but the same Spirit.*[3] But the working of miracles is also accomplished by an unclean spirit, as in *Matthew.*[4] *For false Christs and false prophets will arise and show great signs and wonders.* Therefore the power of working miracles is not necessarily a charism.

3. Miracles are distinguished into 'signs', 'prodigies', or 'portents', and 'wonders'. So it is unreasonable to reckon the working of miracles a charism, any more than the working of signs and wonders.

4. A miraculous healing is done by the power of God. Therefore we should not distinguish the grace of healing from that of working miracles.

5. The working of miracles comes from faith, either in him who works them, as in 1 *Corinthians*,[5] *If I should have all faith so as to move mountains,* or even the faith of others for whose sake the miracle takes place, hence *Matthew*,[6] *He did not do mighty works there because of their unbelief.* If then 'faith' is put among the charisms, it is superfluous to allow another charism for the working of miracles.

ON THE OTHER HAND: St Paul says,[7] speaking of the charisms, *To one is given the grace of healing, to another the working of miracles.*

REPLY: As was said,[8] the Holy Spirit sufficiently provides the Church

---

[a]Note the title of this Question, which is not treating of miracles as such, but of the charisms or special graces, given to men whereby they become God's instruments for the working of miracles. This limits the range of the topic here. It has been already treated in wider terms; 1a. 105, 6 & 8; 110, 4; 114, 4. Vol. 15 of this series.

sufficienter providet Ecclesiæ in his quæ sunt utilia ad salutem, ad quod ordinantur gratiæ gratis datæ. Sicut autem oportet quod notitia quam quis divinitus accepit, in notitiam aliorum deducatur per donum linguarum et per gratiam sermonis, ita necesse est quod sermo prolatus confirmetur ad hoc quod credibilis fiat. Hoc autem fit per operationem miraculorum, secundum illud *Marc.*,[9] *Et sermonem confirmante, sequentibus signis.* Et hoc rationabiliter. Naturale enim est homini ut veritatem intelligibilem per sensibiles effectus deprehendat. Unde sicut ductu naturalis rationis homo pervenire potest ad aliquam Dei notitiam per effectus naturales; ita per aliquos supernaturales effectus, qui miracula dicuntur, in aliquam supernaturalem cognitionem credendorum homo inducitur. Et ideo operatio miraculorum pertinet ad gratiam gratis datam.

1. Ad primum ergo dicendum quod, sicut prophetia se extendit ad omnia quæ supernaturaliter cognosci possunt, ita operatio virtutum se extendit ad omnia quæ supernaturaliter fieri possunt: quorum quidem causa est divina omnipotentia, quæ nulli creaturæ communicari potest. Et ideo impossibile est quod principium operandi miracula sit aliqua qualitas habitualiter manens in anima. Sed tamen hoc potest contingere quod sicut mens prophetæ movetur ex inspiratione divina ad aliquid supernaturaliter cognoscendum: ita etiam mens miracula facientis moveatur ad faciendum aliquid ad quod sequitur effectus miraculi, quod Deus sua virtute facit. Quod quandoque quidem fit, præcedente oratione, sicut cum Petrus Tabitam mortuam suscitavit, ut habetur *Act.*[10] Quandoque etiam non præcedente manifesta oratione, sed Deo ad nutum hominis operante; sicut Petrus Ananiam et Saphiram mentientes morti increpando tradidit, ut dicitur *Act.*[11] Unde Gregorius dicit[12] quod *Sancti aliquando ex potestate miracula exhibent, aliquando ex postulatione.* Utrolibet tamen modo Deus principaliter operatur, qui utitur instrumentaliter vel interiori motu hominis, vel ejus locutione, vel etiam aliquo exteriori actu, seu etiam aliquo contactu corporali corporis etiam mortui.

Unde cum Josue dixisset quasi ex potestate,[13] *Sol contra Gabaon ne movearis,* subditur postea, *Non fuit ante et postea tam longa dies, obediente Domino voci hominis.*

2. Ad secundum dicendum quod ibi loquitur Dominus de miraculis quæ fienda sunt tempore Antichristi; de quibus Apostolus dicit,[14] *adventus Antichristi erit secundum operationem Satanæ in omni virtute, et signis, et prodigiis mendacibus.* Et, sicut Augustinus dicit,[15] *Ambigi solet utrum propterea dicta sint signa et prodigia mendacia, quoniam mortales sensus per phantasmata decepturus est, ut quod non facit, facere videatur; an quia illa ipsa, etiamsi erunt vera prodigia, ad mendacium pertrahent credituros.* Vera

---

[9]*Mark* 16, 20   [10]*Acts* 9, 40   [11]*Acts* 5, 3

with all that is needful for salvation: and such is the purpose of charisms. It is also needful for the transmission of the truth to be confirmed so as to become credible. This is the end envisaged by the working of miracles, as we read in *Mark*,[9] *While the Lord worked with them and confirmed the message by its attendant signs.* And this is reasonable. For it is natural for a man to grasp intellectual truth through sense-perceptible effects. Hence, just as a man can come to some knowledge of God through being led to it by natural reason and through natural effects, so by some supernatural effects, which are termed miracles, a man is brought to a certain super-natural knowledge of truths to be believed. That is why the working of miracles is a type of charism.

Hence: 1. As prophecy extends to all that can be supernaturally known, so the operation of miracles extends to all that can be supernaturally accomplished. The cause of all these is God's power—which cannot be communicated to any creature. So the principle of miracle-working cannot be any permanently abiding quality of the soul.

However, just as the mind of a prophet is moved by divine inspiration to know something supernaturally, so the mind of one working a miracle is moved to do something which results in a miracle—which God does by his own power. This sometimes takes place with prayer beforehand, as when Peter raised the dead Tabitha;[10] sometimes even without any prayer to precede, God simply acts at man's behest, as when Ananias and Saphira lied, and were handed over to death at the reproval of St Peter.[11] Hence Gregory says,[12] *The saints work miracles, sometimes by their power, sometimes by their prayers.* Either way God is the principal worker, and uses as instruments either the inward impulse of a man, or his words, or some outward deed, or even some contact of a body, even dead.

Hence when Joshua had said,[13] as it were of his own power, *Sun stand still at Gibeon,* the words are added, *there has been no day like it, before or since, when the Lord hearkened to the voice of a man.*

2. The Lord there speaks of miracles which are to be done at the time of Antichrist. Of these St Paul says,[14] *The coming of the lawless one by the activity of Satan will be with all power, and with pretended signs and wonders.* Augustine says here,[15] *We might ask why these signs are called deceiving: is it because they will deceive people's senses by phantasms appearing to do what in fact they do not do? or are they real prodigies dragging men down to untruth?* The prodigies would be real, if the things themselves were real.

---

[12]*Dialog.* II, 30. PL 66, 188
[13]*Joshua* 10, 2, 14
[14]II *Thessalonians* 2, 9
[15]*De civit. Dei* xx, 19. PL 41, 687

autem dicuntur, quia ipsæ res veræ erunt, sicut magi Pharaonis fecerunt veras ranas et veros serpentes; non tamen habebunt veram rationem miraculi, quia fient virtute naturalium causarum, sicut in *Prima Parte*[16] dictum est. Sed operatio miraculorum, quæ attribuitur gratiæ gratis datæ, fit virtute divina ad hominum utilitatem.

3. Ad tertium dicendum quod in miraculis duo possunt attendi. Unum quidem est id quod fit, quod quidem est aliquid excedens facultatem naturæ, et secundum hoc miracula dicuntur *virtutes*. Aliud est id propter quod miracula fiunt, scilicet ad manifestandum aliquid supernaturale: et secundum hoc communiter dicuntur *signa*; propter excellentiam autem dicuntur *portenta*, vel *prodigia*, quasi procul aliquid ostendentia.

4. Ad quartum dicendum quod gratia sanitatum commemoratur seorsum, quia per eam confertur homini aliquod beneficium, scilicet corporalis sanitas, præter beneficium commune quod exhibetur in omnibus miraculis, ut scilicet homines adducantur in Dei notitiam.

5. Ad quintum dicendum quod operatio miraculorum attribuitur fidei propter duo. Primo quidem, quia ordinatur ad fidei confirmationem; secundo, quia procedit ex Dei omnipotentia, cui fides innititur. Et tamen sicut præter gratiam fidei necessaria est gratia sermonis ad fidei instructionem; ita etiam necessaria est operatio miraculorum ad fidei confirmationem.

articulus 2. utrum mali possint miracula facere

AD SECUNDUM sic proceditur:[1] 1. Videtur quod mali non possint miracula facere. Miracula enim impetrantur per orationem, sicut dictum est.[2] Sed oratio peccatoris non est exaudibilis, secundum illud *Joan.*,[3] *Scimus, quia peccatores Deus non audit;* et *Prov.* dicitur,[4] *Qui declinat aures suas ne audiat legem, oratio ejus erit execrabilis.* Ergo videtur quod mali miracula facere non possint.

2. Præterea, miracula attribuuntur fidei, secundum illud *Matt.*,[5] *Si habueritis fidem, sicut granum sinapis, dicetis monti huic, Transi hinc, et transibit. Fides* autem *sine operibus mortua est,* ut dicitur *Jac.*,[6] et sic non videtur quod habeat propriam operationem. Ergo videtur quod mali, qui non sunt bonorum operum operativi, miracula facere non possint.

3. Præterea, miracula sunt quædam divina testimonia, secundum illud ad *Heb.*,[7] *Contestante Deo signis, et portentis, et variis virtutibus;* unde et in

[16]1a. 114, 4
[1]cf 1a. 110, 4 ad 2. *In Matt.* 7. *In* I *Cor.* 12, *lect.* 2; 13, *lect.* 1. *In* II *Thess.* 2, *lect.* 2. *De potentia* VI, 5 ad 9; 9 ad 5. *Quodl.* IV, 1 ad 4
[2]above art. 1 ad 1   [3]*John* 9, 31

Thus the Pharaoh's magicians produced real frogs and real serpents. Yet these deeds will not be miracles in the strict sense, because brought about by natural causes, as shown in *Prima Pars*.[16] But the working of a miracle which is ascribed to a charism is accomplished by the power of God for man's profit.

3. Two points should be noted about miracles: the first is that which takes place, which is something exceeding the powers of nature. In this sense miracles are termed 'powers'. The other point is the purpose for which they are worked, viz. to show something supernatural. In this sense they are commonly called 'signs'. Because of their outstanding character they are referred to as 'portents' and 'prodigies', as if demonstrative of something remote.

4. The 'grace of healing' is listed separately because by it some benefit is conferred upon a man, namely bodily health, aside from the common benefit which is manifested in all miracles, which is that of men being drawn to a knowledge of God.

5. The working of miracles is attributed to faith for two reasons. First, because it is directed to the confirmation of faith. Secondly, because it proceeds from the almighty power of God on which faith rests. And yet, if besides a grace of faith, a grace of speech is needed for the instruction of faith, so too a working of miracles is needed for the confirmation of faith.

article 2. can the wicked work miracles?

THE SECOND POINT:[1] 1. It seems that evil people cannot work miracles. Miracles come about by prayer, as was said.[2] But the prayer of a sinner is not to be heard: *We know that God does not hear sinners*,[3] and, *If one turns away from hearing the law, even his prayer is an abomination*.[4] So it seems that sinners cannot work miracles.

2. Miracles are attributed to faith, as is said in *Matthew*,[5] *If you have faith as a grain of mustard seed, you will say to this mountain, move hence to yonder place, and it will move; and nothing will be impossible to you*. But *faith without works is dead*, as is said in *James*,[6] so apparently it has no operation of its own. Hence, seemingly, sinners, destitute of good works, cannot work miracles.

3. Miracles are a kind of divine testimony; thus *Hebrews*,[7] *While God bore witness by signs and wonders*. So, too, in the Church, some come to be

---

[4]*Proverbs* 28, 9
[5]*Matthew* 17, 19
[6]*James* 2, 20
[7]*Hebrews* 2, 4

Ecclesia aliqui canonizantur per testimonia miraculorum. Sed Deus non potest esse testis falsitatis. Ergo videtur quod mali homines non possint miracula facere.

4. Præterea, boni sunt Deo conjunctiores quam mali. Sed non omnes boni faciunt miracula. Ergo multo minus mali faciunt.

SED CONTRA est quod dicit Apostolus,[8] *Si habuero omnem fidem, ita ut montes transferam; charitatem autem non habuero, nihil sum.* Sed quicumque non habet charitatem, est malus, quia *hoc solum donum Spiritus Sancti est, quod dividit inter filios regni et filios perditionis,* ut dicit Augustinus.[9] Ergo videtur quod etiam mali possint miracula facere.

RESPONSIO: Dicendum quod miraculorum aliqua quidem sunt non vera, sed phantastica facta, quibus scilicet ludificatur homo, ut videatur ei aliquid quod non est; quædam vero sunt vera facta, sed non vere habent rationem miraculi, quæ fiunt virtute aliquarum naturalium causarum: et hæc duo possunt fieri per dæmonem, ut supra dictum est.[10]

Sed vera miracula non possunt fieri nisi virtute divina: operatur enim ea Deus ad hominum utilitatem; et hoc dupliciter: uno quidem modo ad veritatis prædicatæ confirmationem; alio modo ad demonstrationem sanctitatis alicujus, quem Deus hominibus vult proponere in exemplum virtutis.

Primo autem modo miracula possunt fieri per quemcumque qui veram fidem prædicat, et nomen Christi invocat: quod etiam interdum per malos fit. Et secundum hunc modum etiam mali possunt miracula facere. Unde super illud *Matt.,*[11] *Nonne in nomine tuo prophetavimus?* etc., dicit Hieronymus,[12] *Prophetare vel virtutes facere, et dæmonia ejicere, interdum non est ejus meritis qui operatur; sed invocatione nominis Christi hoc agit ut homines Deum honorent, ad cujus invocationem fiunt tanta miracula.*

Secundo autem modo non fiunt miracula nisi a sanctis, ad quorum sanctitatem demonstrandam miracula fiunt vel in vita eorum, vel etiam post mortem, sive per eos, sive per alios. Legitur enim *Act.,*[13] quod *Deus faciebat virtutes per manus Pauli: et etiam super languidos deferebantur a corpore ejus sudaria, et recedebant ab eis languores.*

Et sic etiam nihil prohiberet per aliquem peccatorem miracula fieri ad invocationem alicujus sancti: quæ tamen miracula non dicitur facere ille, sed ille ad cujus sanctitatem demonstrandam hæc fierent.

1. Ad primum ergo dicendum quod, sicut supra dictum est,[14] cum de

---

[8]*I Corinthians* 13, 2
[9]*De Trin.* xv, 18. PL 42, 1082
[10]above art. 1 ad 2
[11]*Matthew* 7, 22
[12]PL 26, 50

canonized through the evidence of miracles. But God cannot be a witness to falsehood. Therefore sinners cannot work miracles.

4. Good people are closer than bad to God. But not all good people work miracles. Therefore still less do sinners do so.

ON THE OTHER HAND: St Paul says,[8] *If I have all faith so as to remove mountains, but have not love, I am nothing,* But he who has not love is a sinner: because *the gift alone of the Holy Spirit is what divides the sons of the kingdom and the sons of perdition,* as Augustine says.[9] Therefore it seems that even sinners can work miracles.

REPLY: Some miracles are not genuine but fanciful tricks to sport with man, deluding him by the appearance of that which is not. Others are true deeds, but lack the real character of miracle because they are brought about by some natural cause. These two types can be performed by demons, as was said.[10]

True miracles, however, can only be performed by the power of God; and God does them for the profit of mankind. And this is in two ways: one for the confirmation of the truth preached, another to demonstrate the holiness of someone whom God wishes to propose to men as an example of virtuous living.

In the first way miracles can be worked by anyone who preaches true faith and calls upon the name of Christ: which, at times, is done by sinners. In this manner even sinners can work miracles. On *Matthew,*[11] *Did he not prophesy in your name,* etc., Jerome says,[12] *To prophesy, to work miracles, to drive out demons is not always a proof of the merit of him who so acts. It is the invocation of the name of Christ which obtains all that, so that men should honour the divinity of the Christ in whose name so many miracles are wrought.*

In the second way, miracles are only worked by saints. It is to demonstrate their sanctity that miracles take place either in their life or after their death, either in their own person, or through others. We read[13] that *God did extraordinary miracles by the hand of Paul, so that handkerchiefs or aprons were carried away from his body to the sick, and diseases left them.* In this way, too, there is nothing to prevent miracles being done by a sinner at the invocation of some saint. But then these miracles are not said to be worked by the sinner, but by him in virtue of whose sanctity the miracles were worked.

Hence: 1. As was said,[14] when dealing with prayer, a prayer which is

---

[13]*Acts* 19, 11
[14]2a2æ. 83, 16

oratione ageretur, oratio in impetrando non innititur merito, sed divinæ misericordiæ, quæ etiam ad malos se extendit: et ideo etiam quandoque peccatorum oratio a Deo exauditur. Unde Augustinus dicit,[15] quod *illud verbum cæcus locutus est, quasi adhuc inunctus*, idest nondum perfecte illuminatus, *nam peccatores exaudit Deus.*

Quod autem dicitur, quod oratio non audientis legem est execrabilis, intelligendum est quantum est ex merito peccatoris; sed interdum impetrat ex misericordia Dei, vel propter salutem ejus qui orat, sicut auditus est publicanus, ut dicitur *Luc.*,[16] vel etiam propter salutem aliorum et gloriam Dei.

2. Ad secundum dicendum quod fides sine operibus dicitur esse mortua quantum ad ipsum credentem, qui per eam non vivit vita gratiæ. Nihil autem prohibet quod res viva operetur per instrumentum mortuum, sicut homo operatur per baculum; et hoc modo Deus operatur per fidem hominis peccatoris instrumentaliter.

3. Ad tertium dicendum quod miracula semper sunt vera testimonia ejus ad quod inducuntur. Unde a malis, qui falsam doctrinam enuntiant, nunquam fiunt vera miracula ad confirmationem suæ doctrinæ; quamvis quandoque fieri possint ad commendationem nominis Christi, quod invocant, et in virtute sacramentorum quæ exhibent. Ab his autem qui veram doctrinam enuntiant, fiunt quandoque vera miracula ad confirmationem doctrinæ, non autem ad testificationem sanctitatis. Unde Augustinus dicit,[17] *Aliter magi faciunt miracula, aliter boni Christiani, aliter mali. Magi per privatos contractus cum dæmonibus; boni Christiani per publicam justitiam; mali Christiani per signa publicæ justitiæ.*

4. Ad quartum dicendum quod, sicut Augustinus dicit,[18] *Admonet nos Dominus ut intelligamus quædam miracula etiam sceleratos homines facere, qualia sancti facere non possunt*; et sicut Augustinus ibidem dicit, *ideo non omnibus sanctis ista attribuuntur, ne perniciosissimo errore decipiantur infirmi, æstimantes in talibus factis esse majora dona quam in operibus justitiæ, quibus vita æterna comparatur.*

---

[15]On *John* 9, 32. PL 35, 1718
[16]*Luke* 18, 13

heard does not depend on the merit of him who prayed, but on the divine compassion which extends even to the evil. And so, at times, even the prayer of sinners is heard by God. Hence Augustine says,[15] of the man born blind, *the blind man spoke thus even before being anointed,* that is, before being fully restored to sight, because *God hears sinners.*

The sayings about him who turns away from the law, whose prayer is an abomination, must be gauged in terms of the sinner's merit. Yet at times his prayer is heard from the compassion of God, or because of the salvation of him who prays, as the publican was heard,[16] or because of the salvation of others to the glory of God.

2. Faith without works is said to be dead with respect to the believer himself who with such faith does not live the life of grace. There is nothing to prevent a living being from working with a lifeless instrument, as a man walks with a stick. In this way, God acts through the faith of a sinful man, instrumentally.

3. Miracles are always true witnesses of what they confirm. Hence the wicked who proclaim false doctrine never accomplish true miracles for the confirmation of their doctrine; though sometimes they could do so for the honour of Christ's name which they invoke, and by the power of the sacraments which they administer.

As for the wicked who announce truth, these could sometimes work real miracles to confirm their teaching, but not to witness to their sanctity. Augustine remarks on this subject,[17] *There is a great difference between the miracles of magicians and those of good Christians and those of bad Christians. Magicians work miracles by private compact with demons, good Christians by their manifest righteousness, and bad Christians by the outward signs of righteousness.*

4. Augustine also says,[18] *God does not grant the gift of miracles to all his saints, lest by a most pernicious error the weak be deceived into thinking such deeds to imply greater gifts than the deed of righteousness whereby eternal life is obtained.*

---

[17]LXXXIII *Quæst.* 79. PL 40, 92
[18]loc cit

Appendix 1

PROPHECY AS REVELATION

SOCIETY, says St Thomas,[1] as being ordained to eternal life, can only be maintained on course by a righteousness which comes of faith and whose starting-point is prophecy. By society he means the people of God on their march towards heaven, and he takes prophecy here in its widest sense to include all manner of divine communication, including revelation and inspiration of the Scriptures. Prophecy represents God's initiative; he speaks, and his word arouses a response in the one who comes to believe. Without prophecy, in this very wide sense, faith would not come to be or continue to be. The supposition all through this key text is that prophecy-revelation is for the salvational good of men on their way to God. It is a *social* charism for the good of the pilgrim Church in its eschatological setting.

Let us note that 'prophecy-revelation' does not imply anything new in God. 'Every action or relation which we attribute to God but which has its effect in time or space involves no new reality or entity on the side of God who is Unchanging Actuality, but only a new reality or entity in the created universe.'[2] When God reveals or inspires there is a psychological 'event' in the minds of those affected, a *visio prophetica* of some sort, an awareness of what is commonly hidden from human perception. 'It is not God who is wrapped in veils; the veils are the ignorance and darkness, the unconsciousness which normally envelops our own minds.'[3] Similarly God is not absent from us; but our minds are in greater or less degree absent from him, and must remain so until they possess the final consummation of revelation which is the vision beatific.[4]

Because it is a social gift, i.e. for the good of all mankind focused on God, prophecy has a certain official and public character. It was commissioned by God first for the people of Israel and their tradition, and then for the followers of Christ who followed close on them. We need to stress this public and social character, because there have been 'private revelations' in the long history of the Church. Some of these have indeed been impressive and lofty. Yet it is commonly taught that Revelation proper ceased with the death of the last of the Apostles, St John, about A.D. 100.[5]

All subsequent revelations which God could have or could still grant have not the same social and public character in the matter of doctrine and do

---

[1] *De veritate* XII, 3 ad 11
[2] 1a. 12, 7
[3] 2a2æ. 171, 1 ad 4
[4] ibid 4 ad 2
[5] For the normative rôle of the faith of the apostolic generation, cf K. Rahner, *Inspiration in the Bible*, Quæstiones Disputatæ. 1964

not command the assent of faith. Even saints can produce the fruit of their imagination and mingle errors with vision. But the true prophet or man of God or inspired writer, because he is dispensing the word of God and not his own, is protected from error by God himself. And this word of God is *living and effectual (Hebr.* 4, 12), and *able to build up and to give an inheritance among all the sanctified (Acts* 20, 32). *When you received the word of God which you heard from us, you accepted it not as the word of men but as what it really is, the word of God which is at work among you believers* (1 Thess. 2, 13).

Prophecy in the wide sense teaches the Church's children that the divine plan of revelation is realized in deeds and words that are closely interconnected, so that the deeds wrought by God in the history of salvation manifest and reinforce the teaching and realities signified by the words, while the words proclaim the deeds and cast light upon the mystery contained in them. The profound truth conveyed by this revelation, whether it concerns God or man's salvation, shines forth for us in Christ who is at once the mediator and fullness of its revelation in its entirety (*Mt.* 11, 27; *Jn.* 1, 14, 17; 14, 6; 17, 1-3; 1 *Cor.* 3, 16; 4, 6; *Ephes.* 1, 3-14).

Finally, the Christian economy, the new and definitive covenant, will never pass away, and no other public revelation is to be awaited before the glorious manifestation of our Lord Jesus Christ (1 *Tim.* 6, 14; *Tit.* 2, 13).

Appendix 2

FROM PROPHECY TO SCRIPTURAL INSPIRATION

ST THOMAS sees the gift of prophecy in intellectual terms, in the order of knowledge and as an enlightenment of the mind with a strengthening of its native capacities to reach out to something utterly *other*. But intellectual grasp alone would not be enough; the prophet must transmit and convey to others, and the matter prophesied is for all the people of God. Merely natural means would not suffice for such a supernatural mission. As the prophet's mind has been enlightened by a grace from God, so too will his power of speech or delivery be God-given in the 'gift of tongues' and charisms of speech (176-7).[1] And finally, as it were to compel a more than human conviction, God grants a prophet signs or proofs of his mission: he has the gift of miracles (178).

Prophecy is a showing of hidden truth surpassing the reason (171, 2), supernatural (174, 5), which bears some resemblance to divine knowledge (173, 1 & 174, 1), and is a sort of teaching (171, 6). The hidden, inaccessible character of the truth is essential to prophetic knowledge properly so called. Not so, however, with the inspired writer of Scripture or 'hagiographer', who may often, and, indeed, most often, be handling matter which he has collected and collated by the most ordinary natural means, for instance, the prologues to 11 *Maccabees* or *Luke*.

A prophet's supernatural instruction can be effected in two ways. These two ways correspond to two elements present in all human knowledge: the Aristotelean analysis of knowledge is here pressed into service. Thus in human knowledge there is, first, the *lumen intelligibile*, 'intellectual light', which enables the knowing subject to pass judgment. And, secondly, the *species*, 'appearances', 'representations', 'ideas', which prepare for the judgment.

He is a prophet in the true sense when he receives a light to *judge* (*cf* 171. 3 ad 3). 1. An interesting particular case arises when the *Tertia Pars* treats of the title *prophet* given to our Lord in Scripture. It is argued that in this instance the ignorance is not in him but in his hearers (3a. 7, 8). He is a prophet in a lesser sense, or not at all, if he receives *species* only (cf 173, 2). Thus Pharaoh is not to be called a prophet (*De veritate* XII, 7), and Caiphas is no more a prophet than Balaam's ass (*In Joan.* 11, 51, *lect.* 7). He is a prophet in the fullest sense when he receives both *species* and *lumen*, both the 'appearances' and the judgment (cf 173, 2. 3a. 30, 3).

St Thomas also deals with the instance when *lumen* is received from God but without *species*. Light is given to judge of purely human and naturally

---

[1]References in this style are to Questions in the present treatise

knowable realities 'according to God' (*De veritate* XII, 7 & 13. 2a2æ. 173, 2; 174, 2 & 3 ad 3). This last instance becomes important as explaining the inspired writers of Scripture. Their case is no longer one of true prophecy. St Thomas follows St Jerome, in using the term *hagiographi*, 'sacred writers'. To his mind scriptural writers are, as writers, a cut below the prophets (though of course it can and does happen that the sacred author is also a prophet in the strict sense), but the non-prophets are far more numerous. Most of the many biblical writers were *hagiographi*. (A careful reading of 173, 2; 174, 3 ad 3; and 174, 2 ad 3 is recommended.)

Scriptural inspiration has been termed a prophetic instinct. In the individual writer it is not a permanent disposition or trait of character, but a transient impulse, *motus et passio transiens*, granted by the Holy Spirit for the precise purpose of getting a book or part of a book written. Once the writing is completed, the charism ceases to be operative (171, 2; 174, 3 ad 3).

The written work is the end product of biblical inspiration. Amanuenses, secretaries, redactors, revisers, in any number, who have of their own mind contributed anything to the book or part of a book are *inspired*. But in so far as these furnish purely material labour (e.g. in being dictated to) or provide the matter, they are not then inspired. This becomes important when we remember how biblical writers wrote through secretaries, e.g. Jeremiah used Baruch (*Jer.* 36, 4), and St Paul used Tertius (*Rom.* 16, 22).

Light on the mystery of biblical inspiration has been sought from the notion of instrumental causality. This notion, which has appealed to modern theologians, was in fact used sparingly by St Thomas (cf *Quodl.* VII, 14 ad 3, 2a2æ. 172, 4 ad 1; 173, 4. *In Heb.* II, lect. 7. *De pot.* IV, 1). It is argued that the books are wholly from God, and wholly from a human cause. Hence all books manifest human traits, sometimes very forcibly, and the style, characters, foibles and preoccupations of the various authors; and all the while as they wrote they were borne along by the Holy Spirit to the point of writing what God wanted and as God wanted.

No style, literary form, image, disposition, etc. is repugnant to Scripture: formal error and fallacy alone are excluded. 'No one who has a just conception of biblical inspiration will be surprised to find that the sacred writers, like the other ancients, employ certain arts of exposition and narrative, certain idioms especially characteristic of the semitic languages (known as "approximations") and certain hyperbolical and even paradoxical expressions designed for the sake of emphasis. The Sacred Books need not exclude any of the forms of expression which were commonly used in human speech by the ancient peoples, especially of the East, to convey their meaning, so long as they are in no way incompatible with God's sanctity and truth.'[2]

This is not new, but traditional teaching. Thus it was well recognized that 'Scripture conveys divine things to man in a style that men are wont to use' (*In Heb.* I, lect 4), and that 'to the prophetic truth it is a matter of indifference what figures of speech are used' (2a2æ. 172, 3 ad 1).

---

[2]Encyclical of Pius XII, *Divino Afflante* §41

APPENDIX 2. FROM PROPHECY TO INSPIRATION

As the Word of God was made flesh and like unto us in all things, sin excepted, so the words of God, expressed in human language, are in all ways like human speech, error excepted. The result is an inspired Word which is rich in meaning, richer often than the human author may have imagined (cf 173, 4). Thus we get as consequences of inspiration several senses in a text. This is proper to Scripture; and so is its inerrancy, which needs to be rightly understood in the light of what has been said.

Appendix 3

THE PROPHETIC TRADITION
OF ISRAEL

THE chosen people, small in number and insignificant politically, stand out conspicuously in the ancient world by reason of their faith in the Unique God, by their ideals, and by their tradition of prophecy. They realized, as we do to this day, that God spoke through the prophets. But the Hebrew prophets lived, spoke, and acted over several centuries of very human and very tangled history. It is not easy to trace the origins of prophecy; and the end of prophecy in Israel was mysterious. *I will raise up for them a prophet, like you, from among their brethren; and I will put my words in his mouth, and he shall speak to them all that I command him* (*Deut.* 18, 18)—this text is from a high point in the tradition of Israel, and should be read in its whole context (*Deut.* 18, 9–22). God is to provide an alternative to the consultation of witches, necromancers, mediums, etc. An institution was set up and would assure that, at various points in the sacred history, someone, like Moses, would be at hand, to convey truths about God and about God's will for the human race and more especially for his Chosen People. The word of the prophet was ever to be at hand. The prophet is to meet a permanent need of the people after their settlement in Canaan (v. 9); he is to speak on behalf of God (vv. 16–18) and replace any recourse to divination (v. 14). It is admitted that they may be false prophets, but a means of discernment between true and false is added (v. 21). The argument of the passage in its context shows that the 'prophet' is not so much an individual in the future, but Moses' representative for the time being, whose office it would be to supply Israel with needful guidance and advice whenever necessary. The reference is not so much to an individual but to a prophetical order, a permanent channel.

This text is also Messianic, and the terms of reference are also to an ideal prophet who should be 'like Moses' in a pre-eminent degree, in whom the line of prophets should culminate, who himself should be supremely Prophet. The tradition of Messianic interpretation can be traced back to Nathanael (*John* 1, 45), who is expressing his own and his contemporaries' belief in the prophet (ibid 21) who was awaited by Israel. This commonly accepted belief is appealed to by Stephen in *Acts* 7, 37 and Peter in *Acts* 3, 22, and both quote from *Deut.* 18. Christian tradition subsequently took up the text to show that Christ is Messiah and Prophet. It is expressed by Origen, Tertullian, Cyprian, Eusebius, Epiphanius, Augustine, Chrysostom.

The origins of prophecy are mysterious, but we can profitably consider how the great religions of antiquity had their 'inspired' men who claimed to be speaking in the name of their god. From earliest times seers and diviners existed in the Near East; their task was to ascertain the mind of their divinities and convey it to kings and others. Texts from Mari B.C. 2000–1000 tell of prophetic activity by the banks of the Euphrates and at the very ancient site of Byblos in Syria. On the famous Moabite Stone, Mesha of Moan is spurred on by a message from his divinity Chemosh, *Go take Nebo from Israel.*[1]

Ecstatic prophecy is attested in the experiences of Wen Amon the Egyptian who wandered through Israel and Syria, c. 1100 B.C. He was harried by a 'possessed boy',[2] as Paul was by a girl with a 'spirit of divination' a thousand years later (*Acts* 16, 16–18). Ancient Babylonia too had its mantic priests who pronounced oracles from hepatoscopy. There is also evidence of oracles given during frenzied 'possession'.

The Near East from ancient times knew of prophecy and prophetic phenomena in general: it was generally realized that some men spoke in the Word of God to their fellow men. This fact in no way detracts from the unique character of Israelite prophecy which ever had at its core a whole-hearted adherence and devotion to the Unique Lord, 'Yahweh Ehad'.

The Bible tells us of 'prophets of Baal', 450 of these summoned by Jezabel, a native of Tyre, and discomfited by Elijah on Mount Carmel (1 *Kings* 18, 19–40)[3]. 1 *Kings* 22, 6 tells of Ahab consulting some four hundred; this may represent the whole body 'in practice'. These prophetic groups at times behaved ecstatically while claiming to speak in the name of the Lord. There may well have been a legitimate institution of a group character, such as we find with Samuel (1 *Sam.* 10, 5); *The Spirit of the Lord will come down upon you.* 1 *Sam.* 19, 20 seems to suggest that the spirit is 'catching' as well as lawful (cf 1 *Kings* 18, 4 in the time of Elijah). Elishah too had contact with prophetic groupings; cf 11 *Kings* 2, 3–18; 4, 38; and 6, 1 (where Elishah the prophet is contrasted with *the sons of the prophets*), and 11 *Kings* 9, 1; *Amos* 7, 14.

Music played its part (1 *Samuel* 10, 5; 11 *Kings* 3, 15; *And when the music played the power of the Lord came over him*). So too did symbolic actions and mimes of 1 *Kings* 22, 11, and the striking case of Ahijah of Shilo, 1 *Kings* 11, 29. There are other examples in *Isa.* 20, 2–4; and especially in *Jer.* 13, 1; 19, 1; 27, 2; *Ezek*, 4, 1–4; 12, 1–16, 37, 15.

There were, no doubt, some extravagant behaviour and psychological abnormalities, but such things were quite irrelevant to the proper work of prophets as mouthpieces of God. We can distinguish prophets of Baal, Asherah, etc. and prophets of the true God: yet in their outward actions and practices there might be many similarities. All were called by the same term *Nābī*, which could be used in a good, not so good, and bad sense. *Nābī*, the

---

[1] Ancient Near Eastern Texts. pp. 320–31. 2nd edition, 1955. Ed. Pritchard
[2] op. cit 25–9
[3] 1 *Kings* 18, 9 also refers to four hundred prophets of Asherah—making Asherah into a Canaanite goddess. This has been verified by the finds at Ugarit (Ras Shamra). cf C. H. Gordon, *Ugaritic Manual*, 111, 274. Rome, 1955.

Hebrew word,[4] seems to derive from a root meaning to 'call' to proclaim (Akkadian *nabu* = call, Arabic *nabaa*, Ethiopian, *nababa*). In derivatives it can mean 'be beside oneself' (cf I *Sam.* 18, 10, *he raved* (RSV)). The more essential meaning is 'call', 'proclaim': thus the prophet is bearer and interpreter of the Word of God. Thus too Aaron speaks for, and is the mouth of Moses in *Exod.* 4, 15-16; 7, 1. Moses is to be a *god for Pharaoh and Aaron his prophet* (*Nābī*) (cf *Jerem.* 1, 9, *I am putting my words into your mouth*).

The prophet is essentially a mouthpiece or an intermediary between God and man. Our own word prophet is from the Greek *prophētēs* and is 'one who speaks for', on behalf of, one who not so much foretells but proclaims and relays a message. Historically, at all periods, we see the prophets acutely conscious of *God speaking*. They introduce their messages again and again with 'The Lord says', 'Oracle of Yahweh'. This word of God compels utterance. *The Lord God speaks, who can refuse utterance?*, cries Amos (3, 8) who himself had denied any claim to be a prophet at all. Jeremiah shrinks from the call, but is in the grip of God; *Jer.* 1, 1-10, and for life (cf 20, 7-10). We could contrast the first part of the Jonah story which shows a prophet running away from his vocation. Prophets were to proclaim God's demands, to be signs of the divine will in their own persons. The actions they perform, and often enough their whole lives, are to speak of God. Hosea's unhappy marriage is a symbol (*Hos.* 1-3); Isaiah himself and his children are 'signs and portents' (*Isa.* 8, 18; 20, 3). The life of Jeremiah and the seemingly strange commands of God are all significant (*Jer.* 13, 1-11, and 16). Ezekiel too is to be a *sign for the house of Israel* as he carries out the commandments of God (cf *Ezek.* 4, 3; 12, 6, 11; 24, 24).

The divine message came to the prophet in all manner of ways; most of all perhaps by inward inspiration—for thus we understand such phrases as, 'Word of the Lord to . . .' or 'The Word of the Lord came to me'. The prophet's pronouncement may come from quite ordinary circumstances, e.g. the sight of an almond branch (*Jer.* 1, 11) or of two baskets of figs (*Jer.* 24, 1) or a visit to a potter's workshop (*Jer.* 18, 1-4). The literary forms used to convey the messages are immensely varied. Each prophet has very naturally his own temperament, circumstances, education. But the genuine prophet is always aware that he is a mouthpiece and no more. His own words—and they are his own—are also the Word of God to be passed on to others. The source of this conviction would appear to be in some mysterious experience of God. The divine seizure may provoke abnormalities but these are merely incidental. The prophet, like the mystic, is raised to a supranormal psychological state by divine intervention. There we must leave the mystery. For it is a mystery of faith which we proclaim every time we say God it was who spoke through the prophets.

Though the terms *Nābī* and *prophētēs* do not necessarily imply futurity;

---

[4]An odd historical note in I *Sam.* 9,9 tells us that the older term was *roeh* or 'seer'. Other terms were 'man of God' (I *Kings* 13, 1-31; 'servant' (*Jer.* 7, 25); 'angel' or 'messenger' of the Lord (RSV), (*Hag.* 1, 13); 'shepherd' in *Zech.* 10, 2.

the prophet's message may relate both to present and future. The message very often relates to contemporaries of the prophet, to whom he communicates the will of God, showing unflinchingly their failings and abandonment of God. There is indeed, quantitatively, a great deal of spiritual scolding, in e.g. *Jeremiah*.

Future happenings were often manifested to prophets by means of visions. But then vision-pictures lacked perspective. Events are not presented in historical order, but the future is alongside the present, or present and future are interspersed without any regard for sequence. Events happening at the end of time can appear immediate to the prophet. The older prophets do not distinguish clearly between the preparation for the Messianic kingdom, i.e. the Return from Exile, and the Messianic kingdom itself. For them the inauguration of a Messianic era coalesces with the fall of Babylon. Immanuel is a child during the reign of Tiglath-Pileser (*Isa.* 7, 14–15).

In the Servant poems the Messiah seems destined to liberate Israel from the prison-house of exile (cf *Isa.* 42, 7; 49, 6, 8–9), but in fact the Messiah appeared centuries after the Return from Babylon. But the prophet saw *at one glance* two related events, the liberation from Babylon and the Messiah's work of liberating mankind from sin. John the Baptist saw the Messiah putting the axe to the root of the trees and winnowing the grain (*Mt.* 3, 10–12), that is, he bridges the time between Christ's activity on earth and his Second Coming at the Last Judgment.

At times the prophet foretells some event in the near future which will indicate his words and his mission from God (cf 1 *Sam.* 10, 1; *Isa.* 7, 14; *Jer.* 28, 15; 44, 29–30). At times the prophet will tell of punishment due for crimes or of prosperity to follow on repentance. Prophets of this later period look still farther ahead for the final triumph of God; though there is also a lesson for the present. The prophet's message can be twofold; it can at once threaten and console. Jeremiah was sent *to tear up and to knock down, to build up and to plant.* Menaces and reproaches come thick and fast, and make wearisome reading perhaps. Prophets were haunted by the fact of sin, that obstacle to the will of God. But salvation, and joyous salvation, is never completely forgotten. Even in *Jeremiah* of the Jeremiads, there are chapters 30–3. The Book of Consolation (*Isa.* 40–55) is a peak of prophecy. Future happiness is told of in the older prophets too (cf *Amos* 9, 8–15; *Hos.* 2, 16–25; 11, 8–11; 14, 2–9). In God's dealings with his people pardon and punishment are complementary.

The nature of the prophetic office must be gathered from a number of facts and texts. The fundamental idea is, as has been said, that the prophet is one who has an immediate experience of God; one to whom the holiness and will of God have been revealed. He is one who contemplates present and future through the eyes of God; he is sent to remind men of their duties to God, and to win them back to obedience and love of God. Prophecy thus understood is something peculiar to Israel, a providential disposition of God for the guidance and salvation of his people.

If prophecy and prophets are seen thus, it is natural enough that Moses was accounted father of them all (cf *Deut.* 18, 5, 18) and their most distinguished representative (*Deut.* 34, 10–12; *Num.* 12, 6–8). For he spoke with God face to face and conveyed God's truth to his Chosen People. But this rôle did not die with him, and the spirit dwells with Joshua, *Num.* 27, 18; *Deut.* 34, 9.

It has been usual to speak of classical prophecy, by which is meant the writing prophets of the earlier period, e.g. Amos, Hosea, Isaiah, Micah, Nahum, Habakkuk and Jeremiah; and we should add the non-writing prophets of an earlier period still, e.g. Nathan, Ahijah of Shilo, Elijah, Elishah, etc. These so-called 'classic' prophets illustrate many of the characteristics of the prophets and of prophetic action in the service of the living God. More useful perhaps is to set out the prophets in roughly chronological order: pre-exilic (as above); exilic, to include Second Isaiah, Ezekiel; post-exilic i.e. Haggai, Zachariah, Malachi, Obadiah, Joel—to which we might add Daniel. Daniel illustrates one of the deviations taken by Hebrew prophecy in the later years of that long history, for Daniel is essentially apocrypha rather than prophecy, and there are already apocalyptic sections; e.g. *Isaiah* 24–7, and most of *Zechariah*. At the later and important period of Israel's history (important in its own right and as preparatory for the New Testament) the 'Conscience of Israel' (B. Vawter's striking title[5]) was to find its expression in two very different modes: apocalypse and the wisdom literature of established Judaism.

True prophecy ceased to be, and the sorrows, anguish and hopes of the People of God found an outlet in the plethora of symbols adduced by anonymous writers who would peer into secrets known only to God and plead with Him to indicate his purposes. But true prophecy also resolved itself, and more soberly, into that wisdom literature which was in part more self-conscious as well as more aware of the significance of Israel's historic past: *Happy are we, O Israel, because we know what is pleasing to God* (*Baruch.* 4, 4).

Prophecy came to an end, and the People of God quietly recognized this. There is a story (1 *Macc.* 4, 46) how stones of the altar which had been profaned were stored away *until there should come a prophet to tell them what to do with them.* At least it was realized that a prophet might come.

Prophecy, however, did come back to the world with John the Baptist and him whom he preached, Christ the Lord and Wisdom of God.

---

[5]London and New York, 1961

Appendix 4

PROPHECY IN THE NEW TESTAMENT AND IN THE EARLY CHURCH

PROPHECY was extinct for about two centuries before Christ, and substitutes for the prophetic office seem to have been wisdom writings and teaching, and also apocalyptic works.

With the coming of Christianity came a vigorous and sudden revival of prophecy. St Luke in his gospel of the Holy Spirit brings out the point that Zechariah *was filled with the Holy Spirit and prophesied* (1, 67). The Holy Spirit was abundantly at work in the story of the Precursor and his parents. Zechariah the prophet shared in a knowledge of God's purposing: *Blessed be the Lord the God of Israel for he has visited and redeemed his people* (*Lk.* 1, 68). The same perception is shown in Simeon of Jerusalem (*Lk.* 2, 25) as he goes to the temple in spirit. We are told too of a prophetess Anna the daughter of Phanuel of the tribe of Aser (*Lk.* 2, 36) who spoke of God *to all who were looking for the redemption of Israel* (*Lk.* 2, 38). St Luke is in effect depicting the admirable light of God's kingdom; the day was dawning because Christ was soon to be conceived and born on earth. St Matthew tells of a few who were privileged to sense and know God's loving purposes, among them Joseph to whom it was revealed that Jesus would be born of Mary and would *save his people from their sins* (*Mt.* 1, 21).

St John the Baptist comes on the scene suddenly, dramatically. The interesting point is that he was recognized as a prophet (no one had seen a prophet for 200 years), perhaps because the man in the street had a clear idea of what a prophet should be like, especially if coming in the robe of Elijah, the expected Precursor of the great and fearful day of the Lord (*Mal.* 3, 1; 4, 5; *Mt.* 11, 14; *Mk.* 9, 11–13; *Lk.* 1, 17). Tradition had also remembered this prophet's distinctive garb of haircloth: this had certainly been characteristic of some old *Nābī's* (cf 2 *Kings* 1, 8; *Zech.* 13, 4). Some argue from *Zech.* 13, 6 & 1 *Kings* 20, 38 & 41 that they had other distinguishing marks; not, however, the tonsure, as the *Jerome Commentary*[1] suggests: tonsure had some religious significance no doubt, but was explicitly forbidden by the Law (*Lev.* 19, 27–8; *Deut.* 14, 1).

Characteristically foreshortening time, John the Baptist proclaims that the Messianic judgment was about to begin (*Mt.* 3, 10–12), the day of wrath was near (*Mt.* 3, 2). John Baptist's message was not merely applicable to gentiles but to the Chosen People themselves and their religious leaders. The Precursor immediately precedes the Messiah, but also furnishes the

---

[1] New York, 1969, p. 226

background, the terminology of the new preaching: believe, repent, do penance, be baptized, etc. Our Lord takes up John Baptist's preaching and John's very words as soon as the Precursor was silenced by Herod (*Mk.* 1, 14): the stage was set, our Lord had but to open his ministry. The forerunner had done his work.[2]

Christian prophecy, deeply rooted in the Church at all times, takes its origin and initial expression in the person and work of Christ. Crowds around him in Galilee as in Jerusalem willingly referred to him as a prophet, as it were Jeremiah come to life again (cf *Mt.* 16, 4; *Mk.* 6, 15; *Jn.* 4, 19; 6, 14; 7, 40; 9, 17). Our Lord accepted this view of his mission, partial though it was, for he was eminently 'more than a prophet'. He was to give to the New Israel of God the prophetic spirit which had been the glory of Israel (*Lk.* 2, 49; *Jn.* 16, 12). But it derived from Christ himself the Prophet who was to inaugurate an altogether new line of prophets and a new quality of prophecy which can be discerned in the life of the Church or Christ continued.

On the first Pentecost, prophecy burst on the scene as a fulfilment of hopes and promises: *your sons and your daughters shall prophesy* (*Acts* 2, 17, citing *Joel* 2, 26). Such was the extraordinary gift of Spirit and prophecy (the two going together) which marked the occasion. Prophets seem to have become a recognized institution in Jerusalem as early as A.D. 43-44. Thus Christian prophets Agabus and others went to Antioch and ministered there (*Acts* 11, 27; 13, 1). After the conference at Jerusalem (A.D. 49) we are told of two other prophets Judas Barsabbas and Silas who came from Jerusalem and *exhorted the brethren with many words and strengthened them* (*Acts* 15, 32). Seven years later we read of Philip's four daughters prophesying in or near Caesarea. Agabus predicts a famine under Claudius, and with a characteristic prophetic gesture enacts St Paul's arrest (*Acts* 21, 10-14). St Paul had had other premonitions or warnings from the Holy Spirit (cf *Acts* 20, 23). Prophets seem to be found everywhere in Churches founded by St Paul (cf 1 *Thess.* 5, 20; 1 *Cor.* 12, 28; 13, 2; 14, 3; *Ephes,* 3, 1; *Rom.* 12, 6).

These prophets had a definite rôle: they were to build up the Church which an apostle had founded, to exhort, to console, to strengthen the faith of those who had come to believe, and also to convict unbelievers, laying bare the secrets of the heart. The ideal prophet in theory knew all mysteries, had all knowledge (cf 1 *Cor.* 13, 2; 14, 3-4, 23-4).

There was, from the beginning, an institution and an ideal of prophecy. But prophecy could also be abused and its exercise needed some regulation. St Paul (1 *Cor.* 14) tries to put some due order in the use of prophecy in worship. Thus not more than two or three should speak at the same meeting. And the prophets were not to be senseless automata—indeed *the spirits of the prophets are subject to the prophets* (cf 1 *Cor.* 14, 32).

1 *Corinthians* 14 tells us most about these early prophets, but it was probably at Ephesus that the prophets came to be recognized as an institution.

---

[2]cf St Thomas, *In Joan.* 1, *lect.* 14

The local Church there was to be furnished with apostles, prophets, evangelists, pastors, teachers (*Ephes.* 4, 11), and no doubt all local Churches would have some of these favoured brethren to help, encourage, teach and rule them.

In St Paul's time the utterances and exhortations of the prophets were wholly oral. Later, in the *Apocalypse* prophecy under the new covenant takes a written form. Both the prologue and epilogue claim that the *Apocalypse* is a prophecy (cf *Apoc.* 1, 3; 10, 11; 22, 7, 10, 18–19) and the author is a prophet who has brother-prophets (*Apoc.* 22, 9). The Church, as viewed in the *Apocalypse*, is Spirit and Bride, the charismatic ministry, and a body of believers. No special place is assigned to bishops, priests and deacons— unless they were also prophets, as may sometimes have happened. We read of 'prophets and saints' and 'saints, apostles and prophets' (*Apoc.* 16, 6; 18, 20, 24). Unlike St Paul, the Apocalyptist's view of the Christian ministry is wholly charismatic and prophets are held in high esteem, according to Swete, 'such a view of the ministry is not unnatural in a prophetic book'.*

It is usually thought that prophecy as an institution or element inherent in the life and worship of the Church suffered an eclipse in the second century. Thus for Ignatius who makes much of the office of a bishop, the 'prophets' are invariably those of the Old Testament. Polycarp it is true was remembered as a prophet and teacher, yet Polycarp himself refers (*Phil.*) to prophets of the Old Testament rather than to a present reality.

Apollinarius, cited in Eusebius (*Ecclesiastical History* 5, 17) writes, 'The charism of prophecy must exist in all the Church until the second coming: this is the view of St Paul.'

---

*The Apocalypse of St John, p. xxi. London, 2nd edition 1907.

Appendix 5

THE PROPHETIC ELEMENT
IN THE CHURCH

VATICAN II'S Dogmatic Constitution tells us that 'the Spirit abides in the Church and in the hearts of the faithful as in a temple; that is where he prays and bears witness to the fact of adoption. He guides the Church into all truth; he makes her one in fellowship and service; he fits her out with gifts of different kinds, hierarchical and charismatic, and makes his fruits her adornment. By the power of the Gospel he gives the Church youth and continual renewal.' Such a text reminds us of what has always been known: the life-giving Spirit abides to bring to perfection both in the Church generally and in its individual members. A new and noteworthy stress is in the explicit reference to *charismatic gifts*.

Note first that charismatic gifts can appear anywhere and at any time in the Church's life; their function is to direct and maintain that life. Often we associate charismatic gifts with the dawn and early years of the Church's life, and look upon the charismata as a very special dispensation of the Holy Spirit at a particular time when the faith had to be founded and grounded in a world 'twisted out of its true pattern'. Such a view too easily blinds us to some of the possibilities of the abiding Spirit who is for all time.

But why then until Vatican II was so little said about the charismatic and prophetic element in the Church? Perhaps because ever since the Council of Trent stress was laid upon the hierarchy. This was something of an apologetic stand taken at the Counter-reformation, and lasting up to Vatican II; and with it may have gone a certain suspicion of the charismatic and prophetic as being too often linked with heretical tendencies or aberrant individualisms.

Vatican II has freed us from apologetic preoccupations and has redressed the balance. There is no need to be suspicious of, let alone fear, the charismata. Rather should we in a spirit of faith recognize their presence among us, and acknowledge that the Spirit can be and is very much at work in the hearts of very many, even in our urbanized and technological society. Note too that both the hierarchy and the charismata are termed *gifts* of the Spirit: this is important for all who tend to look upon hierarchy as merely juridical disposition, whereas it too is a work of Spirit and each and every link of the hierarchy is called by the Spirit, and *one does not take this honour upon himself, but he is called by God, just as Aaron was* (*Heb.* 5, 4). Karl Rahner puts the matter in perspective: 'There is a charismatic structure in the Church besides the hierarchical . . . in the constitution of the Church the Spirit as Lord of the Church reserves to himself the power and the right to impart impulses to the Church without always and everywhere directing them through the official hierarchical organs of the Church. The same thing can expressly be said about the relation between the hierarchical organs themselves, i.e. between the Papacy and the Bishops. Because the Bishops embody the Universal Church 'on the spot', and in so far as they do so, being the direct representatives of Christ himself and not simply of the Pope, they are indeed always dependent on and responsible to that unity of the Church in her diffusion which is embodied by the Pope, and hence are subject to him; they must preserve 'peace and communion' with the Apostolic See . . . they are also hierarchical channels for the impulses of the Holy Spirit, who in the first place accomplishes through them what he wishes done at this particular place in the Church, and furthermore possibly some new insight, a new vitality, new modes of Christian life, private or public, that the Holy Spirit wishes to impart via this point to the Church as a whole.'[1]

The Dogmatic Constitution of Vatican II goes on (§35) to speak of Christ, 'the great Prophet who has issued the proclamation of his Father's Kingdom by his life's witness and the power of his word and continually fulfills his prophetic office until his glory is revealed'. Because Christ is supremely Prophet, the Church which is truly Christ continued in time and place must have a prophetic function too. Such a lasting prophetic function was long ago foretold in *Deut.* 18, 18, interpreted of Christ in *Acts* 3, 22 and 7, 37, and then lawfully understood of the whole prophetic history of Israel, and finally of prophecy as an abiding charism in the New Israel of God.

Christ's prophetic work was accomplished 'by his life's witness and the power of his word'. Both these aspects are rooted in the Hebrew prophetic tradition when so often a prophet's life witness caused him to be called 'Man of God' (*'ish 'elohim*) or one whose whole being speaks of God, whose whole action is God's action in him. In New Testament terms, *The Son can do nothing of his own accord but only what he sees the Father doing; for whatever he does, that the Son does likewise (Jn. 5, 19)*. The power of his word is appealed to in the reiterated 'Oracle of the Lord' (*Ne'um Yahweh*) of the Prophets of old, and of course the Gospel is *the power of God for salvation to everyone who has faith (Rom. 1, 16)*.

The hierarchy teach in his name and by his power, because from the beginning the Lord Jesus called to him men of his own choosing, and he appointed twelve that they might be with him and that he might send them forth to preach (*Mk.* 3, 13). Thus, the Apostles were the first members of the New Israel, and at the same time the beginning of the sacred hierarchy (cf Vatican II, Decree of the Church's Missionary Activity, §5.) But it is not only through the hierarchy that Christ performs through all the ages his prophetic task. 'He uses the laity, too, and therefore he appoints them as witnesses and equips them with the discernment of faith and the grace of speech. He wants the power of the Gospel to shine through their daily life in family and in society. They show themselves as sons of promise if they make the most of the present moment with strong faith and hope' (§35). Again, 'the consecrated People of God have a share, too, in Christ's

---

[1] *Mission and Grace*, Vol. II, pp. 27–8. London, 1964

prophetic office, chiefly by spreading a live witness to him by means of a life of faith and charity, and by offering to God a Sacrifice of Praise, the tribute of lips that acknowledge his name (cf. *Heb.* 13, 15).'

Such texts of the Council afford considerable insight into the mode of the Spirit's operations among all the people of God. Other texts of the Council reinforce our first impressions. 'From the reception of these charisms or gifts, including those which are less dramatic, there arise for each believer the right and duty to use them in the Church and in the world for the good of mankind and the upbuilding of the Church. In so doing believers need to enjoy the freedom of the Holy Spirit who *breathes where he wills*' (Decree on the Apostolate of the Laity, §3). 'The advance of age brings with it better self-knowledge, thus enabling each person to evaluate more accurately the talents with which God has enriched his Soul and to exercise more effectively those charismatic gifts which the Holy Spirit has bestowed on him for the good of his brothers' (§30).

'While testing spirits to see if they be of God, priests should discover with the instinct of faith, acknowledge with joy, and foster with diligence the various humble and exalted charisms of the laity (Decree on the Ministry of Priests, §9).

Appendix 6

CHARISMS

THE Greek term *charisma* denotes a gift or favour freely and graciously bestowed, and can be used of any grace or favour of God—from redemption and life eternal to communing with the brethren in faith (cf *Rom.* 5, 15–16; 6, 23). It is used of the privileges granted to the people of Israel (*Rom.* 11, 29), of non-material gifts bestowed upon Christians (1 *Pet.* 4, 10), of the spiritual possession of a believer (*Rom.* 1, 11), of the gift of an office mediated by the laying on of hands (1 *Tim.* 4, 14; 11 *Tim.* 1, 6), and of the power to be continent in matters of sex (1 *Cor.* 7, 7).

Our concern is with a more special use of the term, primarily in the New Testament, when it refers to extraordinary graces given to individual Christians for the good of others around them or Christians generally. Many of these are enumerated in 1 *Cor.* 12, 8–10 . . . *Through the Spirit the utterance (Logos) of wisdom, and to another the utterance of knowledge, to another faith in the same spirit, to another gifts of healing by the one Spirit, to another the working of miracles, to another prophecy, to another ability to distinguish between spirits, to another various kinds of tongues, to another interpretation of tongues.* In verses 23–30 we find added—apostles, prophets, doctors, helpers (literally, 'helps': but we take the abstract for concrete) and administrators. Another list is in *Rom.* 12, 6–8 and in *Ephes.* 4, 11. It is by no means certain that St Paul's lists are exhaustive: and the wording of 1 *Cor.* 12, 4–7 suggests manifold activities of the Spirit . . . *varieties of gifts . . . varieties of service . . . varieties of working . . .* The activity of the Spirit at the dawn of the Church outstripped all precise categories and classifications. Anything like systematization of the charism will probably be distorting. The manifestations of the Spirit are described in terms which at best are analogical. A given term may cover several realities, and a term may not express adequately any one reality. F. Prat[1] arrives at twenty distinct charisms, though he suggests that some are synonymous. More helpful is a precise exegesis of each term that has come down to us, in terms of context, previous history, etc., without any claim to have exhausted the content.

Extraordinary gifts of God had been prophesied by *Joel* (2, 28), and promised by Christ: *and these signs will accompany those who believe; in my name they will cast out demons; they will speak in new tongues; they will pick up serpents, and if they drink any deadly thing it will not hurt them; they will lay their hands on the sick, and they will recover* (*Mk.* 16, 17–18). The Lord's promise was fulfilled particularly on the day of Pentecost when something which transcended all normal experience took place. This is clear from St Luke's narrative (*Acts* 2, 5–11): whatever the limits of

---

[1]*Theology of St Paul.* London. 1958. I, Note D.

language the Spirit was present in power, and 'speaking with tongues' was looked upon as a sure sign of the Spirit's presence (cf *Acts* 2, 4; 10, 46 & 19, 6) and also as a symbol of the reversal of the Tower of Babel story (*Gen.* 11, 1-9). Men then had no common language because they were estranged from a common obedience to God. St Luke wants to show mankind re-created, re-united and speaking one universal language of the Holy Spirit of God. The scene in *Acts* 2 takes place among Jews only, Jews of the Diaspora who normally spoke the languages of their country of residence. St Luke is at pains to show that the Holy Spirit was to come upon Gentiles too: *Acts* 10 shows the Gentile Pentecost, in which the Holy Spirit takes the initiative, comes upon his elect *before* baptism, and thus shows God's intention: there was to be neither Jew nor Gentile but only a People of God.

The Spirit burst upon the world at Pentecost at first intensively and then extensively, for the Church spread with a wonderful rapidity. The Lord's promise was fulfilled as the Church spread to Samaria (*Acts* 8, 18), to Ephesus (19, 6), to Rome (12, 6), in Galatia (*Gal.* 3, 5), and more markedly (or is it because we have more information?) in Corinth (1 *Cor.* 12-14).

When St Paul arrived in a Church, the working of the Spirit became manifest (1 *Cor.* 1, 7). There were miracles (*Gal.* 3, 5); his words were supernaturally powerful (1 *Cor.* 2, 4; cf *Rom*, 1, 17 'the power of God' which is the Gospel). The Galatians, however 'senseless', had at least begun with the Spirit (*Gal.* 3, 3) and had spiritual experiences (*Gal.* 3, 4) which made them realize what a wealth of charismata accompanied the arrival of St Paul in 'Asia'. They as it were saw God at work among themselves, giving witness of his presence. They recognized Paul as envoy of Christ and Angel of God, and were for beginning a new life in the Holy Spirit.

Greeks, or Greek-speaking pagans, wherever Christianity was preached, would be easily inclined to accept the more outward phenomena of the Spirit as corresponding to other religious experiences in the Near East of that period. It would not be difficult for a Corinthian to see an analogy between Christian speaking with tongues and the ecstatic utterances of the initiates of Dionysius. There is, however, no indication of a hellenistic origin for Christian charisms. Yet in practice the 'prophets' of Corinth and other Churches betray a certain familiarity with pagan prophets and usages—which was inevitable. Traces of this appear, cf 1 *Cor.* 12, 1-3, *no one speaking by the Holy Spirit ever says Jesus be cursed, and no one can say Jesus is Lord except by the Holy Spirit.* Thus there are two kinds of utterance or prophetical speech or exclamatory prayer which are as opposite as light and dark. These two types of prophecy or prayer no doubt co-existed side by side in the Corinth of St Paul's day. We could compare the co-existence of the prophets of Baal and the prophets of Yahweh (1 *Kgs.* 18, etc). Both with the prophets of old and with the ecstatics of the New Testament times, the several external resemblances corresponded to a psychological reality. The souls, imaginations and sensibilities of Christians and pagans alike could by charisms and by phenomena externally appear very much akin to charisms.

In Corinth particularly, St Paul worked hard to check survivals of paganism or infiltrations of pagan thought. He laid down a golden rule in 1 *Cor.* 14, 32, *the spirits (pneumata) of the prophets are subject to the prophets.* 'Spirits' here are the inspirations, inclinations and desires which do not necessarily come from the Holy Spirit. Prophets, and all who are moved by the Spirit, should be discerning, and masters of themselves, not losing control over their acts. This was to be quite different from the pagan giving oneself up to the influence of the deity with a surrender which verges on intoxication. Christian charismatics retain their personality and conscious free-will, fully realizing that any gift is from God above: *There are varieties of charisms but the same spirit . . . the same Lord . . . the same God* (1 *Cor.* 12, 4–6).

Still St Paul had to struggle on and teach that authentic Christian charisms come from the Spirit alone. To the Corinthian pagans, the intellectual charisms seemed to provide a gateway to a divine world. St Paul counters this by insisting on their *transient* nature, and the fact that they are surpassed by the theological virtues and notably by charity. Thus 1 *Cor.* 13, the 'Hymn to Charity' is St Paul's answer to misapprehension of charisms. The most sensational charisms (tongues of men and angels . . . prophetic powers . . . all knowledge . . . all faith . . .) are pure ostentation if charity is lacking (1 *Cor.* 13, 1–3). Charity counters all childish rivalities (4–7), charisms are insufficient (8–10); it is even suggested that charisms are like the prattle of a child (11); charisms, the imperfect, the enigmatic, even prophecy, ends with the Parousia; charity will remain when we are 'face to face' (12–13). Apart from charisms there is a religious knowledge which is a mark of Christian maturity; it is hinted at in v. 11, it is set out in 1 *Cor.* 1, 18–2, 16 where we have a whole Christian philosophy, and where, *inter alia*, we read *the unspiritual man does not receive the gifts of the Spirit of God, for they are folly to him, and he is not able to understand them for they are spiritually discerned* (1 *Cor.* 2, 14). This was true of many Corinthians in St Paul's day, as of many contemporaries of our day.

St Paul had not only to set the charisms in their true and theological perspective, but also to regulate some charismatic excesses in Christian services. Everything has to be done in an orderly way. In a 'prophecy-meeting' at Corinth, two or three prophets are allowed to speak, in turn, and separately, so that all the congregation may benefit. If one of the faithful is suddenly inspired, i.e. receives a private 'revelation' (*Ephes.* 5, 20) while the prophet is speaking, then the prophet must keep silent. St Paul is simply making rulings for good order at services, and reminding them as always that 'the spirits of the prophets are subject to the prophets' (1 *Cor.* 14, 32).

There does not seem to have been the same difficulty in other Churches. The work of the Spirit then showed itself more in the inspired chants, hymns, odes, in the solemn language of worship (cf *Ephes.* 5, 18, 20). There are many known fragments of hymns, e.g. in *Phil.* 2, 6–11; *Coloss.* 1, 15–20; *Ephes.* 5, 14; 1 *Tim.* 3, 16, etc. A very real zeal for God found an outlet in such hymns and chants rather than in broken utterances and strange languages.

The *Summa* treatise, after dwelling on prophecy, limits itself to the gift of speech (utterance, *logos*), the gift of tongues, and the gift of miracles; i.e. it treats specifically of those gifts which have most to do with the publishing abroad of God's revealed truth. Prophecy gives us revealed truth, speech and tongues relay, hand on that truth, and the working of miracles makes it effective and convincing. These charisms or gracious gifts of God furthered the progress of God's revelation—in a striking manner at the dawn of the Church, and then in a rather more muted manner in the Church ever since. It would be untrue to say that these gifts have died out. They are with us still, most of all among those of immense faith who can grasp the depths and immensity of revealed truth with ever-increasing firmness.

Appendix 7

THE CHARISMS THAT ATTACH TO SPEECH

'SPEECH' in this context means rather utterance (RSV) or proclamation, teaching, instruction. Underlying St Thomas's *sermo* is the wide-ranging Greek term *logos*, which looms large in St Paul and in the New Testament generally. For the early Christians preaching was *the service of the word* (*Acts* 6, 4), and apostles are *servants of the word* (*Lk.* 1, 2). In this way specifically Christian vocabulary was coming into being.

For the Corinthians, however, this Christian usage might be far from acceptable. They had philosophical or semi-philosophical usages in mind, and would not realize that this Christian *logos* was inspired, a teaching of the Spirit (1 *Cor.* 2, 13); and it had, according to St Paul, two forms, namely the word of wisdom, and the word of knowledge. But these were not a rhetorician's mode of classification, on ways of expressing oneself. Nor was it to be taken as the language of the mysteries which impinged very much upon the pagan minds of that period.

This 'word' of wisdom and 'word' of knowledge (in each case we are to understand 'utterance', 'proclamation') consist of *speeches which contain and convey wisdom and knowledge*, and are accordingly of immense spiritual profit to those who hear them. This contrasts rather forcibly with the gift of speaking with tongues which may often be of little spiritual profit, and anyway calls for an interpreter. The real sense of this charism appears in 1 *Cor.* 2, 13, *We impart this in words not taught by human wisdom but taught by the Spirit.*

The connotation is that of an inspired utterance intended for the perfect or wholly spiritual (cf *Among the mature do we impart wisdom, although it is not a wisdom of this age or of the rulers of this age*, 1 *Cor.* 2, 6). It is interesting to note that St Paul, at the beginning of his first letter to the Corinthians, thanks God that they were *enriched in him with all speech and all knowledge* (1, 5); and in his second letter flatters them, or is it irony?—*You excel in everything—in faith, in utterance, in knowledge, in all earnestness, in your love for us.*

The same teaching about speech or 'utterance' appears in another tradition, that of 1 *Pet.* 4, 10–11, *As each has received a gift, employ it for one another . . . whoever speaks, as one who utters oracles of God.* In this context this gift of speech is represented as a communication of divine oracles, a sort of revelatory discourse.

The basis of inspired locution or Spirit-filled speech is in a tradition stemming from our Lord; *Do not be anxious how you are to speak or what you are to say; for what you are to say will be given you in that hour; for it is not you who speak, but the Spirit of your Father speaking through you (Mt.* 10, 19–20;

cf *Mk.* 13, 11; *Lk.* 21, 15). In the same line comes the description of Stephen disputing with the Jews, who could not resist the spirit with which he spoke (*Acts* 6, 10). This echoes a well-substantiated Old Testament tradition, best expressed in the words of David as he lay dying, *The spirit of the Lord speaks by me, his word is upon my tongue* (II *Sam.* 23, 2); and we can compare *Jer.* 1, 6–9; *Num.* 22, 38; *Deut.* 18, 18; *Acts* 3, 22.

Glossary

abstraction from the senses: not alienation, but a leaving of sensation out of consideration; is called for when a prophet receives infused images (2a2æ. 173, 3); when the soul is to be more easily influenced by spiritual substances (2a2æ. 172, 1); and in ecstasy (2a2æ. 175, 1).

blessed, the: those in heaven who see God as he is (1 *Jn.* 3, 2). The technical term is *comprehensores:* it is adopted from 1 *Corinthians* 9, 24, *katalambanō*, to lay hold of, and does not suggest that the beatific vision comprehends God as he comprehends himself: cf 1a2æ. 4, 3. Vol. 16 of this series.

demons: can convey truths if God so disposes (2a2æ. 172, 5 & 6) and perform pseudo-miracles (2a2æ. 178, 1 & 2).

dreams: in a state of sleep the soul has greater receptivity but weaker judgment than when awake (2a2æ. 172, 1 & 2).

essence: the nature of a being, often its specific nature, signified by the definition. Divine essence, what God is in himself; knowing the divine essence, not merely knowing him as manifested in his effects.

eternal mirror or *mirror of eternity:* not the divine essence in itself, but 'certain similitudes lighted up by a God-given light' (2a2æ. 173, 1).

future contingent: an event which will happen but aside from the determinism of existing causes; contrasted with what must necessarily come to pass given the present nature of things.

hagiographer: one who receives light to judge about naturally knowable truths without necessarily rising to prophecy, which, properly speaking, is of a supernatural truth (2a2æ. 174, 3). Applied to a sacred or inspired writer; and thus a term of particular interest for the theological study of Biblical 'inspiration'.

heavens (third): a part in the geocentric system of celestial spheres which obtained in the Middle Ages. This was taken from Aristotle; later Ptolemy's system was preferred. Beyond the moon, sun, and planets lay the fixed stars. There were fifty-six spheres in Aristotle's system: the various celestial spheres above the material spheres were considered to exert influence on such sublunary dwellers as men on earth. The most manifest of these influences was light, thought of as a quality most proper to the celestial element. For the cosmology of the *Summa,* cf Vol. 10 of this series, ed. W. A. Wallace.

instrumental causality: produces an effect above the nature of the proximate agent and corresponding to the form in the intention of the principal cause, as in the human use of razors, pianofortes, paintbrushes, and so forth. God uses human instruments to produce results surpassing their native capabilities. They retain their human character and action; yet the result is wholly God's as well as wholly theirs.

light: 'a kind of manifestation of truth' (1a. 106, 1 ad 2). God alone gives light to the mind: men and angels communicate species and images. Light from prophecy is conductive to the direction of human acts especially as regards the worship of God (2a2æ. 172, 1).

mediation: the bridging of extremes in the order of being and of knowledge.

revelation: apocalypsis, a laying bare or unveiling of truths about God. But the veils are on us, not on God; the light of truth must be let into our minds. God reveals, and his activity is his very being, so his revealing is his very presence among people. This revelation is far more than a communication of truths: a cardinal point in theology.

species: likenesses of objective things in a cognitive power, of sense, of imagination, of intellect.

Index of Scriptural Texts

General Index

A

B

C

D

E

P

R

S

T

U

V

W

Z

VOLUMES

General Editor: THOMAS GILBY, O.P.

Printed in the United States
62687LVS00002B/107